PREFACE

This Handbook of Christian Theology sets forth the convictions of the author formed and confirmed through fifty years of study, preaching and teaching. If they are in agreement with the long-established faith of the orthodox Church and in harmony with the Lutheran Confessions, it is because the author believes that these all rest upon Biblical and rational grounds. It is not maintained for one moment that the author's views are infallible or that he has invariably expressed the mind of the Spirit. He has honestly endeavored to interpret the Word of God as revealed in the sacred Scriptures of the Old and the New Testaments, whose authority he deems sufficiently established as the basis and norm for rational belief and personal faith.

The Handbook is frankly but, we trust, not offensively dogmatic. It is dogmatic in the sense that it presents a standard by which the student may direct his thinking, giving him some definite points for acceptance or rejection. It is not a full presentation of the great science of Christian theology. Its object is to set forth in simple language the minimum of what a minister should know in order to be a faithful preacher of the Gospel. The author hopes that it may also be read with profit by laymen who desire a plain and orderly statement of Christian doctrine.

The Handbook is not a slavish reproduction of traditional theology. While the author believes that a radical reconstruction of theology is not needed, he is of the opinion that a restatement in the language and thought of today is desirable. Much of the modern reconstruction eliminates the precious "faith which was once for all delivered to the saints," and leaves in its stead merely the vague speculations of naturalism.

The general line of treatment is not new. First of all

is presented an apologetic as the ground of Christian doctrine. This embraces a defence of the reasonableness of the belief in the existence of God and of the acceptance of the Bible as a revelation of His nature and of His relation to the universe, especially to man.

While apologetics in its broad meaning is a distinct branch of systematic theology apart from dogmatics, the belief in the existence and the revelation of God is so fundamental to dogmatics that it is consciously or unconsciously treated in nearly all works on dogmatics. It seems best, therefore, to begin the present treatise with a statement of the ground upon which Christian doctrine rests.

The foundation having been laid in apologetics, the discussion proceeds to dogmatics, which sets forth the Christian conception of God as derived from the Bible, developed in the Church, and realized in Christian experience, and of the way of salvation through Christ.

It should be borne in mind always that the ultimate end of the study of theology is not chiefly a scientific conception of religious truth, but a strong conviction of its saving power. As related to preaching, theology supplies the matter and concept, and gives to the minister the confidence of certainty and of good order in the treatment of his message; but theology cannot impart life and salvation apart from the quickening Spirit, who inspired the sacred writers and who alone can apply the Gospel of Jesus Christ to the salvation of sinners.

A HANDBOOK OF CHRISTIAN THEOLOGY

By

J. A. SINGMASTER

PHILADELPHIA

THE UNITED LUTHERAN PUBLICATION HOUSE

BIOGRAPHICAL

JOHN ALDEN SINGMASTER, D.D., LL.D.

Born at Macungie, Pa., August 31, 1852.

Entered into rest at Gettysburg, Pa., February 27, 1926.

Dr. Singmaster did his most important work for the Church through his connection with the Gettysburg Theological Seminary. He was an active member of the Board of Directors from 1894 until 1900, when he accepted a call to the new chair of Biblical Theology. He also served for several years as financial secretary of the institution. In 1903 he became professor of Systematic Theology and Chairman of the Faculty. In 1906 he was chosen as president of the Seminary. In addition to his duties as a professor, he was instrumental in raising $300,000 for the cancellation of debts, the erection of buildings and for endowment. At the time of his death he was the Henry Singmaster Professor of Systematic Theology and President of the Seminary.

Dr. Singmaster was an experienced pastor, having served congregations at Schuylkill Haven, Lyons and Macungie, Pa., Brooklyn, N. Y., and Allentown, Pa. He was a member of the East Pennsylvania Synod for forty-eight years, and served his synod as president, secretary and treasurer and as a delegate to the General Synod and the United Lutheran Church. He was a former president of the General Synod and an important member of the committee which formed the United Lutheran Church in America. He was for twenty years chairman of the Common Service Book Committee. He was also a member of the Deaconess Board, and of the Foreign Mission Board, and chairman of the United Lutheran Church Committee on Church Papers.

He took a vital interest in whatever engaged his attention and contributed to the furtherance of every work for which he shared responsibility.

This volume, which was practically accepted for publication at the time of his sudden entrance into life, is a monument to his memory and a medium for continuing his theological teaching.

TABLE OF CONTENTS

INTRODUCTION

PAGE

I. THE NATURE OF THEOLOGY 15-21
    1. The Definition of Theology
    2. The Content of Theology—Religion

II. THE NEED FOR THEOLOGY 21-23
    1. The Character of the Bible
    2. The Development of Doctrine
    3. The Nature of the Church
    4. The Idea of Proportion
    5. The Need for Defense

III. THE RELATIONS OF THEOLOGY 23-26
    1. Its Relation to Reason
    2. Its Relation to Science
    3. Its Relation to Philosophy
    4. Its Relation to Modern Thought

IV. THE SOURCES OF THEOLOGY 26-28
    1. The Bible
    2. The Holy Spirit
    3. Religious Experience
    4. The Creeds
    5. Anthropology
    6. The Universe

V. THE METHOD OF THEOLOGY 29-32
    1. Terminology
    2. The Scientific Process
    3. The Point of View of Methodology

APOLOGETICS

INTRODUCTION.. 33-34
    1. Definition
    2. Importance
    3. The Fundamental Purpose
    4. Relation to Dogmatics

A. THE EXISTENCE OF GOD

I. THE WITNESS OF JESUS CHRIST 34-36
    1. The Chief Witness of God
    2. A Character of History
    3. His Ethical Perfection
    4. His Idea of God
    5. Finality of His Testimony

II. THE WITNESS OF MAN 26 41
    1. The Personality of Man
    2. The Religious Nature of Man
    3. The Religious Experience of Man
    4. The Idea of God
    5. The Ontological Argument

PAGE

III. THE WITNESS OF THE UNIVERSE 41-47
    1. The Universe an Effect
    2. The Cosmological Argument
    3. The Conservation of Matter and Energy
    4. The Teleological Argument
IV. THE WITNESS OF THE BIBLE 47-48
V. THE WITNESS OF HISTORY 48-49
    1. The Universality of Religion
    2. The Blessedness of Religion
    3. The Nature of Christianity
VI. SOME ANTI-THEISTIC THEORIES 50-52
    1. Agnosticism
    2. Materialism
    3. Idealism

B. THE DIVINE REVELATION

I. THE PRESUMPTIVE EVIDENCE 52-54
    1. The Possibility of a Divine Revelation
    2. The Probability of a Divine Revelation
II. THE POSITIVE EVIDENCE 54-61
    1. The Bible as a Book
    2. The Bible as an Influence
    3. The Bible its Own Witness
    4. The Evidence of Prophecy
III. THE CANON OF SCRIPTURE 61-72
    1. The History of the Canon
    2. The Test of Canonicity
    3. Non-canonical Books.
    4. The Bible a Divine Revelation
    5. The Bible the Product of Inspiration
    6. Discrepancies in Scripture
    7. The Authority of Scripture
    8. The Use of Scripture in Theology

DOGMATICS

PART I

THEOLOGY (THE DOCTRINE OF GOD)

A. THE NATURE AND ATTRIBUTES OF GOD

I. THE NATURE OF GOD 75-77
    1. The Definition of God
II. THE ATTRIBUTES OF GOD 77-84
    1. Attributes of Personality
    2. Attributes of Absoluteness
    3. Attributes of Holiness
    4. Attributes of Love

B. The Trinity

PAGE

I. THE GROUND OF THE DOCTRINE 84-87
    1. The Faith of the Church
    2. The Postulate of Christianity
    3. The Source of the Doctrine
    4. The Historic Unfolding
    5. The Connotations of the Doctrine

II. THE FORMULATION OF THE DOCTRINE 87-90
    1. Its Necessity
    2. The Preparation
    3. The Progress
    4. The Consummation

III. THE NATURE OF THE TRINITY 90-99
    1. A Mystery
    2. A Threefold Personality
    3. A Matter of Faith in Christ
    4. The Immanent Trinity
    5. The Manifested Trinity

C. The Works of God

I. CREATION 99-103
    1. The Christian View
    2. The Biblical Account
    3. The Biblical Cosmogony

II. PROVIDENCE 103-105
    1. Definition
    2. Proof
    3. Phases of the Doctrine

III. MIRACLES 105-109
    1. Definition
    2. Proof
    3. Purpose
    4. Objections
    5. Old Testament Miracles

IV. PRAYER 110-112
    1. The Nature of Prayer
    2. The Elements of Prayer
    3. The Spirit of Prayer
    4. Encouragement to Prayer
    5. The Value of Prayer
    6. Difficulties in Regard to Prayer

V. ANGELS 112-118
    1. Angels in General
    2. Good Angels
    3. Evil Spirits

PART II

ANTHROPOLOGY (THE DOCTRINE OF MAN)

A. The Nature of Man

I. A COMPOSITE BEING 121-125
    1. A Twofold Being
    2. The Body

PAGE

3. The Unity of Spirit and Body
4. Man's Relation to Animals
II. THE MORAL NATURE OF MAN 125-131
    1. Man an Ethical Being
    2. Man Endowed with Conscience
    3. Proof of the Existence of Conscience
    4. The Office of Conscience
    5. The Domain of Conscience
    6. The Standard of Conscience
    7. The Fallibility of Conscience
    8. False Theories of Conscience
    9. Biblical Teaching Concerning Conscience
   10. The Implications of Conscience
III. THE FREEDOM OF MAN 131-134
    1. The Definition of Will
    2. The Freedom of the First Man
    3. The Partial Loss of Freedom
    4. The Restoration of Freedom
    5. Determinism.
    6. Divine Sovereignty and Free Will
    7. The Nature of Real Freedom
    8. Absolute Freedom in this Life
IV. THE IMMORTALITY OF MAN 134-139
    1. A Postulate of Religion
    2. Scripture Teaching
    3. Rational Arguments for Immortality
    4. The Possible Immortality of Adam's Body

B. THE ORIGIN OF MAN

I. THE BIBLICAL ACCOUNT 139-140
II. THE SCIENTIFIC THEORY 140-143
    1. The Origin of Life
    2. The Theory of Evolution
III. THE ORIGIN OF SOULS 143-145
    1. Pre-existence
    2. Creationism
    3. Traducianism

C. THE FALL OF MAN
(The Doctrine of Sin)

I. THE FACT OF SIN 145-147
    1. The Evidence of Consciousness
    2. The Bible
    3. Human Government
    4. Society
    5. History
II. THE NATURE OF SIN 147-149
    1. The Biblical Terms
    2. The Inherent Character of Sin
    3. The Guilt of Sin
III. THE ORIGIN OF SIN 149-152
    1. The Naturalistic View
    2. The View of Theistic Evolution

3. The View of Bodily Infection
4. The Scripture Teaching   PAGE
IV. ORIGINAL SIN 152-155
    1. Its Nature
    2. Its Extent
    3. Its Denial
    4. Its Transmission
V. THE CLASSIFICATION OF SINS 155-156
    1. Sin a Unit
    2. Forms of Sin
    3. The Unpardonable Sin
VI. THE PROBLEM OF EVIL 156-157
    1. God not the Author of Evil
    2. Evil Involved in Finite Freedom
    3. A Remedy Free to All

PART III
CHRISTOLOGY (THE DOCTRINE OF CHRIST)

INTRODUCTION 161-163
    1. The Promise of Salvation
    2. The Nature of Salvation
    3. The Mediation of Salvation

A. THE GIFT OF CHRIST
I. THE MOTIVE OF THE GIFT 163
II. THE UNIVERSALITY OF THE GIFT 163-167
    1. Affirmed in the Scriptures
    2. Limited by Predestinarians
III. PREPARATION FOR THE GIFT 167-171
    1. The Need for Preparation
    2. Factors in the Preparation

B. THE PERSON OF CHRIST
I. THE TESTIMONY CONCERNING CHRIST 172-176
    1. His Birth and Early Years
    2. His Relations with Men
    3. His Relations with God
    4. His Ministry
    5. His End
    6. Summary
II. THE INCARNATION 176-186
    1. The Meaning of the Incarnation
    2. The Scripture Basis of the Incarnation
    3. The Possibility of the Incarnation
    4. The Purpose of the Incarnation
    5. The Mode of the Incarnation
    6. The Importance of the Doctrine
III. THE CONSTITUTION OF CHRIST'S PERSON........................ 186-198
    1. The Deity of Christ
    2. The Humanity of Christ
    3. The Relations of the Two Natures
    4. The Impeccability of Christ

C. THE STATES OF CHRIST
PAGE

I. THE STATE OF HUMILIATION 198-200
  1. Its Duration
  2. Its Nature
  3. Its Expression
II. THE STATE OF EXALTATION 200-206
  1. Revivification
  2. Descent into Hell
  3. The Resurrection
  4. The Ascension
  5. The Session at God's Right Hand

D. THE WORK OF CHRIST

I. THE WORK OF CHRIST AS PROPHET 207-212
  1. The Prophet
  2. The Teacher
II. THE WORK OF CHRIST AS PRIEST 212-234
  1. The Fact of Christ's Priesthood
  2. The Purpose of Christ's Priesthood
  3. The Atonement by Substitution
  4. The Atonement by Sacrifice
  5. Theories of the Atonement
  6. The Extent of the Atonement
  7. The Intercession of Christ
III. THE WORK OF CHRIST AS KING 234-239
  1. The Fact
  2. The Ground
  3. The Necessity
  4. A Definition
  5. The Characteristics
  6. Its Relation to the Church
  7. Its Relation to the State
  8. The Relation of the Church and State
  9. The Consummation of the Kingdom

PART IV

PNEUMATOLOGY (THE DOCTRINE OF THE SPIRIT)

A. THE PERSON OF THE SPIRIT

I. HIS NATURE 243
II. HIS MANIFESTATION 243
III. HIS RELATION TO CHRIST 244

B. THE OFFICE OF THE SPIRIT

I. WITNESSING 244
II. CONVICTING 244
III. COMFORTING 245

C. The Work of the Spirit

PAGE

1. THE CALL 245-248
   1. The Definition
   2. The Subjects
   3. The Method
   4. The Effect

II. REPENTANCE AND FAITH 248-252
   1. Definition
   2. Contrition
   3. Faith

III. JUSTIFICATION 252-256
   1. The Biblical Teaching
   2. False Views of Justification

IV. REGENERATION AND CONVERSION 256-260
   1. Definition
   2. Nature
   3. The Means
   4. The Relation of Regeneration and Justification
   5. Conversion

V. SANCTIFICATION 260-262
   1. Definition
   2. Nature
   3. Method
   4. Degree

D. Means of Grace

I. THE WORD 262-264
   1. The Fitness of the Word
   2. The Form of the Word

II. THE SACRAMENTS 264-267
   1. The General Doctrine

III. BAPTISM 267-277
   1. The General Doctrine
   2. The Doctrine of Infant Baptism
   3. Sponsors and Confirmation
   4. The Effect of Baptism
   5. The Mode of Baptism

IV. THE LORD'S SUPPER 277-282
   1. Its Institution
   2. Its Definition
   3. Its Names
   4. Its Constituents
   5. Its Administration
   6. Its Design
   7. The Doctrinal Construction

V. THE CHURCH 282-288
   1. Its Nature
   2. Its Origin
   3. Its Marks
   4. Its Design
   5. Its Ministry

PART V

ESCHATOLOGY (THE DOCTRINE OF LAST THINGS)

PAGE

I. DEATH 291-292
    1. Its Nature
    2. Its Cause
    3. Its Effect

II. THE INTERMEDIATE STATE 292-293
    1. Its Character
    2. Purgatory

III. THE PAROUSIA 293-297
    1. Its Certainty
    2. Its Characteristics

IV. THE RESURRECTION 297-300
    1. The Fact
    2. The Nature
    3. The Scripture Details
    4. Relation Between the Natural and Scriptural Bodies

V. THE JUDGMENT 301-304
    1. The Fact
    2. Proof of a Final Judgment
    3. The Judge
    4. The Subjects
    5. The Ground
    6. The Criteria
    7. The Form

VI. RETRIBUTION 304-308
    1. Hell
    2. Heaven

A HANDBOOK OF CHRISTIAN THEOLOGY

INTRODUCTION

I. THE NATURE OF THEOLOGY

1. The Definition of Theology

(1) The word theology was used in ancient times by heathen philosophers in its etymological sense as "a discourse concerning God." The early Christian teachers employed the term in connection with the Christological controversies. Since the time of Abelard, in the twelfth century, it has been applied in its present comprehensive sense, including the study of all Christian doctrine.

(2) Christian theology is defined by Schaff as "the science of the Christian religion, as revealed in the Bible, developed in history and believed and practiced in the Church." Haering defines dogmatic theology as "the scientific exposition of revelation, as it is understood by faith; or as the science of Christian truth, as that truth is believed and confessed in the Church on the ground of revelation." We submit the following: Christian theology is the systematic presentation of the Christian faith, resting on the Bible, developed in the Church, and realized in Christian experience.

2. The Content of Theology—Religion

The subject-matter of theology is religion, of which it is the scientific presentation. Religion precedes theology as the starry sky antedates astronomy, and flowers antedate botany. True religion must ever be not only the content of Christian theology but also its animating principle, without which it becomes a mere academic pursuit.

1) THE DEFINITION OF RELIGION.

The word religion is of uncertain derivation. Cicero found-it in *religere*, which means primarily "to read again" and then "to ponder" or "to reflect." Lactantius derived it from *religare*, which means to "bind back." The ideas underlying both these words are applicable to religion.

Religion in its subjective aspect is the communion of the soul with God. To know Him and to come into gracious relation with Him is ever the hope and the effort of the best of mankind. In its comprehensive sense religion embraces all strivings after God, from the feeble gropings of the pagan to the ripe experiences of the Christian saint. At its best it claims the whole man, soul and body, for time and for eternity.

Religion is true in so far as it embraces a proper knowledge of God and leads to an inner experience and outward life in conformity with God's nature and will. It is essentially first a matter of spirit. It touches and moves the higher life of man and leads him to self-surrender to God, in whom he finds peace and hope.

Religion is also external. It expresses itself in worship, in fellowship with other believers and in a holy and beneficent life. It also necessarily forms organizations and systems, even when it is imperfect and corrupt. Thus we find various religions, heathen, Jewish, Mohammedan, beside the Christian. The last is incomparably superior to all others, as a study of comparative religion plainly shows. It has all the marks of finality. Nevertheless, other religions are not totally without elements of truth which Christianity should recognize in its endeavor to evangelize the world.

2) THE UNIVERSALITY OF RELIGION.

Religion is a universal fact in the life of mankind. Cicero long since observed this truth, which has been abundantly confirmed by subsequent investigation. Practically the whole world has been explored, and yet nowhere has been found a race entirely destitute of religious ideas and practices. It has been mistakenly affirmed, sometimes in the interest of false philosophy and sometimes from a lack of a thorough acquaintance with the facts, that tribes exist in Africa which have no religion whatever. It is true that there are tribes with such a rudimentary conception of religion that it may be overlooked by the cursory traveler. Moreover, the native is often exceedingly reserved in his superstitions from fear either of ridicule or of the wrath of his deity. The universality of religion is now conceded by all competent investigators.

3) The Origin of Religion.

How is religion accounted for? Whence does it arise? The answer to this varies with the attitude toward more fundamental questions, such as "Is there a God?" "Is God to be found?" "Has God spoken?" A negative answer makes religion practically a human invention.

(1) False Theories.

a. Deists, atheists and materialists make religion a political invention, a fraud imposed upon the people by their rulers to keep them in subjection. These lords reason that nothing so well subdues and awes the human spirit as the fear of a Supreme Being. There is certainly this much truth in this statement, that no government is stable without religion, and this implies belief in God. After the French Revolution had outlawed God by edict, and had thus let loose the vilest passions of men to wreak ruin upon society, Robespierre declared that if there were no God, one would have to be invented.

b. Another explanation of religion is that it is the product of natural phenomena. Men having observed the might and the moods of nature, now so beneficent and now so destructive, gradually personified them, and then invested them with living attributes. This explanation was offered by Lactantius at the breaking up of the ancient idolatrous faiths. While it accounts for the erroneous form of religious belief, it fails to explain what prompted men to these superstitions.

c. A third and more popular theory is that religion is an illusion. Feuerbach, for instance, maintained that God is simply a magnified man, enlarged by man's own imagination. He is like the colossal image of a human form reflected on the clouds. Renan declared that life demands illusions; they belong to the adornment of life, which is otherwise barren. All persons are poets, and they revel in creations of their own fancy. Especially is this true of women, and hence they are more religious than men.

These several efforts to account for the existence of religion are unscientific, because they ignore patent facts as well as the philosophy of religion. They ignore the persistent idea of God, which somehow must underlie all religion. They cannot explain the history of religion, which plainly declares its universality. They ignore the psychology of religion, which forbids the idea that man is so constituted that he will believe a lie rather than the truth. They ignore also the unwillingness of intelligent persons to die for a poetical illusion, however freely they suffer martyrdom for a reality.

(2) The True Theory.

Man is naturally a religious being. There can be no doubt of the Bible's teaching that he was made in the image of God. He is a personal being. He is endowed with intelligence, self-consciousness, and self-determination. These qualities connote a personal Creator infinitely greater than man and yet like him. The soul in its longing for fellowship with a Soul higher than itself realizes that it is seeking communion with a Person and not with an abstraction or with impersonal matter.

The existence of man's religious nature is usually taken for granted, except as false philosophy endeavors to dispute it. The Bible is the supreme book of religion. Its pages burn with passionate yearning for God. David cries, "My soul thirsteth for the living God!" Earnest men in all centuries have shared this longing, and have declared with Augustine, "O God, Thou hast made the soul for Thyself, and our heart is not at rest until it finds rest with Thee."

The heathen, no less than the people of God, feel their need of divine help. Their poets speak freely of man's need of the deities. Homer declared that "all men need the gods." Magnificent temples were erected to their honor. The earth, the sea, and the sky were peopled with their presence. In fetish and totem pole as well as in noble pantheon we read the old, the universal, and the irrepressible longing of the soul for God.

4) THE EARLIEST FORM OF RELIGION.

(1) Modern Liberal Opinion.

The earliest form of the idea of God is a matter of greatest importance. Those who are controlled by the hypothesis of evolution as God's only way of working conclude that conceptions of God and experience in religion are the slow growth of centuries from insignificant beginnings. They profess to find through the study of philosophy and the history of religion unmistakable evidence that "religion passes through three great stages. The first and earliest known to us is spiritism, the primitive form of belief, out of which all higher religion has grown. . Then follows polytheism. Finally comes monotheism, a spiritual faith; monotheism transforms worship into a spiritual communion of man and God. These three stages of religion mark an ascending scale of life."[1] It is asserted that "the belief in a primitive divine revelation containing the eternal principles of religion and morality has been completely undermined. Now it is recognized that religion like everything else, has developed from small beginnings; that fetishism and polytheism are older than monotheism, and that the latter has been due to the play and interplay of many and diverse forces."[2]

(2) The Conservative View.

Over against the speculation of philosophy and the history of religions, whose investigations are necessarily limited, the probability that monotheism was the original form of the idea of God is sustained on the ground of reason, philology, and history.

---

[1] Galloway, *The Philosophy of Religion.* P. 242.
[2] McGiffert, *The Rise of Modern Religious Ideas.* P. 178.

a. Reason.

The progenitor of the human race was evidently a man and not a beast. He was endowed with a keen mind and had the capacity of intercourse with his Maker. To a Christian it is inconceivable that Adam was without a knowledge of his Creator and that he should have been left to grope after God if haply he might find Him.

Moreover, it is psychologically and philosophically true that the thought of unity precedes multiplicity. The child grasps one thing at a time, going from unity to multiples, as its observation and mental strength increase. That the childlike, undeveloped primitive man of naturalism should have come to monotheism by way of animism and polytheism does not seem to be in accord with reason. It is certainly more probable that he thought of God before he thought of gods.

b. Philology.

The names for God used by the nations of the Aryan family can be traced back to the same root. "Zeus, the most sacred name in Greek mythology, is the same word as Dyaus in Sanscrit, Jovis or Ju in Jupiter in Latin, Tiw in Anglo-Saxon (preserved in Tiwsday, Tuesday, the day of the Eddic god), Tyr and Zio in old high German. This word was framed once and once only. It was not borrowed by the Greek from the Hindus, nor by the Romans and the Germans from the Greeks. It must have existed before the ancestors of these primeval races became separate in language and religion."[3]

c. History.

The historical records imbedded in the Bible are very ancient. Moses, who lived over thirty centuries ago and who is a trustworthy authority, had no trouble in ascribing a monotheistic belief to our first parents. Moreover, secular history confirms the Bible as to the antiquity of monotheism. "The earlier Greek poetry is more monotheistic than

---

[3] Mueller, *Science of Language*. 2nd Series, X.

the later. There is less polytheism in the Homeric theology than in that of Greece in the time of St. Paul."

Rawlinson maintains that "the primary doctrine of the esoteric religion of Egypt undoubtedly was the real essential unity of the divine nature. The gods of the popular mythology were understood in the esoteric religion to be either personified attributes of the Deity or parts of nature which he had created."[4]

A papyrus discovered in Thebes in the year 1847 and presented to the National Library in Paris is said to be the oldest book extant. It contains a treatise on manners written by Kakimo in 4450 B.C. and in its reference to God, He is spoken of in the singular number.[5]

Dorner says that "numerous historic traces of a monotheistic basis shine through polytheism and its background; and since it cannot be denied that the story of religion, like that of morals, exhibits numerous signs of a fall from a higher stage, of a process of depravation and return to barbarism, there is nothing of a historic character opposed to the theory that fetishism and polytheism are simply afterbirths following upon a better age."

II. THE NEED FOR THEOLOGY

The need for theology is as self-evident as the need for any other orderly statement of facts. Religion, the Bible, and the Church are undeniably facts of primary importance in the history of the race. They are the justification of theology, which has been properly called "the Queen of the Sciences."

1. The Character of the Bible

The most apparent need for theology comes from the character of the Scriptures. The Bible is not a theological treatise. It sets forth truth by way of law, commandment, history, poetry and parable, appealing to every age and every walk of life. It is a progressive revelation in con-

---

[4] Shedd, *Dogmatic Theology*. Pp. 214, 215.
[5] Wright, *Origin and Antiquity of Man*. Pp. 51-53.

tent and in method through centuries and covenants. Through it all runs a clear purpose and a unity of truth and this it is the province of theology to discover and to set forth. We might as well expect a scientific botany in nature as an articulated theology in the Bible. History testifies that the Bible needs to be scientifically interpreted in the light of the best reason and by the aid of the Holy Spirit. How can it be expected that its sacred contents should be comprehensively understood without classification and interpretation?

2. The Development of Doctrine

Moreover, theology deals with religious truth beyond that directly revealed in the Bible. While it bases its deductions upon the Scriptures, it takes into consideration the unfolding and developing of doctrine through the centuries. The Holy Spirit has led the Church to a constantly clearer conception of the truth. Through long struggles, as is evident from church history, the true doctrine has become more and more emancipated from error. It is the province of theology to summarize, to group, and to formulate the various results derived from Scripture, reason and experience. Thus is held the ground that is gained in the ceaseless conflict with error, and thus is conserved the best thought of the Church.

3. The Nature of the Church

The need for theology grows also out of the very nature of the Church, which is the community of all believers. It is vain to decry confessions, or creeds, or theology; they are as unavoidable as the constitutions, written or unwritten, which bind men in the same society. The Church is not organized on mere sentiment, sympathy, or fellowship. It is founded on the truth. It is a community of faith. There can be no real fellowship or coherence where there is no common standard as to the meaning of language or the content of faith. There can be no edifying worship, no consistent teaching in school or pulpit without some kind of theology.

4. The Idea of Proportion

The idea of proportion also demands a proper formulation of belief. No doctrine or phase of doctrine must be maintained at the expense of another. No unessential feature must be magnified; no abnormal development can be tolerated; for undue emphasis placed upon one idea must obscure others equally important. Theology aims at symmetry. It opposes barriers to fads and fanaticism. It strives to present the whole truth in right relations.

5. The Need for Defense

Theology is demanded as a means of defense against aggression. The first age of the Church was that of apologetics, in which the fathers maintained the divine origin and character of our holy religion. Then followed the age of polemics, in which the great question of Christ's divine Sonship was finally settled. Whether the danger comes from heresy within or from assault without, theology seeks to defend the faith. The creeds which it has formulated have been the bulwarks of the Church.

III. THE RELATIONS OF THEOLOGY

1. Its Relation to Reason

Reason or the exercise of the intellectual faculties holds the same relation to theology which it holds to other sciences. A conflict between reason and theology, when both are normal, is unthinkable. Theology can be formed only by the exercise of the mind, and it must always be in harmony with what is true. It is sometimes falsely said that faith is the opposite of reason. Faith is of the nature of a lofty intuition, which may transcend ordinary rational processes; but faith and reason go hand in hand, as is seen in the development of science and the ordinary affairs of life. It is entirely in accordance with reason that theology, which has to do with religion, should have a larger measure of the transcendent than physical science. But theology must always be rational.

2. Its Relation to Science

Theology is a science, and must conform to scientific canons. It is just as truly a science as astronomy, because it recognizes and organizes facts. That it is not infallible its best advocates will at once concede. It has erred in its observations and judgments, as all so-called sciences have. Perhaps it has been, on the whole, more free from error than physical science. It is unfair to contrast the theology of a dark age with the sciences of an enlightened period. The Church has always been the patron of learning. It is true that the Catholic Church has at times restricted investigation, but the Protestant Church promotes and fosters the freest inquiry after truth. The alleged conflicts between science and the Bible are fast disappearing under the more rational treatment of the facts of creation and the language of revelation.

3. Its Relation to Philosophy

What has been said about theology and science is in a large measure applicable also to theology and philosophy. As every man is somewhat of a theologian, so is he also somewhat of a philosopher. Theology and philosophy occupy in part the same ground. They both presume to investigate and to teach what is true concerning God and the world. "There is no province of human experience," says Caird, "there is nothing in the whole realm of reality which lies beyond the domain of philosophy, or to which philosophical investigation does not extend. Religion, so far from forming an exception to the all-embracing domain of philosophy, is rather just that province which lies nearest to it; for, in one point of view, religion and philosophy have common objects and a common content, and in the explanation of religion, philosophy may be said to be at the same time explaining itself."

While the domain and purpose of theology and philosophy are similar, their methods are different. Theology relies for its data chiefly upon the sacred Scriptures, receiving them as true, therefore as an adequate explanation of the universe as the creation of Almighty God. Philosophy seeks to attain knowledge through speculation and induction from data outside of revelation.   Rejecting or ignoring the latter and relying upon unaided reason, philosophy must fight its way through the deep obscurity surrounding our being and destiny.   Moreover, philosophy is largely abstract and impersonal, while theology revolves round a living, concrete personality, Jesus Christ.

At its birth Christianity was greeted with scorn by philosophy.   To the Greek the gospel was foolishness.   Yet efforts were not wanting to amalgamate philosophy and theology.   Philo, the learned Alexandrian Jew, endeavored to reconcile Plato and the Old Testament.   Gnosticism tried to do the same with the New.   The early fathers seem to have profited in some ways by their study of philosophy; nevertheless, in time it became a blight to the Church. Whether on the whole Christianity has gained or lost by contact with philosophy is an unsettled question.   The Reformers, revolting against the scholasticism of the Middle Ages, held philosophy in small esteem.   Luther with characteristic vehemence pronounced Aristotle a neighbor of the devil and a spoiler of pious doctrine.   This condemnation is, however, too sweeping.

Philosophy has, no doubt, rendered important service to religion not only by furnishing a dialectic for its logical presentation, but also by stimulating thought.   "It is only through the activity of the speculative reason," says Flint, "that religion is prevented from becoming a degrading anthropomorphism, that the mind is compelled to think of God not merely as a Father, King, and Judge, but as the Absolute and Infinite Being."

"Philosophy and science, however, are only methods. They cannot create, but only observe and interpret.   In Christianity something is offered for science to observe and for philosophy to interpret."

4.   Its Relation to Modern Thought

As a progressive science theology must be willing to accept all truth pertinent to it.   It must welcome the discoveries of archaeology, the results of scientific investigation in the domain of nature, the findings of history, psychology, and criticism. It need fear nothing which has value for human welfare. But it must reserve to itself the right of judgment, and be not hasty in letting go what is old.

There is much in so-called modern thought that is neither modern nor thoughtful. It is often the recrudescence of ancient error in modern garb. The Church dare not give up what she has found to be fundamental through age-long experience. While she is bound by her very nature to prove all things, she is bound also to hold fast to that which is good. Ancient orders have passed away. Former scientific theories have been rejected. But the Church in her essential and vital beliefs has survived the wreck of mere human institutions, and remains the one stable factor amid the constant changes in the world.

There is a "common assumption," says Illingworth, "that our modern knowledge is universally greater than that of bygone ages and that our opinions, therefore, upon all subjects are more likely to be true than those of the men of old. In certain large departments of thought, such as the physical sciences, or archæology, or critical scholarship, this is of course perfectly true. But there is one region and that for our present purpose the most important region in which it is conspicuously untrue, and that is the region of religious experience, the spiritual history of souls—their hopes and fears, their trials and temptations, their agonies and ecstasies, their heights of faith and depths of love. We, too, have our knowledge of these things, but it is distracted by a multitude of other interests, which had not dawned upon the horizon of the earlier world; whereas the absence of such distraction enabled the leading minds of older days to concentrate their attention upon the interior life and its vicissitudes. We may be scientific experts but they were spiritual experts."

IV.   THE SOURCES OF THEOLOGY

Whatever sheds light upon the problems which arise in the consideration of religion must be regarded as a source of theology.

1. The Bible

The chief source of Christian theology is naturally the record of the founding of Christianity and of its dominant ideas. The Christian religion is the religion of Jesus Christ revealed in the Holy Scriptures. These are the only original record of His life and teachings. In a real sense He is the content of the Bible. Whatever opinion one may have as to inspiration, the Scriptures make a powerful appeal to faith. The rejection of their authenticity leaves theology without any substantial basis and reduces it to vague speculation. The Bible is and must remain the chief seat of authority, not only for theology, but also for personal faith.

2. The Holy Spirit

The Bible is a spiritual book and communicates spiritual truth, which must be spiritually discerned. The natural man is incapable of spiritual discernment. He must be born again of the Holy Spirit, who not only moved men to write the sacred records, but who remains their interpreter, and who is the Guide into all truth. Without His illumination, theology is a mere academic pursuit without saving power.

3. Religious Experience

The chief secondary source of theology is personal religious experience. The experience of the Christian community is of undoubted value, for unless a teaching commends itself to serious and intelligent persons, and produces in them and in their lives the effect which its acceptance promises, it should not be received as true. How far any experience may be taken as authoritative will be considered in another connection.

4. The Creeds

The creeds of Christendom, as the expression of the common historic faith of the Church, are also a secondary but by no means an unimportant source in theology. They epitomize the doctrines which survived in the struggle between truth and error. They are not monuments of a dead past, but landmarks in the progress of truth. Their content bears evidence of earnest thought and deep devotion, while their rhythmic language fits some to be a part of the liturgy of the Church. A refusal to give creeds the proper weight, as testimony to the profound conviction and experiences of centuries, shows an absence of the historic spirit and the presence of a deep-seated prejudice against the aspect of truth which they affirm.

5. Anthropology

Whatever pertains to man—his nature, his history, his achievements, his hopes and his fears—ought not to be considered foreign to theology. Whatever he is, thinks or does, has to do with his eternal destiny. Therefore, anthropology in its widest sense yields rich results to the studious theologian. Above everything else theology must be related to man as he is, and to his daily life wherever he may be found. A theology which ignores the average man fails to utilize its best material.

6. The Universe

The physical universe in which we live must be considered a source of theology, for it bears witness to the existence, power, wisdom and love of its Creator. The psalmist has well said:

"The heavens declare the glory of God
And the firmament showeth His handiwork."

The apostle Paul restrained the Lystrians from idolatry, saying, "God left not Himself without witnesses in that He did good, and gave from heaven rains and fruitful seasons filling your hearts with food and gladness." The Master Himself appealed to the lilies of the field and to the birds of the air as witnesses of God's Providence.

The separation of theology into two distinct divisions, natural and revealed, seems now quite unnecessary and unreal. No doubt much may be learned from nature, much more indeed than the fathers dreamed, but it should be studied as a part of the revelation of the good God which culminated in the coming of our Lord.

V. THE METHOD OF THEOLOGY

Theology is no exception to the rule that all branches of study should be pursued systematically and with a distinct aim. As theology deals with the most important truths, it should be presented in an orderly way.

1. Terminology

First of all, the language of theology should be as simple as possible. Archaic and technical terminology should be avoided, especially in a work intended for students rather than for scholars. A violation of this principle is responsible in part for the misconception that theology is merely a scholastic pursuit unrelated to life. Technical terms cannot be avoided altogether, but their meaning should be evident from the context. The language of the ancients was no doubt the very best for them, but the growth of ideas and the constant change in the meaning of words require language which clearly expresses the present apprehension of truth.

2. The Scientific Process

Theology claims to be a true science, because it follows chiefly the inductive method, which requires (1) exact observation, (2) correct interpretation of observed facts, (3) rational explanation of these facts, and (4) orderly construction coordinating and systematizing these facts. But theology cannot be confined in its treatment of the phenomena of the higher life to the narrow sphere of a natural science. Theology looks toward finality and infinity; science is mundane. Hence theology is more than science though in harmony with it. Theology takes cognizance of intuitions, convictions, and revelations which transcend the facts with which ordinary science deals. Nevertheless, all these must be treated in an orderly manner.

3. The Point of View of Methodology

In the limited and more technical sense, methodology has a particular reference to the controlling principle or the point of view of theology. It is concerned about the central dominating idea, around which the system revolves. Unless a true center be found, theology will be erratic, as was ancient astronomy, which made the earth and not the sun the center of the system. Various methods have been applied in the construction of theological systems. The more important are (1) the anthropological, which makes sinful man the center, (2) the Trinitarian, which emphasizes the divine sovereignty (Calvinism), and (3) the Christo-centric, which makes the Person and the work of Jesus Christ the center (Lutheranism).

The "method" differentiates the two great Reformation theologies, the Lutheran and the Reformed, or the Calvinistic. The Lutheran makes Christ the center of its theology, the Reformed takes the sovereignty of God as its pivotal point and truth.

The advocates of the latter theology deny that the former is logical or natural. They hold that the Trinity is the basis and starting-point, that Christology is only a division of theology, that Christ is only a single person of the Trinity, redemption only one of the works of God, and sin an anomaly in the universe, not an original and necessary fact, and that, therefore, the Christological method is fractional (Shedd). The Christo-centric method has recently been disparaged by a great Calvinistic divine, Dr. Patton, who likens dogmas to blocks which may be built into any shape without affecting the significance of each. "You may build castles or cathedrals," says he, "but however much you may change the relations of these blocks to each other, you do not on that account change the individuality of each." It is true that the individuality is not changed by mere transfer, but the importance of the block may be thus immensely altered. A block may be removed from a solid wall without materially affecting it; but the keystone of an arch cannot be taken away without causing a collapse.

It seems most in accord with the nature of the case that we should approach God as He has approached us, that is, through Christ. For out of Christ God is not truly known, "No man hath seen God at any time: the only begotten Son, who is in the bosom of the Father, he hath declared him"

(John 1: 18). "No man knoweth the Father, save the Son, and he to whomsoever the Son willeth to reveal him" (Matt. 11: 27).

The Christo-centric method does not imply that a system of dogmatic theology must begin with Christology. It rather demands the contrary, for "the center is not the beginning but it throws light on the beginning and on the end. Christology furnished the key for theology and anthropology—the doctrine of God and the doctrine of man" (Schaff).

Theology is greatly simplified by starting with Christ, for here is a concrete fact, a *Personality*. "The doctrine of Christ," says Schaff, "is the soul and center of all sound Christian theology." Moreover, as in the first centuries the conflict waged round the person of Christ, so in the latter years this same question is again uppermost. Even from a philosophical standpoint, Christ must be the determining element. The historical spirit cannot ignore "the Supreme Person of history. He has left the mark of his hand on every generation of civilized men that has lived since He lived, and it would not be science to find Him everywhere, and never to ask what He was and what He did."

Fairbairn, a leading Christian philosopher, says: "The Lutheran theology is essentially a soteriology, a science of the Redeemer's Person and work, profoundly conscious of man's sin and the grace by which he is saved. To it two things were necessary—the Scriptures, the source of all knowledge of the justifying Person—and the Sacraments, means by which His people communicate with Him, especially in the act of His passion and death. The philosophers who have most strenuously handled and most nearly solved the problem (of the Incarnation) have been the sons of the land of the Church of Luther, and the theologians of other lands and churches that have today attempted through the Incarnation to vivify theology and relate it to modern knowledge are only paying unconscious but deserved homage to the faith and insight of the Reformer and his sons."

As the Scriptures are the "formal principle" of the Reformation so the doctrine of justification by faith is its "material principle." This is Luther's doctrine of "a standing or a falling Church." The question is still discussed, What is the distinguishing doctrine of the Lutheran Church? Sometimes it is said to be justification, and again the sacraments. A truer answer is, the emphasis which it places on the Person of Christ. The object of faith in justification is nothing less than Christ, and the union and the communion which are set forth in the sacraments are union and communion with Christ, the living Head.

"This is the most important article of the Christian faith," says Luther, "that the Son is true God and also true man, and that He was sent into the world to save it." Concerning this Koestlin says: "Everything is thus made to depend on the article concerning Christ, the Son of God sent into the world, who has secured forgiveness of sins and eternal life. Whosoever has this Christ has all things. This article and that upon justification are one."

APOLOGETICS

1. Definition

The word apology is derived from the Greek *apologia* which means a defense. Historically the first apologies in the post-apostolic Church were of the nature of explanations of the character and mission of Christianity. Later, when the new religion was attacked, its apology became polemic. It is in the former sense that apology is used here.

Apologetics is that department of learning which investigates and establishes the grounds of Christian theology. Hence, it is antecedent to theology, whose function is to build upon the foundation the super-structure of doctrine. It may be called general or fundamental apologetics as over against special apologetics, which may be invoked to vindicate particular phases of Christian belief. In the light of increasing knowledge, the arguments advanced to establish fundamental truth may require re-statement. Their variety and cumulative power, however, are so great that no fear need be entertained that the foundation will ever be moved.

2. Importance

It has sometimes been urged that it is useless to advance so-called rational proofs for the existence of God, because on the one hand God cannot be known through reason, and on the other mere argument does not convert. A little reflection will show that these assertions are quite unreasonable and, indeed, untrue. Kant affirmed that pure reason is incapable of demonstrating the divine existence. It has been shown, however, that this attitude leads to universal scepticism, and destroys confidence in all mental operations.

In reference to the objection that arguments do not convert it is enough to appeal to the fact that a reasonable statement carries conviction to open-minded persons. The presentation of valid argument may at least prepare the way for the spiritual change which is a divine work in the soul.   One of the chief purposes of apologetics is the confirmation of existing faith and the dispelling of honest doubt.

3. The Fundamental Purpose

The fundamental idea of Christian apology is the vindication of theism.   The word theism in its broadest sense indicates a belief in the existence of God, or gods, as over against atheism or the denial of this belief.   In the present connection the word is used to indicate the belief in the personality and sovereignty of the good God, who has created and governs the universe, and who has revealed Himself supernaturally to mankind.   "Theism," as Dods says, "is simply the declaration that this world cannot be rationally construed without the hypothesis of purpose and of a mind in which this purpose is formed and by which it is guided; that is to say, that God has revealed Himself in the constitution of the world and of man" (The Bible, p. 68).

4. Relation to Dogmatics

The task of apologetics in relation to dogmatics is the establishment of a reasonable ground for the belief in the existence of God, and for the acceptance of the Bible as the revelation of God.

A. THE EXISTENCE OF GOD

The existence of a Supreme Being may be taken as a postulate of theology upon the ground of the universality of religion.   The denial of the divine existence is confined to the few.   The census of India, taken in 1911, revealed that among a population of over three hundred millions only seventeen persons described themselves as atheists and only fifty-one as agnostics.   This is a fair illustration of the general attitude of mankind.   Nevertheless, to make assurance doubly sure and to lay a secure ground for the treatment of the doctrine of God, it is worth while to consider the more important fundamental proofs of the existence of God. We use the word proofs advisedly, because the evidences are so numerous and strong as to dispel all doubts concerning this matter.

I. THE WITNESS OF JESUS CHRIST

1. The Chief Witness of God

God has not left Himself without witness. The heavens declare His glory and the firmament shows His handiwork. He has written His name on all His works. The clearest and most final testimony which He has given is found in Jesus Christ. "God, having of old time spoken unto the fathers in the prophets by divers portions and in divers manners, hath at the end of these days spoken unto us in his Son" (Heb. 1: 1-2).

2. A Character of History

The belief in God as revealed in Christ is a matter of faith and life. It rests, however, upon a historic foundation. The question, What think ye of Christ? cannot honestly be evaded. He must be interpreted. No one would for a moment deny that He came into the world about two thousand years ago, that He was born under humble circumstances, that He went about doing good, that He was the greatest teacher whom the world has ever seen, that He died a martyr to the truth, and on the third day rose again. These undeniable facts invest Him with unique interest.

3. His Ethical Perfection

Even a cursory study of Christ's life and teachings reveals His ethical perfection. One of His followers says that He did no sin, neither was guile found in His mouth (I Pet. 2: 22). In the light of centuries He stands out pure and spotless. He made no mistakes. His moral judgments have stood the test of succeeding generations. He illuminated human life and destiny and made plain the path of duty. His teachings have become the ideal standard for personal and social life. His truth and tenderness, His sacrificial love and power are drawing all men unto Him. In Him was life and His life was the light of men.

4. His Idea of God

All that Jesus Christ was and did and taught was connected with His idea of God. Him He revealed as a loving Father, who gave His only-begotten Son for the salvation of men. He interprets God as a Person, He communed with Him. He knew Him, saw Him, and lived with Him. He proclaimed Him with absolute assurance. There is not a shadow of doubt in His teaching as to the existence and love of God. This is not the place to follow the suggestions as to the Deity of Christ. It is enough to say that the best, the noblest, the greatest, the wisest man that ever lived had a clear consciousness of God.

5. Finality in His Testimony

Jesus Christ is the most convincing, the final argument for the existence of God. We need go no further. In Him we have a complete answer to every problem concerning God. We believe Him when He says, "He that hath seen me hath seen the Father." A historic knowledge of Christ carries with it the inevitable thought of the reality of God, and a personal acceptance of Him as Teacher and Saviour dispels all intellectual doubts as to the actual existence and nature of God, as the almighty Maker of heaven and of earth.

II. THE WITNESS OF MAN

1. The Personality of Man

Next to the testimony of Christ as to the reality of God as an infinite and absolute Person, we would rate the witness of the personality of man.

Man is not a mere animal; he is much more. He is essentially mind. He thinks, reflects, and resolves. He possesses intellect, self-consciousness, and self-determination. He is far above nature about him. He studies to subdue it and use it for his own purposes. He is conscious that he is above matter, that he is a spiritual entity, an ego. He is the highest form of existence of which he has immediate knowledge.

When he reflects upon his origin he is inevitably led to

the conclusion that he cannot be the product of so-called nature, for the less cannot produce the greater by any conceivable process of evolution. He must have come from mind or spirit; not vague and undefined, but a person like himself yet far greater than he. It is impossible to explain human personality without postulating a personal creator. This truth seems so clear and so self-evident that it forms one of the strongest evidences of the existence of a supreme being.

2. The Religious Nature of Man

Man is not only a person, but a person of the highest order. He is a moral personality. He has a sense of right and wrong, of obligation. He has a religious nature. There is that within him which arouses aspirations after One higher than himself. He instinctively worships and prays. He recognizes that the tribunal of his conscience is but the type of an external tribunal of a supreme law-giver and judge. Sir William Hamilton, with these facts in view, declared that the only valid arguments for the existence of God and the immortality of the soul rest upon the ground of man's moral nature.

3. The Religious Experience of Man

The metaphysical proofs offered to demonstrate the divine existence are not to be rejected as Kant rejected them when he declared that "pure reason" is inadequate. Nevertheless, his appeal to what he calls "practical reason" or experience is of the highest value. The final appeal for the acceptance of a teaching lies necessarily in practice. If, therefore, the thought of God and what may be taught concerning Him bring into the life of the believer certain convictions, in which he finds rest, and which help him in the tasks and under the burdens of life, he will have for himself, at least, the best proof of the reality of what he accepts. Our Lord Himself invited a personal test of His doctrines when He says, "If any man willeth to do his will, he shall know of the teaching, whether it is of God, or whether I speak from myself" (John 7: 17).

It is perfectly legitimate to invoke the witness of the experience of evangelical Christians as to the existence and character of God. Millions upon millions of the most advanced and thoughtful members of the most progressive nations unite in the testimony that faith in God not only satisfies their craving after the knowledge of a supreme being, but also fills them with a desire to do what is right, and enables them to triumph over fear and evil. The nobility, intelligence, and number of these believers forbids the explanation that they are laboring under a delusion.

4. The Idea of God

1) ITS EXISTENCE.

The idea of God underlies all religions. Before God can be worshiped He must be thought of, and thought of as real. Religion presupposes the existence of God. The universality of religion, therefore, indicates the universality of the idea of God.

2) ITS ORIGIN.

(1) A primeval revelation.

It has been thought by many that when God created man in His own image He would naturally and necessarily reveal Himself to man, and that such a revelation was supplemented by theophanies, such as are mentioned in the Old Testament. The original knowledge of God, it is maintained, never completely died out. The good would cherish such knowledge and the evil would not be able through fear to divest themselves of it.

This theory has much plausibility with those especially who accept literally the Biblical story of man's creation. It would seem to be in accord with the love of the divine Father that He should make Himself known to His child. Moreover, it is true that no nation or individual today has a clear knowledge of God except through an objective, external revelation.

(2) Intuition.

The origin of the idea of God is attributed by many to simple intuition. By this is meant that man is directly conscious of God, that he has what has been called a "God-consciousness." This certainly is not tenable, for God is not part of man, nor man part of God. Consciousness cannot discover anything apart from the man himself. He can be conscious only of his endowments and states.

There is, however, what is called by Harris the "intuition of reason" by which is meant that the human mind is so constituted that evidences of the divine existence, found in His works, in man himself, and in nature about him, make a direct appeal to him and create an immediate conviction that God exists.

Harris says, "In the intuition of reason we have immediate and self-evident knowledge of universal and necessary principles. Our consciousness is not merely that they are true, but that they must be true. Thought cannot transcend them, but must be regulated by them. When apprehended in reflection they present themselves as judgments and may be formulated in propositions. The knowledge of particular realities is given in sense perception and self-consciousness. Rational intuition does not give knowledge of these realities, but only of principles always and everywhere true of these realities. The reality of our knowledge of God is a primitive datum of consciousness. Man being rational is so constituted that in the presence of God and of His various manifestations of Himself, he will know that he knows God in the act of knowing Him."[1]

Plato found the idea of God in the essential principles of knowledge and not in the phenomena of the visible world. "He denied that sense is knowledge and that visible things can be more than images and indications of truth. He maintained, however, that besides the visible world there is an intelligible world with objects which reason sees and senses. These objects . . . are necessary and eternal in themselves."[2]

Harris and Plato agree practically in the general conception of rational intuition, though not of sense perception.

---

[1] Harris, *The Philosophical Basis of Theism*. P. 114.
[2] Flint, *Theism*. P. 270f.

(3) Inference.

The origin of the idea of God is ascribed by the most profound thinkers to the conclusion which the mind draws and is compelled to draw from the constitution of man himself and of nature about him.   Flint remarks, "Our entire spiritual being is constituted for the apprehension of God in and through His works.   All the essential principles of mental action when applied to the meditative consideration of finite things lead up from them to infinite creative wisdom.   The whole of nature external to us is a revelation of God; the whole nature within us has been made for the reception and interpretation of that revelation."   He holds, therefore, that theism is perfectly explicable without intuition.[3]

5.   The Ontological Argument

This is an argument derived from the idea of God, which implies the necessity of His existence.   It is somewhat in line with Plato's doctrine of ideas.   It received its formulation by Anselm (1033-1109).   Though usually regarded as too abstruse to be of value, the ontological argument may be so construed as to be not only valuable but even convincing.

Put into syllogistic form the argument may be presented as follows: We have an idea of a perfect being.   Existence is a necessary attribute of perfection.   Therefore, the perfect being exists.   This has been ridiculed, because the conception of the alleged perfect being might be purely fanciful and grotesque.   But so profound a thinker as Anselm could hardly have fallen into a transparent error. In fact, he uses his argument merely as a confirmation of faith in the existence of God.

The argument may be restated in a more plausible form as follows: The mind is so constituted that it requires the postulate of a perfect self-existent being as the ground of the universe.   So universal a requirement demands an objective reality—a real perfect being.   Therefore the perfect being exists.

---

[3] Flint, *Theism*.   Pp. 79, 83.

This argument may not amount to an actual demonstration, but it furnishes such a strong ground of probability that it becomes at least a confirmatory factor in apologetics. In the ordinary affairs of life and in scientific experimentation probabilities relatively much weaker than this are grounds of belief and action. It is inconceivable that man's nature is a lie, that he has universal longings, ideas and beliefs without an actual counterpart. Just as the senses demand things to see, to hear, to feel, to smell, to taste, so does the soul demand a God who exists. The psalmist declared "My soul thirsteth for God, for the living God" (Ps. 42:2).

III. THE WITNESS OF THE UNIVERSE
1. The Universe an Effect

Is the universe eternal or temporal? Is it self-existent or is it an effect? These questions must be answered by the universe itself. A superficial examination of the earth readily shows that its present condition is the product of countless ages of steady persistent change. A deeper study of nature reveals the undoubted fact that antecedent to the later and apparently more orderly development in earth and sky there was a chaotic or nebulous state of matter. In the graphic language of Genesis, "The earth was waste and void; and darkness was upon the face of the deep."

2. The Cosmological Argument

The perpetual changes everywhere evident have led to the conclusion that nature is an effect, and that, therefore, it must have been caused. This has led to the formulation of the so-called cosmological or more properly aeteological argument for the existence of God. In syllogistic form it is as follows: Every new thing and every new change in a previously existing thing must have a cause, anterior, exterior and sufficient. The universe being finite and dependent and constantly changing is an effect. Therefore it must have a cause, sufficient and antecedent. James Lindsay holds that "the first cause argument customarily presented as an inference from effect to cause is invalid. As an argument, however, from the contingent character of the world to the necessity for a world-ground, it retains validity and worth. Such self-existent and eternal world-ground or first cause is, by an inexorable law of thought the necessary correlate of finitude. Though we must reason to Him from data of sense, yet the view so gained may be regarded as our first and most fundamental conception of God, as involving an absolute being necessarily existing. God and the world are not to be conceived as cause and effect, for modern metaphysics can by no possibility regard such an expression of the connection between the world of experience and the ground of all possible experience as anything like adequate. The true abiding first cause is God, taken as the ultimate and absolute ground of the possibility of everything that is, the self-existent cause of the ever-present world and its phenomena" (Ency. of Ethics).

Let us look more closely at the syllogism. The major premise is indisputable, being based upon the axiom that every effect must have a cause, and that everything that has begun to be must have been originated.

The minor premise is not self-evident to all, and should be demonstrated in order to be valid and to carry conviction.

The conclusion even if allowed, it is maintained, shows at best that the creator of the universe may after all be finite. The argument contends only for a creator. That being won, the character of the creator becomes the subject of further study and deduction.

In reference to the minor premise, it is asserted that it begs the question, because it assumes what is only apparently but not actually true. The constant change on the face of nature is, of course, undeniable. But it is claimed that beneath these changes there is a "permanent element" which J. S. Mill defined as "the specific elementary substance or substances of which it consists and their inherent properties." "These," says Mill, "are known to us as beginning to exist. Within the range of human knowledge they had no beginning and consequently no cause; though they themselves are causes or concauses of everything that takes place. Experience, therefore, affords no evidences nor even analogies to justify our extending to the apparently immovable, a generalization grounded only on our observation of the changeable."

This implies that matter is eternal. When inquiry is made into the nature of matter, we are told that it consists of molecules, which may be separated into atoms, and these into ions, and these into electrons. It is said also that these are endowed with energy, and that matter and energy are alike indestructible.

For the sake of argument let us accept the alleged "conservation of energy and of matter." Let us inquire whether the orderly arrangement of the universe can be accounted for without mind, to marshal the mighty forces of nature and form the magnificent effect which is apparent on every side.

"Did the atoms take counsel together," asks Flint, "and devise a common plan and work it out? That hypothesis is unspeakably absurd, yet it is rational in comparison with the notion that these atoms combined by mere chance, and by chance produced such a universe as that in which we live. . . It is millions to one that they would never produce the simplest of the regular arrangements which we comprehend under the designation of the course of nature, or the lowest of vegetable or animal organisms; millions of millions to one that they would never produce a solar system, the earth, the animal kingdom of human history."

The evidence of mind in the universe forces the postulate of one supreme intelligence. Otherwise its order and unity are unaccountable. This postulate leaves us for the moment, at least, in the dilemma of dualism, the co-existence of eternal matter and eternal mind which was practically the belief of the ancients, who were without a supernatural revelation. To us, however, such an assumption is intolerable and happily unnecessary.

Spirit and matter undoubtedly exist in the present world but matter is everywhere subject to mind. To deny supremacy to the latter is unphilosophical and untrue. Matter cannot account for mind and personality, in spite of the assertion of materialists. It is inconceivable also that an eternal mind could be bound by eternal matter. Under such conditions there could be no great first cause, free and untrammeled.

The whole subject is complicated by the existence of what we know as energy, which is variously defined. Some regard it as an entity apart from matter and others as a force produced by matter under certain relations or combinations. Whatever it may be, it acts in accordance with certain intelligible laws, such as gravitation. Being subject to law that can be measured, it must have originated in mind and not in inert, dumb matter.

According to all theories the individual atoms or electrons which compose matter are finite, and hence no aggregation however great can be infinite. As mind is sufficient to account for the universe, the conclusion is inevitable that matter is a creature and not an eternal existence. The universe had a beginning. "In the beginning God created the heavens and the earth." The dilemma of dualism vanishes.

3. The Conservation of Matter and Energy

Can it be shown that the universe will have an end? If the doctrine of the conservation of energy be true then the universe will not cease. The form of things may indeed be vastly changed and even chaos may again prevail. But is this doctrine of the future eternity of matter and energy true? Frankly, I do not know. The belief in an absolute creator is not put in jeopardy by the acceptance of the conservation of energy; for it is conceivable that in the creation of the universe God intended that it should henceforth continue in some form.

The disintegration of matter is obvious. Hence it has been contended that nature will finally exhaust itself and go into complete nothingness. After an exhaustive study of the subject a recent writer says: "It is almost certain that the present energy of the universe is the result or effect of this destructive or disintegrating process of so-called matter. Thus, while radium is disintegrating there is a manifestation of energy, and when disintegration has been accomplished its energy has ceased. So as electricity is only the passing of electrons from atoms to atoms, it, too, is the result of disintegration. And when that disintegration has gone to the point of equalization or equilibrium, the current stops and energy disappears. And if the electron is nothing but energy, with its passage into electricity, etc., there must be a dematerialization of matter. What we call matter would thus be only a manifestation of energy, and would therefore disappear when that energy would be spent" (Gruber, Creation Ex Nihilo, p. 232).

Others vehemently contend that in no conceivable way will energy and matter cease to be. To those who deny an absolute creation this contention seems to be justified. It is a necessary corollary of the eternity of matter. If it can be shown that in the attrition of the stupendous forces operative in the universe nothing is lost and everything conserved the Christian believer must interpret these conditions as being in harmony with the divine purpose in creation. The annihilation of matter is not taught in the Scriptures.

The apostle Peter may indeed be quoted as saying, "The heavens that now are and the earth by the same word (which ordained the flood) have been stored up for fire being reserved against the day of judgment and destruction of ungodly men. . . . . The heavens shall pass away with a great noise and the elements shall be dissolved with fervent heat, and the earth and the works that are therein shall be burned up." This might indicate absolute annihilation but for two facts: first the allusion to the flood which did not annihilate, but only changed the face of nature; and secondly, Peter's further language, "But according to his promise we look for new heavens and a new earth, wherein dwelleth righteousness" (II Peter 3:13).

To this may be added the Scripture teaching in reference to the future of the saints, who will possess glorified bodies suited to the spiritual state in which they shall live. Matter is not evil; it has no moral character. It is in harmony, therefore, with Christian faith to believe that the all-wise

God has ordained that in the glorious transformation which will take place when it pleases Him, His children shall have new bodies and live in a new environment, which may be simply a transformation of what was old.

The witness of the universe to a great creator is found also in the realm of life. There is no evidence there that life even in its most primitive form has been produced by energy or matter. Spontaneous generation is no longer seriously held. All investigations and experiments have failed to account for its existence from a purely naturalistic viewpoint. Otherwise sober scientists suggested that life may have found its way to the earth from other planets, as the wind wafts the pollen of the flower. But this theory would not account for life at all, only its diffusion. When life in its highest stages is contemplated, we are forced to accept the simple, ancient story that God created man in His own image.

Should it be demonstrated at any time that life may be produced from matter it would not necessarily contradict theism; it would be only another proof that the infinite creator has lodged extraordinary potency in matter.

4. The Teleological Argument

The witness of the universe for the existence of God is clear and strong not only from the evidence of a first cause, but also from that of a final cause. The latter is known as the teleological argument, and is based upon evidence of design in the universe. Science is based on the presumption that nature is intelligible, that it is controlled by law, that there is nothing fortuitous about it. In a word, nature has been constructed and is regulated by a mind, great enough for so stupendous a task. Not only do stars move in their orderly courses from generation to generation, but atoms and electrons are obedient to the laws to which the supreme mind has attuned them.

Vainly have the objectors to teleology ridiculed this argument. They have tried to show that at best it would prove only a wise arrangement of matter in a finite universe and that the deduction of an infinite creator is illogical. But making even this concession, the step from finitude to infinity in this case is easy. The human mind cannot rest in less than an absolute creator. The objection to teleology by anti-theistic evolutionists is even more puerile. That a fortuitous concord of atoms could frame laws which govern them, and which produce the extraordinary objects in nature with their wonderful properties is inconceivably absurd.

The argument from design is simple and convincing. In logical form it is as follows: Whatever exhibits marks of design must have an intelligent maker. The universe has such marks. Therefore the universe must have an intelligent creator.

The major premise seems to be a self-evident proposition. It is capable of proof within the range of human observation. The minor premise can be shown to be true both in organic and inorganic existence. Two striking illustrations of the former may be found in the construction of the eye and the ear, of the latter in physics and chemistry. For details special works on natural theism should be consulted.

IV.   THE WITNESS OF THE BIBLE

We do not here offer proofs that the sacred scriptures of the Christian are the inspired Word of God, whom they profess to reveal.

There are, however, certain undeniable facts in regard to the Bible which make it a very important witness in the case in hand. Its great age is undoubted. Its newest parts have been extant for nearly two thousand years and its oldest parts probably twice as long. It is the most widely circulated of all books and has influenced as has no other. It has moulded civilization by its lofty ideals and is the inspiration of nearly all great ideas that are invoked to make the world better. The soul of man is conscious that the Bible is the best interpreter of his mind and desires. It offers the best explanation of his origin and destiny, and sheds the clearest light on his history. Its authenticity is being constantly corroborated by scientific investigations.

The history, character and abiding influence of the Bible cannot be accounted for except by its own postulate that it is the message and the revelation of the infinite God. All attacks upon it have failed to remove the presumption that it is true.

V. THE WITNESS OF HISTORY

Atheism, as has already been remarked, is uncommon. A belief in some kind of superior being is the usual faith of mankind. In presenting, therefore, an argument from history for the existence of the true God, the following points will appear most striking.

1. The Universality of Religion

The idea of God, the instinct of worship, rites and ceremonies dealing with things supernatural are as widespread as the human race. The religious beliefs and usages of a people are as much and as real a part of their history as their political institutions, their achievements and their failures. How imperfect would be the history of the ancient people without reference to their mythologies, their altars and their temples, the magnificent ruins of which bear testimony to the earnest faith of those who reared them!

History reveals a moral order, resting upon a universal faith in an infinite arbiter of human destiny. Without a belief in some such "power not of ourselves which makes for righteousness" society could not exist. Even in the rudest form of society, there are abundant evidences of the rudiments of moral law.

A belief in retribution is the common faith of all peoples in all ages. The ancient Greeks believed in an avenging Nemesis, who pursued her victims with relentless fury. The heathen Melitans, when they saw a venomous reptile fastening itself on St. Paul's hand, immediately concluded that he was a murderer whom justice would not suffer to live (Acts 28: 4).

The ancients rightly did not limit rewards and punishments to the present life. They believed in immortality whose character was determined by the kind of life lived on earth.

These vague religious instincts and beliefs are not signs of absolute delusion, but rather of a perversion of a necessary and noble possession. With the growth of culture, the human race has not cast away religion, but recognizes it as a normal and indispensable part of individual and social life. Wherever through false philosophy or absorption in material things a nation has given religion a secondary or nominal place, its own security and perpetuity have been threatened by an inevitable decay of morals.

2. The Blessedness of Religion

All real religion has a beneficent effect. Even in a perverted form, its doctrine of an omniscient God exercises a restraining influence upon society, in moderating passion and in checking impulses which would set the world aflame. In recent years the government of Japan called together leading men of various religious sects and begged them to lay down principles of faith and morality for the guidance of the people. It is doubtful whether any statesman in the world, whatever his personal belief, would advocate the extirpation of religion from his country.

3. The Nature of Christianity

The final and sufficient proof of the existence of God is found in the history of Christianity, whose long trial and inherent character prove it to be the absolute religion. It has given to the world an ethical code which vindicates its claim to be supernatural. Nothing loftier in the relations of men and of nations is conceivable. Its practice establishes confidence in all human dealings and insures abiding peace. It is restorative and ennobling, lifting up men and nations to the highest degree of excellence. The key to human progress must be sought in the Christian faith. Back of the Christian faith is the Christian God, who in the fullness of time sent His only Son into the world to reveal Him as our Heavenly Father.

VI.˙ SOME ANTI-THEISTIC THEORIES

After a presentation of theistic proofs, unanswerable in their cumulative force, it does not seem necessary to discuss anti-theistic theories at great length. However, a casual mention seems to be demanded. There are many phases of unbelief, but they all end in practical atheism, or the denial of an absolute, personal Spirit. Of course, a universal negation is incapable of proof and so might be dismissed as unreasonable. But the positive character of unbelief for evil is undoubted and it should be resisted and exposed.

The three dominant forms of unbelief in our time are agnosticism, materialism, and idealism.

1. Agnosticism

Agnosticism, as a philosophical theory, is the doctrine that God cannot be known to exist because to be known He must be classed. Spencer affirmed that "the first cause, the infinite, the absolute, to be known at all must be classed. To be positively thought of, it must be thought of as such or such—as of this or that kind. Can it be like in kind to anything of which we have sensible experience? Obviously not" (First Principles).

The answer to this is not difficult. The Author of the universe can be classed, because He has given unmistakable evidence that He is a person. He is like us. He thinks; He acts from motive; He loves. He has everywhere expressed Himself as a person and nowhere more plainly than in man. It is true that we cannot know Him in all His fullness, but we can know Him as a child knows his parents. The idea of personality is most potent in the formation of our conceptions of God. The more fully we realize what is comprehended in personality, the more clearly will we be able to understand not only that God is, but also in a measure what He is.

Agnosticism must be rejected because it is purely negative and unreasonable. It rests on nothing and comes to nothing. It is a simple denial of what is apparent to most men. Its ethical effect must be disastrous, because it eliminates a sense of continuity, and of responsibility to a higher power.

2. Materialism

This theory, as expounded by Haeckel, holds that the universe is eternal, infinite and illimitable substance in eternal motion.   Its two attributes are matter and energy. Tyndall declared that "we find in matter the promise and potency of every form and quality of life."   In short, matter is everything or the source of everything.   There is no God, unless the universe itself is God.   Materialism is no longer dominant among the unbelieving, and must be rejected because it is founded on assertion rather than on calm investigation.   Among the more evident reasons for its rejection are the following:

1) It fails to account for personality — for mind and spirit.   In its application of the evolutionary hypothesis it derives the higher from the lower and thus reverses the law of causality.

2) It fails to account for life.   It has produced no evidence that life comes from mere matter.

3) It contradicts the highest instincts of the race and leaves man without incentive and without hope.

4) If thought be a mere secretion of the brain, and consciousness a modification of matter and energy, then all so-called moral obligation is a delusion.

3. Idealism

Idealism or idealistic monism is a philosophic theory of the universe, quite the opposite of materialism, but like it in its denial of a personal God.   Materialism teaches that matter is the original sole substance endowed with eternal energy.   Idealism claims that mind, thought, idea, volition and the like are eternal and the source of all things.   Such terms as "thought" and "idea," however, are not taken as realities but rather as abstract terms.   Clifford speaks of the source of everything as "mind-stuff"—whatever that may be.   Lest eternal mind be interpreted, in the Christian sense, as God, the idealist promptly denies any such connotation.

Idealism is as old as Plato, and has come down to us through Kant and his followers, who sought to stand in friendly relation to Christianity, but who in reality denied its fundamental postulate of a personal God. In these latter days Eucken and Bergson, in their revolt from materialism, have taught the primacy of spirit, but they have come to no conclusion as to the existence of a Supreme Being and they are perfectly sure if He exists Jesus Christ is not His Son.

Idealism must be rejected as a form of unbelief which contradicts Christianity with its explicit teachings of a personal God, of the sinfulness of man, of the need of redemption, and of high moral motives. It is, after all, at its best a mere philosophy, which like all philosophy unaided by revelation gives to the poor aching heart of man no divine bosom to lean upon.

B. THE DIVINE REVELATION

The existence of the absolute person, whom we call God, cannot reasonably be doubted in view of the overwhelming evidence in its favor. The question naturally arises, Has God spoken? Has He revealed Himself? A common reply is that He has certainly spoken through creation and thus revealed His wisdom and power. Another reply goes farther and says that He reveals Himself through His providence in caring for His creatures. But these answers are evasive. Has God spoken in a supernatural way? Has He revealed His purpose concerning man?

The Christian declares that God has spoken as man to man, that He has in this or that way impressed the human mind with a knowledge of religious truth, and that the record of these revelations is found in the Bible. This brings the matter before us in a concrete manner. Is the Bible a revelation of God? Was it given to the world by men to whom God spoke?

Before considering the evidence concerning the Bible as a divine revelation it is well to inquire into the question of the possibility and probability of such a revelation. These form what has been called the presumptive evidence of a divine revelation. The consideration of the positive evidence will follow.

I. THE PRESUMPTIVE EVIDENCE

1. The Possibility of a Divine Revelation

(1) The ground of possibility is found in personality. All our reasoning concerning ourselves assures us that man is a person, endowed with intelligence, self-consciousness, and self-determination. We have seen that personality has its origin in self-existent personality, which is nothing else than God. When we remember that God is an infinite, absolute person, we can no longer doubt that He is capable of making Himself known to His rational creatures, whom He has endowed with like personality.

(2) While this is generally acknowledged, objection is made on the ground of the transcendence of God. It is alleged that the finite is incapable of receiving or comprehending the infinite. This objection misses the point. We argue only that God is not the slave of His own absoluteness. He would not be God if He were not able to make intelligent creatures understand Him in the measure of their capacity.

2. The Probability of a Divine Revelation

(1) Man's need of God is self-evident. Even in a state of holiness man is dependent. He needs guidance and instruction. That he is capable of doing the best possible without divine help is hardly credible, and surely contrary to experience.

If we believe that man has fallen and has to a large degree lost fellowship with the creator, his need of divine compassion and help becomes plain. He is a poor lost sheep, exposed to danger on all sides, and needs the care of the shepherd.

(2) God's love for man must be real and infinitely deeper than the love of a mother for her child. All human love is but the reflection of the divine. God cannot be conceived of as lacking an attribute which is esteemed highest in

His creature. God is love, He loves man, even at his worst. Man's peril must move the heart of God.

If among men it is monstrous for a father to refuse to speak to his son, it cannot be true that the great All-Father will refuse to speak in an intelligible way to His child made in His own image. The probability is a thousand to one that He will speak.

II. THE POSITIVE EVIDENCE

The probability of a divine revelation has been fairly well established. That such a revelation has actually been made is claimed for the Bible, which therefore must be put upon the witness stand.

1. The Bible as a Book

(1) ORIGIN.

The word Bible comes from the Greek *biblion*, plural *biblia*, meaning books or scrolls. The word *biblion* comes from *byblus*, the name of the Egyptian reed or papyrus, out of which paper was first made and from which it took its name. The ancient writings were made on papyrus and later on parchment. The Bible is a collection of scriptures consisting of sixty-six books composed by more than forty authors, during fifteen centuries, in different lands and in several languages. Together they form the library called the Canon of Scripture, in two chief parts, the Old Testament and the New.

(2) ANTIQUITY.

These Scriptures are very ancient, as can be shown by quotations from the writings of men who lived about two thousand years ago, as well as by evidences derived from the Scriptures themselves. The New Testament can be traced to the beginning of the Christian era and the Old Testament to centuries earlier.

2. The Bible as an Influence

The Scriptures are more widely read than any other book. The learned and the unlearned alike find a delight in their perusal, and they are listened to with profound reverence as they are read and expounded week after week. Millions confess that these Scriptures have given them the true explanation of themselves, and have inspired them to lead better lives. There can be no denying that the Bible has an energy and vitality which are unaffected by time, distance or translation, and that it has profoundly influenced the human race for good.

3. The Bible Its Own Witness

The Bible must justify itself if it is to be accepted. It must be self-evidencing. Not what men say about it, but what it says itself must be the final argument. Its history, its vast circulation, its blessed influence form a strong presumption in its favor, but it must submit to rigid examination. Careful investigation yields evidence like the following:

1) ITS AUTHENTICITY.

The Bible professes to be a record of facts; if these facts can be authenticated it should be accepted. Let us investigate briefly the New Testament and its authors.

(1) The authors record their personal observations and experience or that of men whom they knew.

(2) The events recorded were in the main public and were witnessed by many persons.

(3) Statements are confirmed by contemporaneous history and by a verification of their allusions to geography, political conditions and the manners and the customs of the people.

(4) Variation in the narrative shows absence of collusion.

(5) The willingness of the authors to undergo martyrdom in defense of what they wrote proves their sincerity.

(6) The present existence of Christianity, which is in harmony with the New Testament Scriptures and which alone explains its origin and character is incontrovertible evidence that the Scriptures are a record of facts.

2) Its Miracles.

Among the facts recorded and authenticated by reliable witnesses are various miracles, which stamp the Bible as supernatural. The nature and function of miracles will be discussed later. Here we simply desire to affirm the general principle, acknowledged by all reasonable critics, that supernatural action for the good of man is entirely possible. That such action has taken place is clearly affirmed by the men to whom we are indebted for our information concerning Christ and the early history of Christianity.

According to any theory worth considering Christ is man, but much more than man. He is divine. He came into the world by the special act of God. He is a miracle. His resurrection is a miracle. The performance of miracles is entirely congruous with His nature and purpose. To discredit miracles means not only to deny the testimony of numerous honest men, but also to deny His veracity, power and divinity. If the New Testament contained nothing more than the story of wonders, it might be rejected; but the miracles recorded are not mere wonders, but signs authenticating and illustrating the character and purpose of Jesus.

3) Its Ethics.

(1) The acceptance of a book, doctrine or system, social or political, should be invariably conditioned upon its ethical character. Tried by this supreme test, the Bible transcends all other books. Its moral character, as it reaches its climax in the life and teachings of Jesus Christ, is without flaw. It sets up a standard for purity, justice and mercy which must be regarded not only as ideal, but as practical.

(2) The Bible reveals an ethical God, one who is holy and righteous, a judge who always does what is right according to our highest moral conceptions. The God of the Bible loves His creatures. He is compassionate toward the erring, slow to anger and plenteous in mercy. He is unwilling that any should perish and He provides a way of salvation. He carefully protects His honor with His justice, and requires conformity to law. The Ten Com-

mandments, given in the Old Testaments, are the expression of abiding principles for the regulation of human conduct.

4) ITS UNITY.

(1) There is a remarkable unity in the Bible, in spite of its diversity. While progress may be noted in the unfolding of truth from Genesis to Revelation there is a singleness of thought and aim that cannot be explained from a merely human standpoint. The scenes are laid on the banks of the Euphrates, the Nile and the Jordan, in the deserts of Arabia and the rich vales of Palestine. Kings and peasants, plowmen and prophets, saints and sinners have wrought upon it, each in his own way. Every form of literature from the bare chronicle to the lofty poetical and dramatic delineation of creation and judgment is found within its pages. It tells of the petty things of tent life and describes the migrations of millions, the rise and fall of empires. The past, the present and the future are comprehended in the sweep of its thought. The sixty-six books are like the same number of instruments in an orchestra directed by a master mind. Who is the master mind if not the Omniscient?

(2) The unifying spirit is found in Christ. The historical Christ who appeared in Palestine and who is winning a world empire is the real content of the Bible, its great theme. In Genesis He is the seed of the woman. In Exodus He is the paschal lamb. In Leviticus He is foreshadowed in type and symbol. Patriarch and prophet looked toward His coming. His kingdom was the hope of Israel. In the New Testament we have the record of His coming, of His life, His teachings, and His atoning death, of His kingdom on earth and of its consummation in heaven. Christ gives the Bible its unity and continuity.

5) ITS REALITY.

The Bible impresses the reader with a sense of reality. De Quincey said, "The great ideas of the Bible protect themselves. The heavenly truths, by their imperishableness, defeat the mortality of the language with which for a moment they are associated."

This sense of reality is confirmed by the test of Christian experience. "If I am asked," says W. R. Smith, "why I receive the Scriptures as the Word of God and as the only perfect rule of faith and life, I answer with all the fathers of the Protestant Church, because the Bible is the only record of the redeeming love of God, because in the Bible alone I find God drawing near to man in Jesus Christ, and declaring to us in Him His will for our salvation. And this record I know to be true by the witness of the Holy Spirit in my heart, whereby I am assured that none other than God Himself is able to speak such words to my soul" (Quoted in Ency. of Religion and Ethics VII, 347).

4. The Evidence of Prophecy

A prophet is a spokesman of God. His message may pertain to the present, the past, or the future. He may be simply a preacher of a message well known, but not heeded, or he may be the deliverer of a new message concerning existing conditions or concerning things to come. It is in the last sense that he will be considered here. Prophecy is the foretelling of events by divine inspiration. This definition is meant to exclude all predictions by human conjecture or prescience.

If it can be established that certain historic events were foretold by the prophets decades and even centuries before their occurrence, the conclusion must be inevitable that the prophets were men under supernatural influence. As there is abundant evidence that the Scriptures were extant long before the fulfillment of many of the prophecies, this argument for their authenticity is irrefutable.

The Scriptures contain a chain of prophecies from Genesis to Revelation, beginning in the Garden of Eden and extending into eternity. The credibility of the sacred writers having been established, we might cite any prophecy even if its fulfillment is recorded in the Bible alone. We shall, however, pass by all but a few and cite only those whose genuineness cannot be disputed, and whose clearness and magnitude are such as appeal to all.

1) PROPHECIES REFERRING TO THE JEWS.

(1) Abraham. Gen. 12: 1-3, "In thee shall all the families of the earth be blessed." The history of the Jewish people can be understood in the light of this promise. Nothing can be clearer than that it is having its fulfillment in Christ and Christianity.

(2) The Dispersion of the Jews. Deut. 28 and 29, reciting the curses and blessings at Ebal and Gerizim. Hosea 9: 17, "They shall be wanderers among the nations." Jer. 24: 9-10, "Tossed to and fro among all the kingdoms of the earth for evil."

2) PROPHECIES REFERRING TO THE GREAT EMPIRES IN DANIEL.

Dan. 2: 31-45, Nebuchadnezzar's vision of the image. Chaps. 7, 8 and 9, Daniel's vision of the four empires: Babylonian, Medo-Persian, Greek and Roman. While there is some difference of opinion in reference to the date of composition and of interpretation, there is agreement as to the remarkable setting forth of great historic sequences.

3) PROPHECIES REFERRING TO ANCIENT CITIES.

(1) Babylon. This city was the metropolis of a vast empire and a city of great magnificence. Its overthrow and desolation seemed as impossible to its people as a like fate would seem to the present inhabitants of London. Yet Jeremiah said, "The wild beasts of the desert with the wolves shall dwell there" (50: 39). "Thou shalt be desolate forever, saith Jehovah." "Babylon shall become heaps, a dwelling place for jackals, an astonishment, and a hissing, without inhabitant" (51: 26, 37). Isaiah speaks in a similar strain (13: 19-22). The striking fulfillment of these predictions is a matter of common knowledge.

(2) Nineveh. This was "an exceeding great city." Its destruction was foretold by Nahum (1: 8, 9; 2: 8-13; 3: 17-

19) and Zephaniah (2: 13-15). It has shared the fate of Babylon.

(3) Tyre. This rich and flourishing city on the Mediterranean became very wicked, in consequence of which the prophets were commanded to foretell its destruction. Ezek. 26: 3-5, "Thus saith the Lord Jehovah, Behold I am against thee, O Tyre, and will cause many nations to come against thee, as the sea causeth its waters to come up. . . She shall be a place for the spreading of the nets. . . She shall become a spoil to the nations." "Nothing now remains of the strength and splendor of the island fortress, except that on a calm day one may look from a boat, and see in the water along the rocky shore great blocks of the ancient breakwater and tumbled pillars of rose-colored granite" (Hastings).

(4) The Cities of the seven Churches of Asia Minor. Rev. 1, 2, 3. The churches at Smyrna and at Philadelphia received God's commendation and are still flourishing, while Ephesus, Sardis, and Laodicea are in ruins. Pergamos and Thyatira, praised in part, are still places of some consequence.

4) PROPHECIES IN THE OLD TESTAMENT REFERRING TO CHRIST.
    (1) The time of His advent. Gen. 49: 10.
    (2) His birth-place. Micah 5: 2.
    (3) His mother. Is. 7: 14.
    (4) His office. Prophet, Deut. 18: 15; Priest, Ps. 110: 4; King, Zech. 9: 9.
    (5) His miracles. Is. 35: 5, 6.
    (6) His sufferings and death. Is. 53.
    (7) His resurrection. Ps. 16: 10.

There are scores of references to Christ in the Old Testament, all of which accurately describe Him, or set forth His words, acts or experiences.

5) PROPHECIES MADE BY CHRIST HIMSELF.
    (1) His betrayal, condemnation and death. Matt. 16: 21; 20: 18, 19; 26: 23, 31.

(2) His resurrection. Matt. 16: 21.

(3) The descent of the Holy Spirit. Luke 24: 49.

(4) The destruction of Jerusalem. Matt. 16; 28; Mk. 13: 2.

These examples of prophecy taken from both Testaments might be greatly multiplied, but they are sufficient to prove that the sacred writers must have been divinely endowed and that their record is true. Scepticism may pervert and garble, but candid minds will not deny the facts set forth, for they are undeniable. The whole fabric of Christianity rests upon the foundation of the apostles and the prophets, who have spoken in the name of the Lord.

III. THE CANON OF SCRIPTURE

We have hitherto assumed that the collection of writings called the Bible was made by competent authority under special divine guidance. While this general statement is undoubtedly correct, its specific proof in all its bearings is not by any means simple.

1. The History of the Canon

1) The Canon is a term applied to the sacred writings, ordinarily known as the Bible. The word canon is derived probably from the Hebrew word "kane," meaning reed or cane. The transition to walking stick and measuring stick and rule was easy. Hence the word canon means rule or standard, and finally a list or collection of writings that have been approved by the rule or that measure up to the standard.

2) THE OLD TESTAMENT CANON.

This must necessarily have been slowly and gradually formed. Modern critics place its completion near the beginning of the Christian era. The very existence, however, of sacred writings suggest that there must have been very early groupings of books.

The Pentateuch was evidently the starting point. Ezra recognized these books as sacred (Neh. 8). It was but natural that to this group should be added another, namely, the prophetic writings. Thus we have "the Law and the Prophets." Finally, the miscellaneous sacred writings were added under the name of Hagiographa. The Old Testament canon was practically completed a century before Christ, though the canonical character of at least Ecclesiastes and the Song of Solomon was a matter of dispute as late as A.D. 70. That the canon was substantially settled in its present form before the birth of Christ is evident from Josephus, who mentions 22 books, corresponding with the 39 in the Old Testament.

3) THE NEW TESTAMENT CANON.

The Old Testament was the Bible of the first Christians. They had no other Scriptures at the beginning. In course of time, however, Christian writings were associated with the ancient Bible. The Epistles to the Churches would naturally be cherished, and later, when eye-witnesses had disappeared, the gospels now committed to writing would be added. Thus gradually the New Testament canon was formed. There is abundant evidence from the writings of friends and foes that the canon was practically settled by the close of the second century. There was some dispute about several books, but by the close of the fourth century the doubts concerning the disputed books had been settled.

4) In the Reformation the canonicity of several books was questioned by Luther on the ground that they bore no evidence convincing to experience, or that they did not teach the doctrine of justification by faith. He was on his guard against Romish errors and was, therefore, somewhat one-sided. The Formula of Concord recognized the existing canon.

5) Even at present the canonicity of Second Peter is disputed, not on the ground of its teachings so much as of its genuineness. The Church, however, accepts all the books of the canon as authentic. While theoretically the canon is always open, practically it is closed. It is conceivable, but hardly probable, that hidden away in some obscure monastery or elsewhere, undiscovered writings of

apostolic authorship may still exist and that they will in time be brought to light. But we may rest assured that the character of the canon will never be disturbed by any additions. After these long years there is no prospect that any of its present books will be eliminated.

6) To the devout student of the canon, especially of the New Testament, it is amazing that out of the vast number of writings of the apostolic age no unworthy book crept in and no worthy book was excluded. This fact seems plainly to indicate that the Christian consciousness of the early Church discerned clearly what was of God and edifying to the believer.

2.. The Test of Canonicity

Upon what grounds were the various books admitted to the canon and by whom? It was the consensus of the Church at large rather than the decrees of councils which decided the matter. Formal ecclesiastical action followed rather than created Christian consciousness concerning the canonicity of the books.

In reference to the Old Testament the acceptance of the existing canon by Christ and His apostles must be final. His fine spiritual discernment would have detected and rejected any unworthy book. His quotations from every part of the Old Testament are an approval of the collection made by the fathers long before.

In regard to the New Testament the problem is somewhat different, for we have no arbiter to decide for us. It is necessary therefore, to seek for general principles by which to test the claims of canonicity. The Reformers, emancipated from the mere external authority of the Church, were compelled to take up anew the question of the canon, for the Roman Catholic Church based some of its doctrines (purgatory) upon the Apocrypha. Luther found his test of canonicity in the witness to Christ, and particularly as to the doctrine of justification by faith. Calvin made the appeal of a book to spiritual experience the test. These are comparatively fair tests if impartially applied. But the tests proposed by Dods and Bruce are broader, and were no doubt practically applied to the formation of the canon.   These tests are: (1) Congruity with the main end of revelation, and (2) antiquity or direct historical connection with the revelation of God in history.

Congruity naturally embraces the testimony of Christ and the appeal to Christian experience.   Historical connection with the apostles makes such writings apostolic.

3.   Non-canonical Books

Various spurious books and others of a lower standard than the canonical books have in the past been thought worthy of a place in the Bible.   In the Septuagint fourteen books appear which are not found in the Hebrew canon, but which were admitted into the Vulgate and are still printed in many of the German versions, though rarely in the English.   They were known as the Apocrypha, which means "hidden."   Cranmer thought they were so called because they were not read publicly but secretly.

The Protestant Church repudiates their canonicity, but in some cases authorizes readings from them.   They are denied a place in the canon because (1) they are not found in the Hebrew, (2) they are not quoted in the New Testament, (3) they are not accurate historically, (4) they are superstitious and trivial.

The Old Testament Apocrypha, however, are by no means valueless, for their allusions, language and doctrines throw light upon the age in which they were written.

4.   The Bible a Divine Revelation

1) ITS NATURE.

The chief characteristic of a canonical book is that it was given under divine influence.   When, therefore, we speak of the Bible as a revelation of God we mean that it is the record of the disclosures made by God, as well as the record of His providence in history, especially to His chosen people. Naturally such a record would include some matters purely incidental and of minor importance which should not be magnified.   Moreover, the divine disclosures would be adapted to the age and the circumstances of those to whom they came.

2) ITS PURPOSES.

In order to understand the Bible as a revelation, its main purpose must be kept in view. The purpose is evidently redemptive in character. The Bible, it is true, starts with creation, but it is not the creation of the physical universe that is contemplated so much as that of man, happy in the presence of his maker and his beautiful environment. The sad story of his fall follows, and then through centuries the effort of God to save mankind fills the record from Genesis to Revelation. The hope of a Messiah lights up the dark pages of Israelitish history in the Old Testament and the glory of the realized hope the pages of the New Testament.

3) ITS INTERPRETATION.

Read in the light of the Cross of Calvary, much of the mystery of the Bible vanishes. The shortcomings of patriarchs, prophets and apostles no longer astonish us, when we remember that God took men as they were, and made them the vehicles of His abounding grace in appointing them to pass the illuminating torch from hand to hand and from generation to generation.

5. The Bible the Product of Inspiration

1) THE RECORDERS.

We have spoken of the Bible as the record of the disclosures and providence of God. But clearly God did not make the record Himself. It was made by men, of whom some received the message of God directly, and others received it indirectly. Paul often records revelations made to him, while Luke records those made to others, from whom he received them. Sometimes the recorder received directly and indirectly different parts of his record. Moses must have used traditions or writings as well as personal revelations.

2) THE QUALIFICATION.

The capacity to receive a divine message is inherent in the human spirit, otherwise there could be no real religion. The power, however, to apprehend a revelation must come from a special quickening of the spirit of man by God, who is spirit. Hence we need not look for any mechanical method in the reception or the recording of the revelations of God; but we are ready to accept the Scripture which declares that the prophets spoke as they were moved by the Holy Spirit (II Pet. 1: 21). This action or energy of God on the human spirit is called inspiration. It is usually exercised upon devout persons engaged in prayer or meditation. For instance, while certain prophets and teachers at Antioch were ministering to the Lord the Holy Spirit gave them a certain commission (Acts 13: 2). The word inspiration occurs but once in the New Testament as an adjective — "inspired" (*Theopneustos*), II Tim. 3: 16. "Every Scripture inspired of God." The idea of inspiration however is expressed in many passages.

3) THE INSPIRATION OF THE OLD TESTAMENT.

Concerning the Old Testament it may be said that the writers claim inspiration whenever they declared "Thus saith the Lord" (Amos 3: 7, 8). The prophecies must all rest upon the presumption of inspiration. The apostles testified to the inspiration of the Old Testament (II Tim. 3: 16). In II Pet. 1: 21 we read "For no prophecy ever came by the will of man: but men spake from God being moved by the Holy Spirit." "Moved" is, literally, borne along. Christ evidently teaches the same truth when He declares (Matt. 5: 17) "Think not that I am come to destroy the law or the prophets." In His conversation with the disciples on the way to Emmaus He reproves them for being slow to believe all that the prophets had spoken. He makes allusion to "all Scriptures" of the Old Testament in Luke 24: 25-27. He also declares in John 10: 35: "The Scripture cannot be broken." These testimonies undeniably indicate the belief of the prophets, of apostles and of Christ Himself that the Old Testament is inspired.

4) THE INSPIRATION OF THE NEW TESTAMENT.

The same line of argument may be applied to the New Testament. Jesus promised the disciples the Holy Spirit, who should guide them into all truth. He would even inspire them to make proper answer before the authorities (Matt. 10: 19, 20). Paul (Gal. 1: 11, 12) declares that the gospel which he preached came to him not from man "but through the revelation of Jesus Christ." Peter puts the writings of Paul on an equality with the "other Scriptures" (II Peter 3: 15, 16). Even when Paul seems to disclaim inspiration in a few instances he actually affirms it (I Cor. 7:40).

The same proofs which establish the authenticity of the Scriptures are in force in respect to inspiration. The character and the contents of the Scriptures preclude the possibility of imposture and deception. ·

5) THEORIES OF INSPIRATION.

(1) Various theories of inspiration have been advocated. The most popular and fallacious of these is the dictation theory, which holds that the writer is merely an instrument which the Spirit used as a player does the organ, or that he is merely the stenographer of God. The error is apparent from the fact that the individuality of the writer is nowhere suppressed. Peter, Paul and John each writes in his own way, in his peculiar style and according to the measure of his knowledge and experience. It is also evident from the diverse reports which the apostles give of the Sermon on the Mount, the Lord's Prayer, the several miracles and discourses of Christ, that they were not unconscious media for the Spirit. Moreover, it is clear from the manner in which the Old Testament is quoted in the New that verbal mechanical inspiration does not exist. Of two hundred and seventy-five quotations comparatively few are literal, the purpose being to give the sense rather than the language.

Another startling fact contradicts the dictation theory, and that is the numerous various readings in the several manuscripts. While these do not vitiate the Scriptures in the least, they do show that God did not seem to require that every word must be miraculously preserved as originally written.

(2) If by the plenary theory is meant that every word of Scripture was suggested by immediate inspiration, then the same objections hold against it that are urged against the dictation theory. If, however, the theory means that the Bible is fully adequate for its redemptive mission then the plenary theory may be allowed.

(3) A dynamic theory has also been proposed. According to this, inspiration extends only to the purely religious teachings of the Bible. If this means that the other statements of the Bible are untrustworthy, the theory goes too far in the negative. If it means that the inspired writers were so intent upon the presentation of their spiritual message that they were somewhat indifferent as to externals the theory seems to have some grounds.

6) DEFINITION OF INSPIRATION.

Inspiration has been defined by some as elevation and stimulation of mind regardless of the subject discussed. Great poets and orators are said to be inspired. Hymn-writers and preachers, it is said, are only less inspired than the prophets and the apostles. In regard to the former, it is plain that they were not inspired to perform the peculiar function of Biblical writers, who were raised up to show the way of salvation. The latter would insist that their inspiration came chiefly through a contemplation of the Bible.

The tentative definition of inspiration which is suggested by Professor Wood seems to be better than the foregoing theories: "Biblical inspiration is the personal influence of God, who so guided all who took part in producing the Bible that they made a body of literature unique in religious value, and so far as we can now see final in religious teaching." (See "A Tenable Theory of Inspiration.")

Whatever theory may be accepted in regard to the production of the Bible none can be true which fails to recognize the divine and the human elements in its composition.

The abounding evidence of the supernatural dare not

be ignored, for without it the Bible becomes utterly inexplicable.

6. Discrepancies in Scripture

1) THEIR EXISTENCE.

The Bible is recognized by the orthodox churches as the only infallible rule of faith and practice, the final arbiter in matters of doctrine and life. Those who deny the authority of the Bible declare that this attitude is unreasonable, because of evident and acknowledged discrepancies. These are usually magnified out of all proportion. Some are really not discrepancies at all, as modern discoveries in Bible lands show. Others can be harmonized. But there are undoubtedly some which can be explained only by urging errors in copying manuscripts or allowing that the sacred writers were themselves in error.

As illustrations there may be mentioned the variations in the sum paid by David for Araunah's threshing floor (Compare II Sam. 24: 24 and I Chr. 21: 25) ; the variation in the genealogies of Christ as given by Matthew and Luke; the title on the Cross, as reported by the four evangelists; the several accounts of the resurrection; and the chronological errors in Stephen's address.

2) THEIR EFFECT ON DOCTRINE.

These apparent inconsistencies, it is to be remembered first of all, do not in the least affect the moral or religious teaching of the Bible. They are entirely incidental and do not influence the purpose intended. Second, they do not vitiate the historicity of the record any more than the slight errors that may be found in any historical writing discredit its authors. Third, literary inerrancy is not asserted when the infallibility of the Bible as a guide to faith is claimed. It was evidently not the intention of God to give mankind a book written by rhetoricians, historians, scientists or orators. He gave us a better book which makes a universal appeal.

3) THEIR RELATION TO FAITH.

No one ever became a Christian because he believed the Bible records the accurate history of the Jews or contains a geography of Palestine or relates the story of the beginnings of Christianity. No one will ever lose saving faith when he discovers trifling errors in these records. It is utterly preposterous that one should give up Christ when he finds out that someone made a mistake in a date or in the price of property! Faith rests upon a much more secure foundation than the inerrancy of transcribers, of translators and of printers. It rests upon a personal experience which finds its verification in every part of the Bible. "Amid all the controversies about the Bible and the attacks upon it, the Christian heart may rest secure in this conviction, that the unique character and value of the Bible are as secure as the unique character and significance of the person of Christ." G. B. Stevens.

7.   The Authority of Scripture

1) UNDERESTIMATED BY LIBERAL THEOLOGY.

Modern liberal theology endeavors to displace the Bible as the chief authority in matters of religion, and endeavors to substitute for it something which it calls "experience," but which really is nothing but reason or human opinion. It uses the word faith to signify something which is to test all teachings. As a fact this is not the nature or function of faith. This use of the term makes it equivalent to reason. Faith is confidence in God, awakened in the believer by the Holy Ghost. It does not judge anything. It receives and takes hold of. To speak of faith as a moral judgment is, therefore, absurd. When it is said that Jesus commends Himself to our faith, the language is incoherent. In a real sense faith is the gift of God. Jesus lays hold on us.

It is asserted, as though a discovery had been made, that God alone is the final authority in religion. No one for a moment disputes this. But has God not revealed His authority in some tangible way? Has it not been proved to the satisfaction of millions that the Bible is the record of His revelation? And has not their religious experience been in entire accord with the Scriptures?

2) SUSTAINED BY VALID ARGUMENT.

Considerations like the following establish the authority of Scripture as final in matters of faith.

(1) The Bible is the only record of the birth, life, labors, death and teachings of Jesus Christ. This cannot be accidental; it is providential. It is inconceivable that God would be indifferent to the preservation of the story of the coming of His only-begotten and well-beloved Son. Nor can we for a moment believe that the noble men who made the record were either deceived or deceivers.

(2) The Bible is the record of the religious experience of the Christians who lived in immediate touch with our Lord while He was on earth. Their experience in any other department of life would be taken without question as normative. Their claims to knowledge and illumination cannot be discredited. Under God they produced a book which has commended itself to the best of men through centuries to be exactly what it professes to be.

(3) It is the experience of multitudes living today that the Bible is the way of salvation. They have put it to the test and have never found it wanting. It is their united testimony that in proportion as they have conformed to its requirements they have found peace and happiness. Their experience, however, in no sense affected the reality of the Bible. It stands on its own merits.

(4) The history of Christianity shows that the rise or the decline of true religion is always coincident with the acceptance or the rejection of the Bible as the book of God. In ancient Israel the discovery of the lost oracles created a return to God. In the time of Luther the restoration of the Bible produced the Reformation. Renewed Bible-study always results in a genuine revival of religion.

(5) The Scriptures make an immediate appeal to man. They are the power of God unto salvation to everyone who believeth. Cold, critical analysis, untouched by spiritual sympathy, cannot judge the Scriptures; they must be spiritually discerned. The experience of the humblest saint is more reliable as a value-judgment of the Bible than the learning of the worldly-wise.

(6) By analogy objective standards in religion are as imperatively demanded as measures, weights and laws in civil and social life. Standards have been fixed not as arbitrary tests but as expressing what is just and useful in daily life. The Bible is the religious standard approved beyond reasonable dispute by Jesus Christ and the Holy Spirit. It has remained unchanged for centuries. The result of ignoring the Bible is vague subjectivism.

8. The Use of Scripture in Theology

1) THE CHIEF SOURCE.

The Bible is the chief source of theology; it is a rich mine from which may be taken a wealth of information and inspiration. Every verse of the one hundred and seventy-six composing the 119th Psalm is a glowing tribute to some phase of God's word—law, testimony, precepts, statutes, commandments, and ordinances. "Thy word," exclaims the psalmist, "is a lamp unto my feet, and a light unto my path." The theologian may sincerely adopt this language, for without the Bible he would be in the dark concerning the most vital questions which arise in the soul.

2) ITS RATIONAL APPLICATION.

The Bible must be used, however, with reason. It is not a thesaurus of texts which can be strung together regardless of their context. Care must be taken to give each Scripture its proper background. The author and his environment must be considered. The age in which he lived, the people to whom he spoke and his purpose in speaking must be taken into account. Moreover, deductions must be in harmony with "the analogy of faith"—with the general purpose and teaching of the Bible. It must be evident at a glance that while all Scripture is valuable, some parts are more so than others, and that our Master's own words stand highest of all. No text is to be discredited as teaching falsehood, but no text can be made to serve as proof of a doctrine simply because of a word which may suggest some relation.

DOGMATICS

PART I

THEOLOGY

THE DOCTRINE OF GOD

A. THE NATURE AND ATTRIBUTES OF GOD

I. THE NATURE OF GOD.

A man's conception of God is determinative not only of his theology but also of his religion. It is highly important therefore, both from the standpoint of knowledge and of faith, that one have a clear view, within the bounds of reason, of the Supreme Being. Theology finds one of its chief functions in setting forth the Christian view of God, as derived chiefly from the Scriptures, confirmed by nature, and verified in experience. The testimony of the Scriptures must be regarded as fundamental, because they contain the revelation of and by Jesus Christ.

1. The Definition of God

As a matter of course it is impossible adequately to define the Supreme Being whom the heaven of heavens cannot contain and who is God from everlasting to everlasting. Nevertheless, it is proper to express in human language such a conception as revelation and experience warrant.

(1) The nominal definition of God is that which is derived from the various names by which He is known or has been pleased to reveal Himself. Caution, however, is to be observed in laying stress upon mere etymology, for the meaning of words is constantly changing.

The English word God expresses the generic idea of deity and is applied to the only real God as well as to false or unreal gods. It is equivalent to the Hebrew word *Elohim* and the Greek *Theos* and the Latin *Deus*. Some have derived it from an Anglo-Saxon root meaning "good." This seems untenable, however suggestive; for the root exists in various modifications in older languages. It has been traced to the word "ghu" in the Aryan tongue, now repre-

75

sented by the Sanscrit, and it is said to mean "to call." Hence God is the one upon whom men call.

Deus and *Theos* evidently came from the same root, *thes,* meaning to implore. Thus these words are closely related to the root idea of God.

The Hebrew has two generic words for God: *El* (plural *Elohim*) and *Jehovah* or *Yahve.* The former is derived from a root meaning "to be strong," thus setting forth God as the Almighty. The latter is the personal name of God by which He revealed Himself to His covenant people. Its root idea is "being" or self-existence. He is the eternal "I am," without age or change, and thus the ground of assurance that His word will not fail.

Besides the names of God, the Bible gives Him various appellations such as Lord, the Almighty, and the Most High, the meaning of which is entirely clear.

(2) The real definition of God attempts a comprehensive statement of His nature as an Infinite Person.

The Augsburg Confession (Art. I) represents Him as "eternal without body, without parts, of infinite power, wisdom and goodness, the Maker and Preserver of all things, visible and invisible."

Dr. A. A. Hodge defines Him as "an intelligent personal Spirit, infinite, eternal, unchangeable in His being, in His wisdom, in His power, in His holiness and in all perfections consistent with His being." W. N. Clarke says, "God is the Personal Spirit, perfectly good, who in holy love creates, sustains and orders all."

Of the many brief definitions we prefer that of Luthardt: "God is absolute Personality and Holy Love." While this may appear somewhat metaphysical, it is really simple and comprehensive. Four fundamental ideas are included: personality, absoluteness, holiness and love. These great ideas are not to be mechanically separated, for each expresses a distinct phase of an inseparable Unity.

"Personality" relates God to man as a Being whom we can, in a measure, understand as possessed of intelligence, self-consciousness, and self-determination. He is like us; or rather we are like Him, though He transcends human personality to an infinite degree. Only by conceiving of God as a spiritual personality can we understand Him at all. When He would reveal Himself most fully, He sent His Son in the person of the God-man, Jesus Christ, who declared, "he that hath seen me hath seen the Father."

"Absoluteness" includes the thought of perfection and infinitude. He is the ground and cause of all things. He is conditioned by nothing outside of Himself—self-determined, unlimited, unchangeable.

"Holiness" indicates that God is moral and spiritual, the source and pattern of all that is right and good. Righteousness, justice and truth belong to Him.

"Love" is an expression not simply of His attitude and act, but of His very essence. God is love. All that is noble, beautiful and good in human character illustrates God's nature.

"God is absolute Personality and Holy Love."

II.   THE ATTRIBUTES OF GOD.

By an attribute is meant a distinct conception of God. The sum of these conceptions constitutes our idea of His nature and character. The attributes are really but an amplification of the brief definition of God, and may accordingly be classified as attributes of Personality, Absoluteness, Holiness, and Love.

1.   Attributes of Personality

1) SPIRITUALITY.

God is represented in Scripture as having hands and feet and other members of a human body, but this is figurative language intended to convey to the immature the reality of God. He is defined by Christ as Spirit (John 4: 24). He is a person above matter. He is mind. Reason demands that He be untrammeled by flesh and blood.

2) LIFE.

As Spirit, God cannot be conceived as lifeless or inactive. He is the ever-living God. "The Father hath life in himself" (John 5:26). He has all the attributes of personal life—thought, initiative, activity. He is not only life but the giver of life, natural and spiritual. He imparts Himself to man in love, with the purpose of making human life a life in God.

3) UNITY.

There is but one God. Polytheism is philosophically and Scripturally inconceivable. Dualism, the eternal coexistence of mind and matter is equally untenable, as we have seen elsewhere. A God at variance with Himself, undecided, inconsistent like the gods of mythology, cannot be a true God, but is a creature of the imagination. God must necessarily be a perfect personality, eternally in harmony with Himself.

This conception corresponds with Bible teaching. "Hear O Israel: Jehovah our God is one Jehovah" (Deut. 6:4). "Thou shalt have no other gods before me" is the first of the Ten Commandments (Ex. 20:3). Paul speaks of the "one God and Father of all" (Eph. 4:6).

2. Attributes of Absoluteness

1) SELF-EXISTENCE.

The first cause of the universe must be uncaused. He exists in and of Himself. There is no other explanation, however staggering to the finite mind must be this stupendous fact. He is the "I am," without beginning or end. In Isaiah 43:10, 11, Jehovah declares, "Before me there was no God formed, neither shall there be after me. I, even I am Jehovah."

2) ETERNITY.

As self-existent, God must be eternal, without past or future. To Him there is no time, but an eternal "now." "From everlasting to everlasting thou art God" (Ps. 90:2). He is "the King eternal, immortal, invisible" (I Tim. 1:17).

3) IMMUTABILITY.

God is unchangeable in essence, character and purpose —"the incorruptible God" (Rom. 1:23); "the Father of lights with whom can be no variation neither shadow that is cast by turning" (Jas. 1:17). Mutability in God would connote deficiency in knowledge or weakness of will, both of which are inconceivable. He cannot change because He cannot be inconsistent with Himself and His perfect wisdom.

Several difficulties have been suggested in regard to immutability. First, God is said to have repented that He made man and that He failed to carry out His threat to destroy Nineveh. These cases illustrate the anthropomorphic manner of speech often used in the Bible. Moreover, the threats are conditional in their very nature. They are intended to provoke unto repentance and good works. The change in God is only apparent, resulting from man's change of attitude.

A second difficulty has been sought in the incarnation. This grows out of a misconception of the nature and power of God, who cannot be limited in His manifestations. Instead of offering a difficulty, the incarnation exhibits the immutable purpose of God to open a way of salvation to His erring children. Only through His becoming man can we really know Him and His matchless love.

4) INFINITY.

When it is affirmed that God is infinite we understand that He is unrestricted and unconditioned in all His activities and powers. He transcends men in an infinite degree. He is not circumscribed by time, distance, location or infinity. His infinity appears in the consideration especially of His ubiquity, His knowledge and His power.

(1) God is omnipresent, not in the sense of filling space with matter, but as a personal being is present in a place. We cannot think of any part of the universe in which God is not. Well has the psalmist expressed this idea. "Whither shall I go from Thy spirit? or whither shall I flee from Thy presence? If I ascend up into heaven, thou art there: if I make my bed in Sheol, behold thou art there. If I take the wings of the morning, and dwell in the uttermost parts of the sea even there shall thy hand lead me, and thy right hand shall hold me" (Ps. 139:7-10).

The Christian faith demands and rejoices in the immanence of God, whose loving eye is upon His children always and everywhere. Faith in His providence rests upon the truth of His immanence. An absentee God, as the deists regard Him, cares nothing for man beyond the institution of law and order, with whose operations He never interferes. In such a God there is no affection, mercy or forgiveness. Happily this view is not in accordance with the revelation which He has made of Himself in His works and especially in Christ.

(2) God is omniscient. He knows all that was and is and will be or can be. Without knowledge, order in the universe is inconceivable, and without it God would not be God. His knowledge extends to the minutest constituents of matter, the humblest forms of life, and to the thoughts and intents of the human heart. "He knoweth our frame; He remembereth that we are dust" (Ps. 103:14).

The divine knowledge may be thought of (a) as intuitive, without process of reasoning; (b) as simultaneous, not successive. Light does not dawn on the Infinite, who is Himself Light. It is also (c) infallible, without error. It is complete and perfect.

Omniscience implies foreknowledge of all future events, not simply those which come as the result of irrefragable law in nature, but also those which take place in human life. Apart from certain events which are clearly ordained, God knows what man gifted with freedom will do.

All contingencies are known to the omniscient God. It has been denied by Calvinists that God knows what might happen under certain circumstances which do not materialize. This denial is based upon the proposition that God ordains all things and hence the things which may be thought of but not actually occur have no tangible basis of existence. But this objection seems to be clearly contradicted by such passages as "If the mighty works had been done in Tyre and Sidon which were done in you, they would have repented long ago in sack-cloth and ashes" (Matt. 11: 21. See also I Sam. 23: 3-13).

(3) God is omnipotent. This is a characteristic of His absoluteness. He is able to enforce His laws, keep His promises and govern His universe. When it is said that He is omnipotent it is implied that He can do what He wills, but not that He can do what is contrary to His nature. He cannot lie; He cannot contradict Himself. He has abundant power to overthrow all opposition and cause truth to triumph. In His omniscience He knows how to apply His strength in order best to meet His ends. The majesty of His might may be seen in the frightful convulsions of nature, and much more in the glorious order visible in the earth and sky.

The doctrine of the divine omnipotence is of the greatest comfort to the believer, who knows that in His own good time God will deliver him from all his trials. He recalls "the strength of his might which he wrought in Christ, when he raised him from the dead, and made him to sit at his right hand in heavenly places far above all rule, and authority and power and dominion, and every name that is named, not only in this world, but also in that which is to come" (Eph. 1: 19-21).

(4) Wisdom. God is absolute not only in His knowledge but also in its application. He is unerring in His judgments. Nothing better than His plans can be thought of. "O the depth of the riches both of the wisdom and knowledge of God" (Rom. 11: 33).

3. Attributes of Holiness
1) THE DEFINITION.
The holiness of God signifies His infinite moral perfection. It is a comprehensive attribute. It stands for the whole character of God, in whom there is a union of all excellencies. He is ethical to an infinite degree. The Judge of all the earth does what is right. There is nothing unreasonable or arbitrary in His dealings with men. His will is the expression of His character in all its fullness.

2) SEVERAL ASPECTS.
Holiness has various aspects. It includes righteousness, justice, and moral purity. It is also the source of the divine

majesty. The seraphim cry, "Holy, holy, holy is Jehovah of hosts: the whole earth is full of his glory" (Is. 6: 3).

3) THE DIVINE STANDARD.

The holiness of God is the standard for human conduct. "Be ye holy for I am holy," says the Lord (Lev. 11: 44). He has revealed His will and purpose in the Scriptures and especially in Christ. From them we learn that He is well pleased with right doing, that His wrath is upon the children of disobedience and that "at the revelation of the Lord Jesus from heaven" He will render "vengeance to them that know not God" (II Thess. 1: 7, 8). The wrath of God is the reaction of His holiness against sin, which is offensive to His character.

4. Attributes of Love

1) ITS NATURE.

No characteristic of the soul is more attractive than love. How beautiful and how sacred is the love of a mother! Love is the greatest thing in the world. It glorifies the humblest life. It reflects the love of God. We love because we are made in the image of God; and we can measurably understand Him by fathoming human love.

"Love suffereth long and is kind, seeketh not its own, . . . rejoiceth with the truth, . . . Love never faileth, . . . Now abideth faith, hope, love, these three; and the greatest of these is love" (I Cor. 13). Nothing can atone for its absence. The greatest gifts and the finest achievements are valueless without it. The most splendid palace furnished in the most luxurious manner, adorned by the hand of genius, its walls covered with the work of the masters, its floors with the costliest rugs, its books, its statuary and all its appointments—what is it but a prison, if there be no love?

"God is love" (I Jno. 4:8). He not only loves, but is the embodiment of love. It is His nature to love. He is always love. In this He far transcends human beings whose love may at times be impaired by passion or weakness. His love is changeless from age to age.

2) ITS MANIFESTATION.

The manifestation of God's love is seen in history and in individual lives. It reaches its climax in Christ. "God so loved the world that he gave his only begotten Son" (Jno. 3: 16). The soul may rest in the contemplation of this supreme sacrifice. Whatever doubt may be suggested by a hard lot or by so-called "inscrutable providence," it dissolves in the light of the cross. Love is the explanation of Bethlehem, Calvary and the New Jerusalem.

3) ITS FORMS.

Love has been analyzed and classified as complacency, benevolence and grace.

(1) By complacency is meant first of all the delight of God in His own perfections. Self-love is not wicked in men when it is equivalent to self-respect, nor is it out of harmony with the deepest humility. In a perfect being, self-love must exist to a perfect degree. We cannot think of God as underestimating Himself. In infinite holiness there must be immeasurable delight.

God must also regard those who love and obey Him with peculiar satisfaction. The "disciple whom Jesus loved," as John calls himself, was not the only disciple whom He loved. If He regards any of His disciples with more than ordinary affection, it must be because they respond to His love.

(2) The love of benevolence is the universal love which God cherishes toward all men and by which He seeks to win them. Only by forgetting that He is love can we believe that He does not love all men. Even this severity is the expression of His love to drive men from evil. Nothing in the Bible can warrant any teaching to the contrary.

(3) Grace is the expression of the divine love in the plan and process of salvation. It is the unmerited favor of God toward the sinner. It is the divine attitude of forgiveness through Christ.

The love of God has sometimes been questioned on account of the presence of suffering and cruelty in nature, and especially on account of the existence of sin in man.

Why should the good God permit these dark things in His otherwise beautiful world?

In regard to the presence of natural evil, we may say that in the evolution of nature the final issue is for good; and as for spiritual evil, whatever its origin and purpose, we know that God has provided a sovereign remedy for sin. His ways are sometimes "past finding out," but we may be sure that in the end all things work together for good to them that love Him.

The attributes of God blend into the beautiful symmetry of a perfect being, and are not out of harmony with one another. We need not perplex ourselves with their mutual relations. The holiness of God is not in conflict with His love. We are assured by Christ that God, the righteous Father, desires to save and not to destroy. There is no debate in the divine mind whether justice or compassion shall triumph; in His wisdom the reconciliation between them is complete. He is "just and the justifier of him that hath faith in Jesus" (Rom. 3: 26).

How inadequate are man's best efforts to present a view of God in words! They can be at best, under the divine blessing, the guide to a more earnest study of the Bible, a more profound contemplation of the goodness of God, and a more complete submission to the leading of the Holy Spirit resulting in the experience of the peace of God which passeth all understanding.

B. THE TRINITY

I. THE GROUND OF THE DOCTRINE.

1. The Faith of the Church

It is the universal faith of the Protestant and the Catholic Churches that there is one God, and that this one God is Father and Son and Holy Spirit. Into this one Name of the Triune God all Christians are baptized. When they are gathered for public service they say with one accord, "I believe in God the Father Almighty . . . and in Jesus Christ His only Son our Lord . . . and in the Holy Ghost," and as they part the blessing of a triune benediction rests upon them.

2. The Postulate of Christianity

The fundamental postulate of Christianity is the existence of the Trinity, embracing the everlasting Father, the pre-existent Son, and the eternal Spirit. So interwoven with the life, thought and language of the Church is the doctrine of the Trinity that its removal from the faith and the confession of the Church would cause the Church to collapse. Christianity might remain for a while an ethical cult, but it would cease to be a religion.

If there be no Trinity, the story of the manger is a myth, that of Calvary a cruel deception, and that of Pentecost a pure invention. Then God has not manifested Himself supernaturally, the Bible is a cunningly-devised fable, and the mighty host of good and intelligent people have for twenty centuries followed a delusion. The probabilities are enormously against such a supposition. That the Church should hold to a doctrine which has been pronounced unreasonable and even puerile is certainly remarkable, and demands satisfactory explanation.

3. The Source of the Doctrine

The doctrine of the Trinity is not the invention of theologians, for it was believed and taught before they existed or attempted its formulation in creeds. It is not the product of metaphysical thinking, for the metaphysical never appeals to the plain man. Neither was it derived from the Scriptures, for it was the faith of the disciples before the Scriptures were written.

It is true that we now get our information and doctrine principally through the Scriptures, which the Christian believes, upon satisfactory ground, to be divinely given for his guidance, wholly credible as the record of facts, as well as of the explanation of facts as made by competent witnesses. We accept the doctrine of the Trinity, therefore, in the first place as we would accept any other well-authenticated facts.

4. The Historic Unfolding

In the Old Testament we have the teaching of monotheism as over against prevailing idolatry and polytheism. It was needful that fallen man should be brought back to the conception of the unity of the God-head, and therefore God reveals Himself as the Jehovah or only and ever-living God. The great leader Moses cries, "Hear, O Israel: Jehovah our God is one Jehovah and thou shalt love Jehovah thy God with all thy heart and with all thy soul and with all thy might" (Deut. 6: 4, 5). So thoroughly was the monotheistic conception instilled that to this day the Jew is a monotheist and anti-trinitarian.

In the fullness of time, when the world was prepared to receive a larger revelation, God manifested Himself in the person of His only Son. His coming and life are undeniable historic facts, recorded in the New Testament, handed down in tradition and preserved in institutions traceable to Him. In Christ our knowledge of God is greatly enriched; indeed, we cannot understand Him except as revealed by the only-begotten Son who dwells in the bosom of the Father. Jesus declared that He and the Father are one and that He is the revealer of the Father.

The revelation of the Son, so long delayed according to human reckoning, was speedily followed by the manifestation of the Holy Spirit, who though eternally existing did not appear in former times as a distinct personality. At the close of His brief ministry our Lord reveals the nature and the coming of the Spirit, "another Comforter." On the day of Pentecost, the Spirit came upon the Church in a most unmistakable and extraordinary manner.

The historic manifestations of God to Israel through theophanies, the history of our Redeemer, and the historicity of Pentecost are the sure objective ground of the Christian belief in the Trinity of God. The sacred Scriptures are the record of these facts. It is the task of theology to construct out of simple fact a consistent system.

The historic revelation of the Trinity experienced by God's people and recorded in the Bible is the first ground of the doctrine. The second and final ground is the present experience of the regenerate. To those who are not regenerate or who explain away the alleged experience of those who are, these arguments mean nothing. Here is an illustration of the subtle error which denies reality or truth to anything which has not fallen within the narrow limit of an individual experience.

Graven deeply into the consciousness of the Church and begotten of experience is the truth that God, in His infinite Fatherhood, has so loved the world that He gave His only Son to redeem man, and His only Spirit to regenerate him.

5. The Connotations of the Doctrine

This brief statement has a broad connotation. It presupposes the Incarnation and the Atonement, both demanded by the soul of man, and also the fellowship of the Spirit with His quickening power. However deep and inexplicable may be the meaning of these great truths, they are believed and cherished by the Church, because they satisfy the heart and inspire the life. They are a part of that glorious Christian faith which exalts God and yet brings Him near.

II.   THE FORMULATION OF THE DOCTRINE.

1. Its Necessity

The formulation of an important belief is inevitable, for the mind demands a clear statement of that which asks for its assent. Not only is formulation needed for faith but also for defense. The doctrine of the Trinity is no exception to this rule. Its formulation, however, was fraught with considerable difficulty because in some respects the Trinity transcends reason.

"Faithful souls," says St. Hilary of Poitiers, "would be contented with the word of God, which bids us 'Go teach all nations, baptizing them into the name of the Father, and of the Son and of the Holy Ghost.' But alas! we are driven by the faults of our heretical opponents to do things unlawful, to scale heights inaccessible, to speak out what is unspeakable, to presume where we ought not. And whereas it is by faith alone that we should worship the

Father, and reverence the Son, and be filled with the Spirit, we are now obliged to strain our weak human language in the utterance of things beyond its scope, forced into this evil procedure by the evil procedure of our foes.   Hence, what should be the matter of silent religious meditation must now needs be imperilled by exposition in words."

2. The Preparation

Between Malachi and Christ, Jewish theology made some progress toward a trinitarian view of God but reached no conclusion. The "logos" was conceived in Jewish and Greek thought as a vague principle or spirit, but rarely reached the status of personality.   The effort of Philo to reconcile Greek philosophy with Judaism was paralleled later by the attempt of the Gnostics to reconcile it with Christian teaching, but with indifferent success.   The apostle John in a few brief sentences clarifies the logos idea, by giving it a personal meaning and identifying it with the pre-existent Christ.

The apostolic Church undoubtedly received and taught the doctrine of the Trinity.   John and Paul teach it in the most explicit manner.   The baptismal formula and the benediction summarize it in a practical and liturgical way, and became the basis of the Apostles' Creed, which underlies all the other creeds.

The ante-Nicene Church as a whole accepted the doctrine; but speculation was not wanting as to the relation of the Three Persons.   Numerous sects naturally arose in the early centuries.   Certain Jewish believers denied that Christ was eternally God's Son, but asserted that He first became the Son when the Spirit descended on Him at baptism.   Gentile Christian Gnosticism, "an astonishing spectre, begotten by the rising sun of Christianity in the evening shadows of departing heathendom," forced the Church to define its view of God as over against the grotesque fancies which predicated two Gods.

3. The Progress

Tertullian (A.D. 160-230) and Origen (A.D. 182-251) more than all others, shaped the doctrine of the Trinity for the third century and in a measure for later times. Nevertheless, these illustrious teachers did not escape the taint of subordination, without, however, meaning to deny the deity of the Son and of the Spirit.

The third century also witnessed the attempt to reconcile monotheism with the deity of Christ, without resorting to the expedient of "the second God." Under the general forms of Modalism, Sabellianism or Patripassianism it was taught that the three Persons of the Godhead were really only separate manifestations of the one God, who appeared to men successively as Father, as Son, and as Spirit.

4. The Consummation

The fourth century witnessed the climax of the Trinitarian controversies. In the person of Arius, a British monk, was represented the error that Christ, though far above man, was a creature through whom God made the world. The time was now at hand for the Church, once for all to set forth the true view of God. The Council of Nice (A.D. 325) after a mighty struggle sounded the death-knell of Arianism and Unitarianism. Its conclusions, with some slight later changes, are embodied in what is known as the Nicene Creed, which is still confessed in most of the churches, and which in beautiful rhythmic language expresses the profound truth that God is Father, Son and Spirit.

THE NICENE CREED.

I believe in one God, the Father Almighty, Maker of heaven and earth, And of all things visible and invisible.

And in one Lord Jesus Christ, the Only-begotten Son of God, Begotten of His Father before all worlds, God of God, Light of Light, Very God of very God, Begotten, not made, Being of one substance with the Father, By Whom all things were made; Who, for us men, and for our salvation, came down from heaven, And was incarnate by the Holy Ghost of the Virgin Mary, And was made man; And was crucified also for us under Pontius Pilate. He suffered and was buried; And the third day He rose again, according to the Scriptures; And ascended into heaven, And sitteth on the right hand of the Father; And He shall come again with glory to judge both the quick and the dead; Whose kingdom shall have no end.

And I believe in the Holy Ghost, The Lord and Giver of Life, Who proceedeth from the Father and the Son, Who with the Father and the Son together is worshipped and glorified, Who spake by the Prophets. And I believe one holy Christian and Apostolic Church. I acknowledge one Baptism for the remission of sins; And I look for the Resurrection of the dead; And the Life of the world to come. Amen.

III. THE NATURE OF THE TRINITY.

1. A Mystery

In attempting to explain the nature of the Three in One we are at once aware that we are dealing with unique relations and supernatural facts. It is not surprising that finite thought and human language should fail to comprehend and to express what is necessarily mysterious. Moreover, the constant change in the meaning of words may mislead us. Thus the words "person," "being," "essence," and the like do not express to us quite what they did to the early theologians. The word "person" as applied to the Trinity does not connote precisely what it conveys when applied to man. The latter is a distinct, individual entity, but even human personality is not devoid of mystery. We cannot explain the undoubted fact that our personality is closely united with a material organism.

2. A Threefold Personality

In asserting that there is one God and also that there are three distinct Persons, we do not mean that the latter have their personalities apart from one another or that they unite in forming a fourth person. The truth has been stated by Dorner: "The one absolute personality is present in each of the divine distinctions in such a way that, though not of themselves and singly personal, they participate in the one divine personality, each in His own manner. The one absolute personality is the unity of the three modes of the divine existence which share therein. Neither is personal without the others. In each in His own manner is the whole Godhead."

3. A Matter of Faith in Christ

The consideration of the Trinity leads into the realm of mystery, but not of unbelief. It may make us less sure of attempted logic but not less confident in our faith. The Christian must do here as he must always do; hold fast to his divine Lord. His person, His word, and His work for us and in us are the absolute guaranty of the existence of the Trinity. The fact is patent, the full explanation can wait. We are after all but children when it comes to the understanding of the supernatural. The child knows his parent somewhat as we know God, more by what he does than by what he is. As the child grows older and begins to reflect about himself, he begins to wonder also about the nature and motive of his parent.

The contemplation of God leads to the recognition of two related aspects of His nature as a Triune Being; first, God as He is in His internal relations, and second, God as He has revealed Himself in His word. The former is expressed under the term, the immanent or essential Trinity, the latter the manifested or economic Trinity.

4. The Immanent Trinity

1) SET FORTH IN THE CREED.

In the Nicene Creed, in which was attempted the first authoritative presentation of the inter-relations of the persons in the Trinity, the crucial word is *homoousion*, translated *of one substance* or *of one essence*. This identifies the Three as of the *same* nature, essence or substance, and not as of *like* nature, *homoiousion*, as some contended. The distinction is vital and not nominal as can easily be seen. The contention was for a fact and not for a word or letter. The former asserts according to the Scriptures the eternal deity of Christ, and His equality with the Father; the latter opens the way to the doctrine of the creation and the subordination of the Logos.

We may turn away from these words like Luther, who expressed his dislike for *homoousion* and *trinity* as being too cold to convey a real idea of God. But he confessed that, in controversy at least, he had no better terms to suggest.

2) EXPLAINED BY LOVE.

Man knows with the heart as well as with the head. He knows by loving as well as by thinking. Does not this throw light upon the whole matter? Should we not with Sartorius study the doctrine of the Trinity and indeed all doctrines as "The Doctrine of Divine Love"?

God is love—love personified, love in substance, love in essence, love in expression. We cannot conceive of God, the absolute, the perfect, as other than love. He would not be God otherwise, for He would lack what is supreme and fundamental in personal life.

The doctrine of the Trinity is illuminated by the nature of love, which sheds its beautiful light not only upon the divine manifestation, but also upon the divine relations and constitution. This thought relieves us immensely of the oppressive conception of the eternal and forbidding solitude of God. It is true that there may be a man here and there who has such extraordinary resources in himself as to be contented without society; but he is abnormal and really not happy.

A "person" must be blessed, he must love in order to be normal. Hence it is inconceivable that our God could be blessed without a Son. We do not wish to deny the fact of a complacent love in which God may find supreme satisfaction in the contemplation of Himself; but we insist that love implies more than one, and that the doctrine of the Three in One makes such love possible and comprehensible.

3) REVEALED IN SCRIPTURE.

The internal relations of the Trinity are in part revealed in the Bible. John speaks of Christ as "the only begotten

Son." The word translated "only begotten," *monogonos*, should probably have been rendered simply *only*, as it is in other passages. The widow of Nain had an "only" son (Lk. 7: 12). Jairus had an "only" daughter (Lk. 8: 42). The emphasis in the Johannine passages is clearly not on "begotten" but on "only," indicating that Christ is the one Son of God; so also when He is spoken of as "the first born," *prototokos*, in contrast with the angels (Heb. 1:6). His unique sonship and honor is asserted rather than His eternal birth.

At all events the term "begotten" has no reference to physical generation, but evidently indicates an identity of essence, and therefore also an ethical and spiritual identity. Even among men the sonship consists not chiefly in the fact of birth but of moral likeness in nobility of character.

We must beware also of making the "generation" of Christ temporal. "It is written in the second Psalm," says Paul, "Thou art my Son, this day have I begotten thee" (Acts 13: 33). Paul applies this passage to Christ's resurrection. The writer to the Hebrews applies it to Christ's superiority to the angels as above noted. As far as the word generation can be applied to the relation between God the Father and God the Son it expresses an eternal relation.

Of the Holy Spirit it is said by our Lord, "When the Comforter is come whom I will send unto you from the Father, even the Spirit of truth, which proceedeth from the Father, he shall bear witness of me" (Jno. 15: 26). Upon this passage is based the doctrine of the procession of the Spirit from the Father. The Nicene Creed declares also that He proceeds "from the Son," because the Spirit of the Father (Matt. 10: 20) is also the Spirit of the Son (Gal. 4: 6). The *spiration* or breathing forth and the *procession* or proceeding are like the begetting, spiritual and eternal, indicating the closest possible personal relation.

4) ILLUSTRATED BY ANALOGIES.

Various analogies have been suggested to illustrate the Trinity. The best and most familiar is that of love in its threefold nature: love itself, the one who loves, and the one who is loved. The family, father, mother and child is a trinity. Sight is supposed to illustrate the idea: the thing seen, the vision, and the will to see; so also the threefold activity of the mind: thinking, feeling and willing. These and many other supposed analogies are all defective; they do not bring personalities into unity. They merely combine functions, acts or objects. It is not needful to seek exact parallels in the natural life. The great truth is a historical revelation, confirmed by religious experience; and this is sufficient.

5. The Manifested Trinity

For the fullest knowledge of the Trinity the sacred Scriptures must be consulted, for they are the historic record of the divine revelation and of the founding of the Church. Without this record there would be no substantial basis for the doctrine. The passages teaching the deity of Father, Son and Spirit are too numerous to quote, but a convincing selection may easily be made.

1) THE NEW TESTAMENT TEACHING.

The New Testament witness to the Trinity is much clearer and fuller than that of the Old Testament and should be considered first.

(1) The Threefold Name.

The culmination of the Gospel teaching concerning the Trinity is found in the last commission of our Lord, which is utterly inexplicable without the presumption that God is One in Three. The unity of the Godhead is expressed in the phrase "into the Name," which is in the singular number; and the Trinity is expressed in the three Persons, Father, Son and Spirit. Their association without any qualification implies their equality.

This combination of three Persons occurs repeatedly. The following instances will suffice. At the annunciation the angel Gabriel mentions the Most High, the Son of God and the Holy Spirit (Lk. 1: 31-35). At the baptism of

Christ, the Father speaks and the Spirit descends upon the Son of God (Jno. 1: 32-34). At His temptation He was led by the Spirit and is called the Son of God (Matt. 4: 1-4). In His promise of the Comforter, the Three appear (Jno. 14: 13-16). In His interview with Nicodemus, God, the Son, and the Spirit are mentioned (Jno. 3: 5, 16). In the apostolic Epistles Peter speaks of the elect "according to the foreknowledge of God the Father, in sanctification of the Spirit unto obedience and the sprinkling of the blood of Jesus Christ" (I Pet. 1: 2). Paul speaks "of peace with God through our Lord Jesus Christ" and of "the love of God" shed abroad in our hearts by the Holy Spirit (Rom. 5: 1, 5). His Epistles to the Corinthians close with the triune benediction (II Cor. 13: 14). John writes of the witness of the Spirit, and of God concerning His Son (I Jno. 5: 7-9). In the closing words of the New Testament he speaks of the call of the Spirit, of the judgment of God, and of the grace of the Lord Jesus (Rev. 22: 17-21).

To the above striking testimony may be added the conclusive evidence which ascribes deity equally to the Three.

(2) The Deity of the Father.

To the Father's deity the passages already quoted afford abundant witness. Moreover, the fatherhood of God is not denied by any theist. In the Scriptures the term Father is applied not only to the First Person but also to the Godhead.

(3) The Deity of the Son.

To the Son, divine titles are given in both testaments. The psalmist exclaims "Thy throne, O God, is forever and ever" (45: 6) and the writer to the Hebrews applies this to Christ, "Unto the Son, he saith, Thy throne" (1: 8). Isaiah (9: 6) calls Him "The Mighty God," and (40: 3) "Jehovah" (Jno. 1: 23). John writes that the eternal Word, Christ, is God, "the only begotten Son" (Jno. 1: 1, 18). Paul speaks of Christ as "over all, God blessed forever" (Rom. 9: 5).

Divine worship is accorded to the Son and accepted by Him. At His ascension "they worshipped Him" (Lk. 24:

52). Thomas called Him, "My Lord and my God" (Jno. 20: 28). Stephen prayed to Christ (Acts 7: 59, 60). Paul declared that "In the name of Jesus every knee should bow" (Phil. 2: 10). Peter writes "To him be the glory both now and forever" (II Pet. 3: 18). John heard a great voice from heaven ascribing the highest glory to the Lamb (Rev. 5: 12).

Divine works are attributed to the Son. "All things were made through Him (Jno. 1: 3), and all things are upheld "by the word of his power" (Heb. 1: 3). Miracles without number and the forgiveness of sins as well as final judgment are ascribed to Him.

Divine attributes are mentioned making Him in all respects God. He has self-existence, is spirit, a person, is omniscient, omnipotent, and omnipresent, and in Him "are all the treasures of wisdom and knowledge hidden" (Col. 2: 3). He is holy, loving, just and true, even as the Father.

Christ claims equality with God. At the feast of dedication at Jerusalem He said to the Jews, "I and the Father are one," "I am the Son of God," "The Father is in me and I in the Father" (Jno. 10: 22-38). Elsewhere He declares, "All things whatsoever the Father hath are mine" (16: 15); and "he that hath seen me hath seen the Father (14: 9). The records also show that He was condemned because He claimed to be the Son of God and to be on equality with Him.

The cumulative force of the above passages is irresistible; the Scriptures teach the deity of our Lord.

In spite of what seems to the evangelical Christian the unmistakable testimony of the Scriptures to the deity of Christ, there are those who, rejecting the doctrine of the Trinity on rationalistic grounds, profess to find in the Bible arguments to sustain their contention. These arguments are based on certain passages affirming the apparent inferiority of Christ to God. For instance, Christ said, "My Father is greater than I" (John 14: 28). He confesses His ignorance of the day of judgment. He learned by experience in the things of daily life.

Only misunderstanding of what was involved in the Incarnation, through which Christ voluntarily denied Himself temporarily the exercise of some supernatural functions, can construe the several passages as affirming personal inferiority. They must be explained as official submission to God in the work of redemption, to accomplish which our Lord took upon Himself the form of a servant.

(4) The Deity of the Spirit.

The Holy Spirit is mentioned on an equality with the Father and the Son in various passages already cited.

His personality is affirmed in the plainest possible manner. Personal pronouns are applied to Him. He is "another Comforter" (Jno. 14: 16). "And he, when he is come, will convict" (16: 8). "When he, the Spirit of truth is come, he shall guide you into all truth" (16: 13). "He shall glorify me" (16: 14). The masculine pronoun *ekeinos* refers to the neuter noun *pneuma,* thus deliberately violating a grammatical rule so as to leave no doubt as to the personality of the Spirit.

Personal acts are ascribed to the Spirit. He teaches, bears witness, speaks, guides, comforts, works, wills and intercedes. The unpardonable sin against Him implies that He is personal.

Divine titles are given to the Holy Spirit. Lying to the Spirit is lying to God (Acts 5: 3, 4). Divine attributes are ascribed to Him: eternity (Heb. 9: 14); omnipresence (Ps. 139: 7, 8); omniscience (I Cor. 2: 10). He moved upon the face of the waters at the creation (Gen. 1: 2). He endows believers with divers gifts and the power to work miracles (I Cor. 12: 11).

2) THE OLD TESTAMENT TEACHING.

The older theologians were wont to find in the Old Testament numerous and explicit references to the Trinity. Later theologians denied that any traces of the doctrine existed, in proof of which they cited the Jews and the Mohammedans, who to this day reject it as teaching polytheism. If, however, the Christian postulate of the Trinity be well founded, it is entirely reasonable to expect some foreshadowing of it in the Old Testament. We believe that the revelation of the Trinity is latent in the Old Testament and patent in the New.

(1) The Name *Elohim*.

In the first verse of the Bible the name of God occurs in the plural form, *Elohim*, which however is construed with a verb in the singular number. Linguists affirm that this is simply the plural of majesty. Nevertheless, the mention of God and the Spirit of God in the immediate context inclines one to see a hint of plurality in *Elohim*. Moreover, when we interpret Genesis by John who declares of Christ, the eternal Word, that "all things were made through Him," we must refer the repeated "And God said" to Christ. Father, Son and Spirit surely participated in the creation, as appears from other passages; and it is not incredible that this truth underlies the account in Genesis.

(2) The Benediction and the Trisagion.

The Aaronic benediction (Numbers 6: 24-26) and the Trisagion of the Seraphim, "Holy, holy, holy is Jehovah of hosts: the whole earth is full of his glory" (Is. 6: 3) strongly suggest the Trinity.

(3) The Messianic Promise.

The Messianic passages which inspired Israel with a passionate hope, occur here and there through the Old Testament and evidently point to a second Person in the Godhead. "The angel of the Lord" frequently mentioned must be differentiated from the Father and according to eminent scholars is identical with the Son.

(4) Allusions to the Spirit.

References to the Spirit and to the Spirit of God are also numerous. Job echoes Genesis when he says "By his Spirit the heavens are garnished" (26: 13). The Psalms declare of the works of nature, "Thou sendest forth thy Spirit, they are created" (104: 30). When David pleads so earnestly "Take not thy Holy Spirit from me" (51: 11), it sounds like an anticipation of a New Testament prayer. Who can deny in the light of Pentecost that when God promised through Joel, 2: 28, "I will pour out my Spirit upon all flesh," He meant that He would send the Holy Spirit, who together with the Father and the Son is worshiped and glorified?

C. THE WORKS OF GOD

I. CREATION.

1. The Christian View

According to the Christian view, God, the Father Almighty, is the "Maker of heaven and earth and of all things visible and invisible." The universe bears undoubted evidence that it is the product of an infinite, personal Spirit. All theories to the contrary are untenable and false. Materialism in any form cannot account even for the existence of matter, much less of spirit. Dualism is false because it postulates the bondage of spirit to matter and accounts for nothing. Emanation is absurd because it attributes the universe to a mechanical effluence from the divine Essence regardless of divine will.

The Christian view of the origin of the universe is derived from the Scriptures, from reason and from experience. The Bible teaches in the most unqualified way that the universe was called into being by God, and that it shows forth the divine glory in its structure and movements. Reflection confirms the noble conception of the law-giver, the psalmist and the prophet. Everywhere are seen the wisdom and goodness of a great Creator.

The personal experience of the best men indicates that they are dependent on a Supreme Being. They see a teleology in the world whose wonderful adaptation to human need suggests that it exists for man. When they remember that God sent His only Son into the world, they are constrained to regard the world as the sphere in which man is undergoing a probation to fit him for a higher life.

2. The Biblical Account

1) An Absolute Creation.

The Old Testament plainly affirms that God called the universe into being, *ex nihilo*, by His will and word. The Hebrew word *bara* used in Genesis, indicates an absolute creation and denies eternity of matter. This word is evidently deliberately and discriminately used.

The psalmist declares that "the earth is Jehovah's and the fulness thereof; the world and they that dwell therein" (Ps. 24: 1). He cries, "O Jehovah how manifold are thy works. In wisdom thou hast made them all: the earth is full of thy riches. . . . Thou sendest forth thy spirit, they are created" (104: 24, 30). "By the word of Jehovah were the heavens made" (33: 6).

In the book of Job, Jehovah is represented as demanding of the ancient saint an answer to the question, "Where wast thou when I laid the foundations of the earth. . . . when the morning stars sang together and the sons of God shouted for joy?" (Job 38: 4, 7).

The New Testament accepts the Old Testament teaching concerning creation, resting its most practical directions for life upon the postulate that "the earth is the Lord's and the fulness thereof" (I Cor. 10: 26). The writer to the Hebrews expresses the acceptance of the doctrine of divine creation when he says, "By faith we understand that the worlds have been framed by the word of God, so that what is seen hath not been made out of things which appear" (11: 3).

2) A Trinitarian Creation.

The Bible teaches that the three Persons in the Trinity cooperated in the creation. In several passages creation is ascribed to each one of the Persons. Paul says "There is one God the Father of (*ex*) whom are all things and we unto him, and one Lord Jesus Christ through (*dia*) whom are all things" (I Cor. 8: 6). "Thou sendest forth thy spirit and they are created," says the psalmist (104: 30). Hence it may be said that creation is *of* the Father, *through* the Son, and *in* the Spirit. The apostle John declares that creation was the particular function of the Son, or Logos. "All things were made through him, and without him was not anything made that hath been made" (Jno. 1: 3).

3) THE METHOD OF CREATION.

In regard to the method of creation the Scriptures are silent. They affirm the absolute creation by God's will. "In the beginning God created the heavens and the earth." Thus opens the Bible. In the rapid sketches which follow there is no intimation of the process except that it was orderly and progressive. Wonderful potency was lodged in Spirit and matter as is still evident.

The Christian may leave the study of the processes of world formation and development to the scientist, as long as God is postulated as the Almighty Maker of heaven and earth. The question of evolution is one of science rather than of theology. No doubt many untenable theories have been advanced in the name of evolution which the Christian cannot accept; but many great and wonderful truths have been the result of a theistic evolutionary theory of the universe.

3. The Bible Cosmogony

1) ITS SOURCE.

Of all the ancient stories of creation, that recorded in Genesis is alone rational and credible. The myths of Babylon are at best grotesque distortions of an original account of a divine creation. The ultimate source of the Biblical account must be sought in primeval revelation. It is incredible that without illumination the human mind can have thought out and arranged so sane and so beautiful a theory of creation. The sages of Greece were unequal to the task. To what extent Moses may have been inspired we cannot tell, but the influence of the Holy Spirit no doubt enabled him to select from traditional accounts what was true and to construct a narrative which remains after centuries the most rational, popular account conceivable. It commends itself to the mind as being in harmony with facts. The magnificent panorama of creation, as seen by the author of Genesis, must be interpreted not by cold reason alone, but by reason touched by the fire of a devout imagination. Evidently the purpose in the Genesis account is to furnish a background for the history of man, especially of his redemption, and this is admirably achieved.

2) ITS RELATION TO SCIENCE.

Some contend that the Biblical cosmogony is hopelessly at variance with science. It is not needful here to attempt a reconciliation, for whether or not discrepancies can be removed the Bible story must be recognized as substantially true in presenting the world as the product of a creative will, progressive in its activity. First is the creation of matter in a chaotic state; then follows order and, in successive periods, life in a constantly rising scale, culminating in man.

3) OBJECTIONS CONSIDERED.

Unreasonable objections to the narrative are readily answered. For instance, when it is declared that geology makes it plain that the universe was not created in six days, the answer is easy. A day in the Bible often stands for a period of indefinite length, and this must be the interpretation of its meaning in Genesis.

Some have stumbled at the apparent contradiction which is involved in the creation of light on the first day and of the sun and moon and stars on the fourth. Whatever the explanation may be, the statement was evidently deliberately made; for it is inconceivable that so intelligent a person as the author of Genesis could have fallen into a palpable error. It is at least supposable that he had knowledge that light is not limited to our present luminaries. If we may accept the scientific statement that matter existed in the beginning as a fiery vapor we have light before the sun took form.

Objection has also been made to the statement that God "rested on the seventh day from all the work which he had made," on the ground that God needs no rest and that His work goes on day and night, perpetually. In reply it may be said that complete cessation of God's activity cannot be intended. Our Lord, whose interpretations and application of the Old Testament Scriptures must be taken as final, wrought miracles on the Sabbath, declaring "My Father worketh even until now and I work" (Jno. 5: 17). The message in Genesis speaks after the manner of men and indicates the completion of a particular cycle of work.

II. PROVIDENCE.

1. Definition

By providence is meant the Creator's constant sustaining and preserving care of the works of His hands.   It involves the immanence of God, who is present always and everywhere.   The deistic doctrine that God has established fixed laws which regulate all things and that His personal supervision is not necessary has no ground in reason or Scripture.

2. Proof

1) BIBLE TEACHING.

The whole tenor of Scripture implies the nearness and love of God.   Paul declared at Athens, "He is not far from each one of us, for in him we live and move and have our being: as certain even of your own poets have said" (Acts 17: 27, 28).

The incarnation, character, works and words of Jesus Christ dispel all doubt as to the providence of God.   In the Sermon on the Mount He gives the most explicit assurance of divine care extending to the most minute concerns of life.

The Psalms echo with expressions of confidence in God as the great provider for man and beast.   The Old Testament is the record of God's dealing with the Jews.

The apostolic teaching harmonizes with the rest of Scripture.   In Him, in the Son of God, "all things consist" or are held together (Col. 1: 17).   In Hebrews 1: 3 we read of the Son as "upholding all things by the word of his power."

2) EXPERIENCE.

The teaching of Scripture is confirmed by human experience and by faith.   History bears witness to the providence of God.   The most conspicuous examples are the people of

God—the chosen people, and the Christian Church. The former have been preserved though scattered among all nations. The growth of the latter in spite of all obstacles cannot be accounted for except as a special object of God's care.

Biography abounds in incidents of extraordinary providential dealings. Paul attributes his remarkable career altogether to special divine guidance. There are innumerable living witnesses who believe with David that the steps of a good man are ordered by the Lord. "Though he fall he shall not be utterly cast down for Jehovah upholdeth him with his hand. I have been young and now am old; yet have I not seen the righteous forsaken, nor his seed begging bread" (Ps. 37: 24, 25).

3. Phases of the Doctrine

Providence may be considered from several points of view, as general and special, causal and permissive, and the like. These divisions are proper, but require no extended dogmatic discussion. There can be no general procedure which does not embrace the individual and vice versa. It is also evident from the nature of a wise and good God that His government must be rational and parental, and that in the exercise thereof He establishes certain immutable decrees, and permits to beings endowed with freedom of will certain choices freighted with corresponding consequences.

Another suggested division of the subject, ordinary and extraordinary providence, requires more consideration.

Ordinary providence refers to the regularity of nature and the usual course of events in which goodness is rewarded and evil punished. The ordinary experiences of life, full of comfort and blessing, are really extraordinary when one stops to consider all that is involved. There is every reason to believe that God makes nature so subservient to man that when properly used the millions on earth need not suffer for lack of sustenance. Even the rigors of nature may be and often are blessed to the development of man.

It is the unusual, however, that is more noticeable than the ordinary, and this calls for comment. The Christian faith embraces a belief in Miracle and Prayer.

III. MIRACLES.

1. Definition

The word *miracle* signifies something wonderful, something out of the ordinary. In Scripture and theology a miracle is an event in the natural world or in human life produced by the intervention of divine power and not to be explained by the ordinary operation of known laws. The miracles wrought by Christ are illustrations.

2. Proof

1) POSSIBILITY.

The possibility of miracles—special divine actions—is not denied even by those who refuse to accept them. God would not be God if it were impossible for Him to manifest His power in extraordinary ways. It is preposterous to limit God.

Miracles are not repugnant to the mind of man. On the contrary, especially in heathen religions, the immanence of God has been over-emphasized rather than denied. To the Christian nothing is more natural than that God should reveal Himself in extraordinary ways.

2) NATURE OF CHRISTIANITY.

Christianity is itself a miracle, an extraordinary coming of God into human history. A denial of this destroys the unique and supernatural character of Christianity and especially of Jesus Christ. We cannot stop to prove that the history of Christ as related in the gospels is authentic. This has been done elsewhere.

Christ is the supreme miracle of history. He cannot be explained by ordinary laws. According to the record, His advent was prophesied centuries before His manifestation; He was conceived by the Holy Ghost; born of the Virgin Mary; heralded by angels. In infancy He was preserved and protected by supernatural intervention. During His ministry He wrought extraordinary cures, and even raised the dead. He Himself rose from the dead and after a sojourn of forty days, during which He showed Himself repeatedly, He visibly ascended to heaven. A denial of these facts puts one outside of the Christian Church. An acknowledgment of them makes belief in miracles not only easy, but necessary.

3) TESTIMONY.

The establishment of an alleged miracle is subject to the law of evidence. The underlying principle of worthiness and congruity must, of course, not be overlooked. The testimony of reliable witnesses is undoubtedly indicated in the well-authenticated record of the Bible. Here is an appeal, not to prejudice, but to the consensus and to the consciousness of the best and most intelligent of mankind. The acceptance of miracles is not dependent altogether upon testimony, but upon a precedent attitude. If the impossibility of miracles be made a postulate, as was done by Hume, no amount of testimony can establish them. To the Christian a miracle is an act of infinite love and power which God exercises in behalf of his children; and therefore a miracle is not only congruous, but is to be expected.

3. Purpose
1) DEFINED BY THE NAMES.

The miracles wrought by Christ or by His authority are defined by three terms: signs, *sameia*, wonders, *terata*, and powers, *dunameis*. These words are combined in a striking passage in Hebrews 2:4, "God also bearing witness with them, both by signs and wonders and by manifold powers, and by gifts of the Holy Spirit, according to his own will." Miracles are "wonders" in their character and manifestation, "powers" in their source, and "signs" in their purpose. It is significant that the word wonders, *terata*, never occurs in the account of a divine miracle without the accompanying word signs, *sameia*. This is evidently significant of the fact that the real meaning of a miracle is teleological. It has a purpose; it presents or illustrates some important truth; it is a parable.

2) BY THEIR CONTENT.

"We accept the miracles of Christ because they embody the very thing to be proved. Miracles are not gratuitous, superfluous, inconvenient and irrelevant credentials; they are themselves didactic and revealing. They were not credentials of the kind that can be examined, approved and then laid aside that the substance of the mission may be gone into. They were something very different from the seal on a letter, which, as soon as recognized, is torn off and thrown away that the contents may be read. They were rather like the very contents of the letter, which in every line reveal and certify the writer. They were like the munificent gift which suggests but one possible giver, the far-reaching benefaction which guarantees its own authorship" (Dods).

3) CREDENTIALS.

Miracles are the credentials of Christ and His apostles. God bore witness to His message through miraculous endowment of the apostles (Heb. 2: 4). Our Lord distinctly appeals to His miracles as confirmatory of His divine mission. He says, "the very works that I do bear witness of me, that the Father hath sent me" (Jno. 5: 36). "If I do not the works of my Father, believe me not" (10: 37). "Believe me for my very works' sake" (14: 11). That miracles are included in the "works" of God is evident from numerous passages (Matt. 16: 9, 10; Jno. 5, 10). In healing the paralytic (Mark 2: 10) Christ confirms His power to forgive sin by the miracle. When John the Baptist sought assurance as to Christ's claims to the Messiahship, Christ appealed to His miracles as fulfilling prophecy.

The evident value of miracles is a distinct asset of faith and cannot be yielded at the demand of unbelief. It may be freely acknowledged that the continuance of miracles is not needed now, because the religion of Jesus Christ has been fully established and its claims vindicated. Moreover, it may be also conceded that the gift of miracles is of less value than that of teaching, for Paul distinctly states that "God hath set some in the Church, first apostles, secondly prophets, thirdly teachers, then miracles" (I Cor. 12:28).

4. Objections

Perhaps the usual objections to miracles have been sufficiently anticipated in what precedes. Nevertheless, they may be briefly enumerated here.

1) The objection that miracles are impossible and unthinkable is mere assertion, because they are neither. To an absolute Person nothing is impossible. What is a miracle to us is just what we expect from Him.

2) The uniformity of law is supposed to rule out miracles, but natural law is not so rigid that it can resist the law governing free creatures, much less the free Creator. A higher law may displace a lower one. God, acting in accordance with the eternal purposes of holy love, may intervene whenever He thinks it important to do so. Such actions may be difficult to class and formulate but they are regular nevertheless. God is too good to be the servant of the laws which He has wisely framed for ordinary purposes.

3) It has sometimes been urged that the present absence of miracles discredits them altogether. If Christ fed multitudes why does He not feed the starving today? Our inability to explain why God does not act in accordance with the ideas of men does not justify the charge of inconsistency. God never promised to feed multitudes by miracle. He has made it possible that every soul in the world be fed and cared for in obedience to the law of love and brotherhood. Surely no wise ruler would put a premium upon lawbreaking and idleness. God might do many things to establish Himself in the confidence of His people, but He would not constantly interfere with the working of ordinary law. Our Lord, when challenged to perform miracles at Nazareth as He had done elsewhere refused to comply and cited the case of Elijah who "when there came a

great famine over all the land" relieved only one poor widow though there were many widows in Israel. The God of Elijah knows what is best.

4) It is also said that miracles make it impossible for a man to adjust himself to his environment. This might be so, if they were constant; but no man expects that God will miraculously feed him, though he has a right to believe that God through the exercise of His providence will rule and overrule that in the end the believer's highest interests will be served.

5) Fraudulent miracles have been cited to discredit alleged miracles of the Bible, but it is contrary to all experience that frauds should be counterfeited. False miracles are easily detected and exposed and do not militate against the true, but rather confirm them.

6) An old objection is that reliable evidence cannot be adduced to establish the authenticity of miracles. Hume very illogically says that miracles are contrary to human experience, but that false testimony is not: hence miracles cannot be proved! He begs the question, and then tries to substantiate his position by trying to discredit all history! In the final analysis the evidence for miracles must be accepted as any other historical events are accepted. When in the case of miracles their intent, their connection, and their relation to Christ and Christianity are considered one is forced to the conclusion that facts of the New Testament, especially Christ, cannot be accounted for if miracles be excluded.

5. Old Testament Miracles

The foregoing remarks contemplate the miracles of the New Testament rather than of the Old Testament; but the principles involved are alike in both cases. All are the expression of God's benevolent powers. The history of the Jews shows forth the providence of God. Its most extraordinary events are pedagogical as far as later generations are concerned. Our Lord applies the story of Jonah as a "sign" of His own resurrection.

IV. PRAYER.

1. The Nature of Prayer

The doctrine of providence involves prayer. Prayer is the outstretched hand of the soul towards God. It is the expression of man's need, and of his communion with his Maker and Father. Prayer is universal. It is not only natural to pray, but unnatural not to pray. The reality of prayer is attested by its universality. It is co-extensive with religion, partakes of its nature, and can be explained away as little as religion.

2. The Elements of Prayer

Prayer is not chiefly petition, as the word seems to indicate. It has the elements of adoration and thanksgiving as well as of confession. Petition, however, is an essential part of prayer and is as natural as the cry of the hungry child. This very figure of speech is used by our Lord when He encourages His disciples to ask God to satisfy their physical and spiritual needs. "Give us this day our daily bread" is the warrant for praying for earthly and heavenly bread.

3. The Spirit of Prayer

True prayer is characterized by faith and submission. On the one hand the believer has confidence that God hears prayer, and that He is attentive to the cry of His children; and on the other he has the feeling of humble submission to the will of God. He can say with his Master, "Thou hearest me always," and also "not my will but thine be done." It would be useless, preposterous and impious to insist upon having one's own way instead of submitting to the infinitely wise and loving God.

4. Encouragement to Prayer

The Bible is the book of prayer. The word is used about three hundred times; and the word praise about as often. Our Lord not only taught His disciples how to pray, and exhorted them with many promises to pray, but He Himself while on earth was in constant communion with His

Father and spent whole nights in prayer. He was transfigured during prayer on the mountain. In the garden He agonized in prayer, and He expired on the Cross with prayer on His lips.

The saints of all ages have been men and women of prayer. The apostles made "supplications and prayer night and day" and admonished their hearers to pray without ceasing. The soldier of the cross is exhorted to put on the whole armor of God and go forth "with all prayer and supplication praying at all seasons in the Spirit, and watching thereunto in all perseverance and supplication for all the saints" (Eph. 6:18).

5.   The Value of Prayer

There can be no doubt that prayer has an important reflex influence. Experience shows that serenity of soul is one of the direct and immediate blessings of prayer. Faith is strengthened by the very act of committing its concerns to the loving God. Through years of trial and disappointment many a believer has been sustained by prayer. The child feels relieved when it has poured out its troubles into the ear of its mother.

But is the value of prayer only reflexive, or does it have objective worth? Does the sincere soul receive what it prays for? The testimony of many reliable witnesses in Biblical and subsequent times confirms faith in the objective value of prayer. Volumes have been written on answered prayer.

6.   Difficulties in Regard to Prayer

Doubt and unbelief suggest inherent difficulties on account of the supposed inflexible reign of law. They may admit that prayer may bring even an objective spiritual blessing, but they deny an external physical answer. The God of nature however is also the God of spirit, and if He be bound by unchangeable fixity in the former, He must also be bound in the latter; for one is just as real as the other. If He can originate, combine and adjust spiritual forces, why should He not do something similar with natural forces?

It may be said here as elsewhere that God is not the slave of His own law. He is a free personal Spirit who can do what seemeth Him good, and this in a perfectly orderly way. It is after all a question of what we call the miraculous. Our ignorance of how God can do this or that does not prevent His doing it.

V. ANGELS.

1. Angels in General

The works of God cannot be limited to that which is discernible by the physical senses. Man himself is really spirit, but spirit embodied. Hence it is evident that there is a spiritual as well as physical creation. There are things terrestial and things celestial, things visible and things invisible.

1) THEIR EXISTENCE.

The existence of other rational beings besides man is extremely probable. The denial of this by Sadducee and materialist is most presumptuous, without proof and without the possibility of proof. We learn from the Scriptures that God created rational beings who are called angels or messengers, who dwell in His immediate presence. The most explicit statements as to their existence, nature and office are contained in both Testaments, from which comes indeed all our information concerning them. It must be confessed that the testimony of the present religious experience concerning angels is vague; but this does not militate against the witness of our Lord. It is conceivable that a more highly developed spiritual experience might make us clearly conscious of their presence.

2) THEIR ORIGIN.

The origin of angels must of course be ascribed to a divine creation, which took place before that of man, for the "sons of God" shouted for joy when Jehovah laid the foundations of the earth (Job 38: 4-7).

3) THEIR NATURE.

These angels or sons of God are personal beings richly endowed (Job 1: 6). They are not mere personifications of wind and fire which are often spoken of as messengers of God, but creatures like man and made in the image of God. They differ from men in being pure spirit, that is incorporeal, and hence invisible, except as God empowered them to assume a human form. They are unlike man, being without sex, and neither marrying, nor being given in marriage. Their number is great, but stationary.

4) THEIR PROBATION.

The angels seem to have undergone a probation as man has and as probably all finite moral beings must. While a vast multitude stood the test; others kept not their first estate but fell from God. Hence there are two. classes: good angels and evil angels or devils.

2. Good Angels

1) THEIR CLASSIFICATION.

The Scriptures represent the good angels as a heavenly hierarchy, or present an orderly division of them into thrones, dominions, principalities and powers (Col. 1: 16; Rom. 8: 38; Eph. 3: 10). Their chief is the archangel Michael (I Thess. 4: 16; Jude 9). Cherubim and seraphim are apparently of the angelic order, whether real or symbolic is not clear. The latter seems the more probable.

Cherubim stood at the gates of the Garden of Eden after the expulsion of man. They have four wings indicating swiftness in obedience, and they stand in the presence of God. Carved images of cherubim ornamented the lid of the ark in the holy of holies, and representations of them appeared in the decorations of the tabernacle and the temple.

Seraphim are distinctly mentioned by Isaiah only (6: 1-7), and are apparently alluded to by John (Rev. 4: 6). They are winged creatures standing in the divine presence singing "Holy, holy, holy is Jehovah of hosts," and sanctifying the prophet for his mission.

The Angel of Jehovah is mentioned a number of times in the Old Testament in connection with striking events.

He appears to Hagar in the desert. Abraham intercedes with him in Sodom. He intercedes to save Isaac. Jacob wrestles with him. He appears to Moses in the burning bush, leads Israel out of Egypt, and directs Joshua. A study of the several passages shows that this theophany is a fuller revelation than that which is given by angels in general. In some cases the Angel is identified with Jehovah. Oehler and other Old Testament scholars are of the opinion that he was none other than the Son of God.

2) THEIR EMPLOYMENT.

The employment of angels includes their celestial and terrestial occupations. In heaven they appear as (a) a vast host or army (Lk. 2:13, Mt. 26:53); (b) a choir (Rev. 5:8, 9; 8:3); and (c) a court. The Son of Man is seated on a throne, surrounded by principalities and powers (Mt. 19:28; Rev. 5:11; 7:11).

On earth the angels appear to bear messages to the faithful. They appear to Joseph, Mary and Zacharias and to the women after the resurrection. They give help to the saints. They deliver Peter from prison and bear the soul of Lazarus to Paradise. They appear to Paul to give him guidance in perplexity. Their relation to our Lord is most beautiful; they announce His advent and comfort Him in His agony.

The ancient belief that each person on earth has his guardian angel has no direct warrant in Scripture, but it is in harmony with the teaching that they are "sent forth to do service for the sake of them that shall inherit salvation" (Heb. 1:14). There is great consolation in the thought that round about the faithful God's angels are keeping perpetual watch.

3. Evil Spirits

1) THEIR EXISTENCE.

The existence of evil spirits is as inherently possible and probable as that of good spirits, and of good and evil men. Their existence is accepted by practically all religions, true and false.

(1) Taught in the Old Testament.

This belief finds ample warrant in the Bible, on the earliest pages of which is recorded the temptation of our first parents by "the serpent," the old serpent, he that is called the Devil and Satan, the deceiver of the whole world (Rev. 12: 9). Evil spirits are alluded to in other parts of the Old Testament, thus affording ground for the somewhat elaborate development of doctrine by the rabbis.

(2) Taught in the New Testament.

That the New Testament teaching confirms the belief in the existence of evil spirits is evident from the numerous allusions to good and evil angels. The words angel and angels occur one hundred and sixty times. The word devil occurs over one hundred times, the word Satan thirty-two times and the words evil spirits forty-five, making one hundred and seventy-seven in all.

(3) Accepted by Christ.

The decisive conclusion of the whole matter must be sought in the attitude of our great Teacher. It is a vain subterfuge to assert that the sayings of Jesus concerning evil spirits are all interpolations, for they are as well substantiated as the other Scriptures. No language could be more explicit than His sayings and injunctions concerning the devil and his angels. Not in a single case is doubt cast upon their reality. In His denunciations of the traditional beliefs of the Pharisees, there is not a word contradicting their belief in the existence of evil demons. On the threshold of the New Testament stands the record of the great temptation in which the reality and personality of Satan are affirmed. An examination of the numerous passages forces the conclusion that our Lord means us to accept the doctrine that there is a devil with a vast body of superhuman followers, that he is the prime authority of evil and that finally he will be punished. To this end Christ became incarnate and made the atonement, "that through death he might bring to nought him that had the power of death, that is the devil" (Heb. 2: 14).

Three alternatives have been suggested in regard to Christ's attitude on the subject of demons: First, that He shared the superstitions of His age, and accepted honestly the traditional though false views; second, that He accommodated His teaching to these views, knowing that they were false, but using them in the interest of higher truth; third, that He knew and experienced the power of evil spirits, as actual and terrible realities. The first of these alternatives is untenable because it denies His omniscience and deity; the second likewise because it would make Him dishonest. The third alone can be true and must be accepted as final.

2) THEIR ORIGIN.

The origin of evil spirits must be traced to the fall of once good angels who like man failed to stand some great moral test. This is implied by Jude when speaking of angels that kept their own principality but left their proper habitation; he says God "hath kept in everlasting bonds under darkness unto the judgment of the great day." In II Pet. 2:4 the apostle says, ". . God spared not angels when they sinned, but cast them down to hell, and committed them to pits of darkness, to be reserved unto judgment." Christ after the return of the Seventy, who declared "Even the demons are subject unto us in thy name," exclaimed, "I beheld Satan fallen as lightning from heaven."

3) THEIR FALL.

The cause of the fall of evil spirits must have been opposition to the Almighty. Paul warns Timothy against receiving into the ministry "a novice, lest being puffed up he fall into the condemnation of the devil" (I Tim. 3:6). From this it appears that pride was the cause of the fall of the evil spirits. Shakespeare makes Wolsey say:

"I charge thee, fling away ambition,
By that sin fell the angels." (Henry VIII.)

Pride, conceit, and ambition to supplant the authority of God are all rooted in unbelief.

4) THEIR PERSONALITY.

That evil spirits with Satan as their leader are personal is evident from the name, Satan, meaning adversary, and devil, meaning accuser, as well as from the personal endowments and acts attributed to them. Our Lord unequivocally deals with Satan as a person. Moreover, the suggestion that Satan stands simply for evil influence is untenable, because the abstract existence of influence apart from a person is not conceivable (Matt. 4: 1-11; Jno. 8: 44).

5) THEIR CLASSIFICATION.

There are ranks of the evil angels as there are of the good. Jesus speaks of the devil and his angels (Matt. 25: 41). Paul mentions principalities, powers, world-rulers of this darkness and spiritual hosts of wickedness (Eph. 6: 12; Col. 2: 15).

6) THEIR POWER.

The power of evil spirits appears to be very great. Nevertheless it is finite and restricted by the will of God and man. Evil suggestions and deep craftiness are among the characteristics of the devil. Taking advantage of man's weakness, he creates great havoc in the world if unrestricted.

Concerning demoniacal possessions the teaching of the New Testament is very plain. Our Lord repeatedly cast out devils and commanded and empowered the apostles to cast them out. To deny this is to put serious imputations upon Him.

Objection is made to the doctrine of demoniacal possessions on at least two grounds; first, that the phenomena exhibited by so-called demoniacs are those of well-known disease, physical and mental; secondly, that no such cases exist today.

In regard to the first objection it may be said that satanic influence might be expected to manifest itself through a disordered mind or a diseased body. Moreover, superhuman knowledge was often present. At all events our Lord could not have been deceived by the symptoms.

In reply to the second objection it may be said that the frightful wickedness of some persons is still strongly suggestive of demoniacal possession. Missionaries report that among non-Christian people the phenomena attendent upon possession at the beginning of the Christian era are still evident (Nevin's Demoniacal Possession). Should these be unauthentic, it nevertheless remains true that the coming of Christ, the second Adam, aroused satanic activity, even as the creation of the first Adam did.

PART II

ANTHROPOLOGY

THE DOCTRINE OF MAN

The Christian view of man is derived from Scripture, from the life and teachings of Christ, and from history and experience. It is of the highest importance that man should endeavor to know himself as he is, as well as his origin and his destiny. No light that can shed knowledge upon man in any aspect should be considered foreign to the theologian; nevertheless, he must confine his inquiries chiefly to the religious nature of man. Modern anthropology is comprehensive in its purpose, embracing archæology, ethnology, and the manners, customs, history and language of the several races. Theological anthropology deals particularly with the Nature, the Origin and the Fall of Man.

A. THE NATURE OF MAN

I. A COMPOSITE BEING.

It is evident that man is not simply matter, but that he is also and chiefly spirit; he is a composite being. To differentiate between the several elements and to analyze them exactly is not easy. Nevertheless, the consensus of the best students of man is that he is a twofold being.

1. A Twofold Being

The materialistic conception that matter is the sole substance, the source and origin of everything, would make man merely developed matter and therefore a monad. But matter cannot account for spirit, and therefore materialistic monism must be rejected. This is equally true of atheistic idealism, which postulates impersonal mind or spirit. But personality cannot arise from impersonality and hence this form of monism must also be rejected.

1) THE SPIRIT.

The Scripture teaching is that God created first the human body and then breathed into it the breath, *neshamah*, of life, and so man became a living soul, *nephesh* (Gen. 2: 7). Thus man is constituted of two parts—body and soul. This accords with our Lord's teaching in the Sermon on the Mount (Matt. 6: 25) where He speaks of body, *soma*, and soul, *psuche*.

However, in several passages of the New Testament a three-fold nature of man is intimated. Paul writes to the Thessalonians, "May your spirit, *pneuma*, and soul, *psuche* and body, *soma*, be preserved entire" (I Thess. 5: 23). The Epistle to the Hebrews speaks of the word of God dividing the soul and spirit (Heb. 4: 12). The words "soul" and "spirit" when used separately in connection with the mention of the "body" are evidently used synonymously. Thus Christ speaks of those who kill the body but not the soul (Matt. 10: 28). James 2: 26 says that "the body without the spirit is dead." The language of the Bible is popular rather than scientific when a three-fold division of man is mentioned.

An appeal to consciousness seems to confirm the idea that man is two-fold, *dichotomous*, rather than three-fold, *trichotomous*. In endeavoring to realize himself, a person is not conscious of a distinction between soul and spirit, except in so far as soul may stand for animal life. The higher soul-life of man is spiritual, and in this lies his likeness to God. Man as mind, *nous*, embracing the faculty of thinking, feeling and willing, cannot be differentiated from man as spirit, *pneuma*. Should the mind of man become impaired he ceases to be "normal man."

The phrase "soul and spirit" regards man as viewed in two different aspects. All through the Scriptures "spirit" denotes life as coming from God; "soul" denotes life as constituted in man. He is a soul or has a soul. He is an ego or person.

When soul and spirit are contrasted, the earthly and the heavenly tendencies or attitude of man are contemplated. Thus Paul speaks of the unconverted or worldly man as the natural man, the soul man, *psuchikos*. "The natural man receiveth not the things of the spirit of God" (I Cor. 2:14). The converted or spirit-man, *pneumaticos*, alone discerns spiritual things. Hence the soul-man becomes the spirit-man when he yields to God; but he does not thereby lose or change his identity. As a natural man he looks downward; as a spiritual man he looks upward.

2. The Body

The material part of man is not mere flesh, *sarx*, but an organized body, *soma*, endowed with life and subject to the spirit. The word flesh when applied to man by the Scriptures stands for his lower nature. The unregenerate man is fleshly, carnal, worldly. He is more animal than spiritual. Even the converted realizes the struggle between the fleshly and the spiritual forces within him. Flesh and body, however, are not the source of sin or inherently sinful. They may be the servant of sin or of holiness. Paul exhorts the Romans, saying "Let not sin therefore reign in your mortal body that ye should obey the lust thereof; neither present your members unto sin as instruments of unrighteousness; but present yourselves unto God, as alive from the dead, and your members as instruments of righteousness unto God" (Rom. 6:12, 13).

The body as the organ of the spirit is to be honored and kept meet for the Master's use, and to be presented a living sacrifice, holy, acceptable to God "as a spiritual service" (Rom. 12:1). The "body is a temple of the Holy Spirit," and "if any man destroyeth the temple of God, him shall God destroy" (I Cor. 6:19; 3:16, 17).

3. The Unity of Spirit and Body

The unity of spirit and body is apparent, but not easily understood. They are closely knit together, act and react on each other in a very remarkable manner, and are mutually dependent. We have no experimental knowledge of the existence of the two apart from each other. The soul receives most of its knowledge through sense perception and it expresses itself through the bodily organs. The body needs the directing counsel and guidance of the spirit.

These things are true not merely of our earthly state, for when this earthly house of our tabernacle is dissolved, we have a building from God, a house not made with hands, eternal in the heavens (II Cor. 5 : 1). "If there is a natural, *psuchikos*, body, there is also a spiritual, *pneumatikos*, body" (I Cor. 15 : 44). The first body is suited to the earthly state; the latter to the celestial, but it is none the less a body; that is, something material.

4. Man's Relation to Animals

Man's possession of a body similar to that of the lower animals suggests a relation between them. Man is really an animal, but that of the highest order. The distinction between them has been expressed by saying that while man is guided by reason, mere animals are directed by instinct, which Paley has defined as "propensity prior to experience and independent of instruction." But man also possesses instinct, and the rudiments of minds are not wanting in animals. They possess memory and can be taught to do things. They possess affection and are capable of resentment. They also exhibit will power, especially stubbornness.

There is, however, a great gulf between men and mere animals. The mental endowments of the latter are only rudimentary and incapable of development beyond narrow limits. They have gregarious instincts and habits, but they have only the rudiments of language and no literature, and are incapable of cultivating art or architecture. Skillful in providing shelters, they do not vary them in a thousand years except as circumstances compel trifling changes. They have no moral character or conscience. A vicious brute is put to death not because it has broken a law, but because it is a menace to human life.

The chief end of creation is found in man, as is clearly seen in his endowment as well as in his dominion over all brutes, and animals exist chiefly for the sake of man. Their contribution to human life and comfort in furnishing food, clothing, transportation and even companionship should be gratefully recognized, and they should be treated with mercy and kindness.

II. THE MORAL NATURE OF MAN.

1. Man an Ethical Being

The highest conception of personality embraces morality, or conformity to a proper ethical standard. Man is a personality endowed with a sense of right and wrong and with the feeling of obligation to do the former and to abstain from the latter. This endowment is implied in the fact that he was made in the image of God. Though he is a fallen creature he has not totally lost the power of moral discernment. When he is regenerated by the spirit this power is quickened and the feeling of obligation strengthened.

2. Man Endowed With Conscience

The common name by which we know this power of discrimination is conscience, which indicates a moral consciousness or recognition of a moral standard. Conscience has been regarded by some as a distinct faculty of the soul; but there is no evidence of this either in consciousness or psychology. It is simply the mind acting in a particular sphere. Conscience is the attitude and the activity of the mind in the domain of morals, accompanied by a sense of obligation. Man has but one mind or soul; and its functions are to think, to feel, and to determine. The intellect, the sensibilities, and the will are the faculties which deal with the affairs of men.

3. Proof of the Existence of Conscience

1) CONSCIOUSNESS.

The existence of conscience as an original endowment and not an acquisition or accommodation seems to be practically self-evident. Reflection places it among the powers of which we are immediately conscious.

2) CHILDREN.

While the evidence of conformity to moral requirements —too often alas! artificial and arbitrary—is not very decided in most children, the moral capacity is there and can be developed very early in life. This is equivalent to saying that man is naturally religious, that he has the capacity to know God, to have fellowship with Him, and to desire to please Him.

3) CONSENSUS.

The consensus of the race affirms the existence and the universality of conscience. In the Greek mythology the Furies followed the criminal—the breaker of the law, took away all peace of mind and led him to disaster. Seneca warns the guilty that remembrance of the past and terror of the future are the furies ever present in the mind of the impious. He illustrates the power of conscience in the case of a man who rejoiced when he discovered that the cobbler whom he owed for a pair of shoes was dead, but who found no rest until he returned to the cobbler's shop, and casting the money in, cried "Go thy way; for though he is dead to all the world, yet he is alive to me."

There are numberless examples in history and every-day life of the existence and power of conscience. So frequent are restorations of unlawfully secured money to the United States Government that it accounts for them in a "conscience fund." It is a proverb that murder will out. Criminals frequently surrender to the authorities, preferring legal punishment to the torment of conscience.

4. The Office of Conscience

The office of conscience is evidently the recognition and enforcement of moral obligation. The question therefore at once arises, Whence the obligation? Upon what does it rest? It has already been intimated that it lies in the constitution of man. He instinctively recognizes obligation to do this or that. This sense of obligation is the plumbline of his being. He cannot be happy unless he lives and acts in harmony with it.

5. The Domain of Conscience

The domain of conscience is as broad as human life. It cannot be arbitrarily limited to what is known as the purely moral realm. The apostle Paul shows a right apprehension of duty and service when he says, "whether, therefore, ye eat or drink or whatsoever ye do, do all to the glory of God" (I Cor. 10:31). The line between what is morally important on the one hand and morally indifferent on the other is hard to draw. One's whole life ought to be lived conscientiously from the standpoint of principle.

In a sense, conscience is a purely personal matter. It passes judgment upon a man's own immediate obligations. It is his conscience and not that of another that rules him. "To his own lord he standeth or falleth" (Rom. 14:4). Yet conscience is also social. Man is influenced by his associates; his apprehension of right and wrong are modified and formed by the society of which he is a member. Its standard, derived from this or that source, becomes the common rule of conduct and of law. However, no merely human standard can be perfect, and society can at best only reflect a divine ideal. Even in a Christian community the social standard does not measure up to that of the Bible.

The realm of conscience also embraces abstract questions as to what one should do under circumstances over which he has no control. One's attitude toward persons and events, public and private, even remote from his power to influence, involves a moral judgment which is really a revelation of character.

6. The Standard of Conscience

The soul of man necessarily acknowledges some authoritative standard of conduct. It may be the product of his own reason or experience or may simply be adopted from the community in which he lives. To the Christian the ultimate source of authority is God, who has expressed himself through the Bible.

God is just and righteous in all His ways. He is a holy God and expects His children to be like Him. His will must be their will.   His laws, precepts, commands and actions in history reveal His will, which is after all only the expression of His character as an infinite and loving Father. Jesus Christ is the revelation of that Father and the invitation to follow Him is gladly accepted by all who would do what is right.   Conscience responds to the Master's call and finds in Him a perfect model.

It is true that the teaching of the Bible has been misunderstood or grossly perverted, but this is true also of every other good gift.   There can be no mistaking its plain meaning by normal persons; and its influence as a correct moral guide is illustrated wherever its standards are accepted and applied.

7.   The Fallibility of Conscience

It is needless to say that conscience is no more infallible than man's judgment in general.   Man is not perfect in any particular.   He suffers from weakened powers and from lack of knowledge.   History records the frightful delusions and cruelties of honest men.   Paul, after his conversion, saw his wickedness in persecuting the Church, and offers no extenuation that he was acting conscientiously under imperfect knowledge.   Conscience is like a watch which however good needs to be adjusted to a standard. Our moral judgment must be brought into harmony with the divine ideal and our faculties strengthened and ennobled by regeneration and a life of fellowship with God.

When the question is asked whether a man should always follow his conscience, the answer must be that if his conscience is properly adjusted and informed he has no alternative but to obey its dictates.   Nevertheless, the greatest care must be exercised in taking extraordinary steps, lest delusions be followed and wrong committed.   Consultation with trusted advisers should precede all actions involving serious consequences.

8.   False Theories of Conscience

Hedonism, the theory that pleasure and not virtue is the end of life, was taught by the ancient Greeks.   The

Epicureans were the principle advocates of this doctrine, the effect of which was to make them mere lovers of pleasure and to lead them into gross excesses. They were vigorously opposed by the Stoics, who made virtue the end of life and who, in spite of their noble purposes, failed in practice because of the lack of the high moral sanctions of true religion.

Utilitarianism is a modified form of hedonism, propounded and named by the late J. Stuart Mill, who taught that "the ethical value of an action depends on, and is derived from its utility." This utility is to be measured by the greatest good to the greatest number. That, therefore, which brings the greatest satisfaction and yields the best results is ethical in the highest degree.

Hedonism and utilitarianism contain elements of truth. Lasting pleasure and ultimate good are proper ends of life when brought into harmony with the Christian spirit, but they do not create conscience. There is a specious error underlying these ideas. Conscience does not stop to weigh a course of action in the scales of pleasure and usefulness; it acts immediately upon the ethical value and decides in favor of the right, regardless of immediate results. Often these are exceedingly painful and unprofitable. If by some subtle alchemy of thought pain can be construed into pleasure utilitarianism might be justified. As a fact, however, the basis of these theories is selfishness, either individual or social, and this is intolerable to the Christian and contradicts the precepts and examples of our Lord.

9. Biblical Teaching Concerning Conscience

The Bible presents no formal teaching concerning conscience, but everywhere assumes its existence, just as it assumes the existence of God.

The word conscience is not mentioned in the Old Testament though the idea of conscience is embraced in such expressions as "heart" and "inward parts." Illustrations of the power of conscience are seen in Adam and Eve who hid themselves after the first sin, in Pharaoh's butler, in Joseph's brethren and in Nebuchadnezzar, whose thoughts troubled him. The Psalms abound in language expressive of the deepest regret and sorrow for sin. The thirty-second reveals conscience at peace, while the fifty-first voices its distress in humble confession and fervent petition.

In the New Testament the word conscience occurs about thirty times, chiefly in the Epistles of Paul, who has been called the apostle of conscience. It plays a large part in his own life, lived in rigid accordance with its dictates. He constantly appeals to the conscience of his hearers. He affirms the universality of conscience when he speaks of the judgment of the Gentiles according to "the law written in their hearts, their conscience bearing witness therewith" (Rom. 2: 14-15). Various aspects of conscience are alluded to in the New Testament such as "a good conscience" (I Tim. 1: 5, 19; 3: 9; I Pet. 3: 16) ; "a weak conscience" (I Cor. 8: 7-12) ; an "evil conscience" (Heb. 10: 22) ; "a seared conscience" (I Tim. 4: 2).

10. The Implications of Conscience

The apologetic as well as the practical value of the implications of conscience should be considered.

1) AN IMMUTABLE MORAL LAW.

Graven upon the nature of man, in all ages and in all lands, is a conviction that a moral order exists in the world. This law may indeed be blurred and its interpretation erroneous, nevertheless its universality connotes the existence of a moral law as real as that of the law of gravitation.

2) AN INFALLIBLE LAWGIVER.

The universal existence of the idea of law and order implies a lawgiver, just as truly as the order in the material word implies a supreme, personal intelligence. Moral order could hardly be conceived without postulating an infinite moral being.

3) AN INEVITABLE JUDGMENT.

A law implies penalty and protection; it vindicates itself whenever it is wisely conceived and fairly administered.

Conscience is itself in a sense a tribunal, which however is not final in its verdicts. These may be referred to a final court from which there is no appeal. In short, conscience implies a judgment to come.

4) A FUTURE EXISTENCE.

Right and truth rarely receive vindication in this life. Conscience reaches beyond the confines of the grave and demands a future life for the retribution deserved in this.

III. THE FREEDOM OF MAN.

1. The Definition of Will

The moral nature of man implies volition; conscience demands it. The will is that power within man which determines action. It is the soul's power of choice. It is the ego that deliberately acts with an end in view. The relation between the will on one hand and the intellect and the feelings on the other is expressed by Seth as follows: "Feeling mediates between intellect and will, converting the cold intellectual conception into a constraining motive of activity. In ends then, there is always an element of feeling as well as of thought; it is the fusion of these two that constitutes the interest of the voluntary life" (Ethical Principles, p. 65).

2. The Freedom of the First Man

The first man must have been created a free being, otherwise he could not have borne the divine likeness. To hold that one is a person is equivalent to saying that he is free. This endowment inherent in man is usually denominated normal or formal freedom. The first man was not only formally free, but also possessed real or actual freedom.

3. The Partial Loss of Freedom

Human experience, however, reveals man as no longer perfectly free; and indeed, often in bondage. The Scriptures explain this loss as having been incurred in the fall of Adam, through disobedience. It is, however, evident from the Bible, as well as from experience, that man retains the power to exercise his will in purely natural matters and also the capacity for moral restoration. When it is said that man is dead through trespass and sin (Eph. 2: 1) it cannot mean that he is either bodily or mentally dead, but that he is spiritually dead, that he has lost fellowship with God.

4. The Restoration of Freedom

Quickened by the Spirit of God the power to use his will returns to man, and he must choose whom he will serve. A man is not swept into the kingdom, *nolens volens.* He may grieve the Spirit and resist Him to his own destruction, or he may yield to the divine call. This is implied in our Lord's charge against the Jews, "Ye will not come to me that ye may have life" (Jno. 5: 40) and in His lament over Jerusalem (Matt. 23: 37).

5. Determinism

In spite of what seems so plain—that man must be free in order to be man—the freedom of the will is disputed on philosophical grounds. Determinism is "the common name for all theories of the human will which represent it as absolutely determined by motives which lie entirely outside of it, thereby reducing its freedom to a mere delusion. There is a dogmatic determination, which in order to glorify the majesty of God, excludes all other causality from human action but God Himself; and there is a philosophic determinism which explains all human actions as results of surrounding circumstances. There is a fatalistic determinism, which places God Himself in the grip of an iron necessity; and there is a pantheistic determinism, which makes even the faint gleam of human freedom vanish into the darkness of a natural process" (Schaff-Herzog Enc., III, 412).

6. Divine Sovereignty and Free Will

It is impossible to enter into the intricacies of a discussion of freedom in general. The problem for us is to reconcile absolute divine sovereignty with human free will. We accept both. Those who in their theological systems have approached the problem from the divine standpoint alone apart from redemption in Christ have fallen into the error of extreme predestinarianism. Augustine, Zwingli, Calvin are the great representatives of this school, which teaches that human destiny is settled by divine decree regardless of what man may do. Calvin calls it from the human standpoint, a *horrible decretum*, which nevertheless is prompted by divine wisdom and love.

Those who approach the subject of human freedom from the standpoint of the experience of redemption through Christ maintain that God in the exercise of His sovereignty in making a creature like unto Himself made him a free, responsible being. This preserves divine sovereignty and human freedom. The sovereignty of God is not impaired by man's disobedience because God's supremacy in punishing still remains. The conditions imposed are those evident in paternal government—blessing for well-doing and punishment for wilful disobedience.

In spite of the ingenious explanation and defence of extreme Calvinism, it is difficult to differentiate it from fatalism. Says W. N. Clarke, "if predestinarians hold to real freedom, they do so by an inconsistency."

7. The Nature of Real Freedom

The nature of real freedom must not be overlooked. In a metaphysical sense freedom implies the power of contrary choice. In practical life good and evil are set before men as objects of choice. It must be evident, however, that only a perverted nature can deliberately choose that which he knows and believes to be wrong. When men yield to temptation to do what is wrong, they do so because they are morally weak. They have grown weaker through inadvertence and abuse, and have refused divine grace until they have become impotent. The so-called ability to choose the wrong is really inability to resist it.

True freedom consists in choosing the right and living consistently with it. In this sense there is no power of contrary choice. The wrong appears to the regenerated man as something sinful, wicked, horrible. He will no more take to it than he would drink a cup of poison. All this is evident when we consider the absolute freedom of God, who cannot sin, or lie, or do any other wrong, because He cannot deny or contradict His holy nature.

8. Absolute Freedom in This Life

Perfect conformity to a perfect ideal and therefore real freedom is not possible to a human being in this life. Nevertheless, it is true that "Whosoever is born of God doeth no sin, because his seed abideth in him; and he cannot sin because he is begotten of God" (I Jno. 3: 9). However, this must be understood in the sense that no regenerated soul, living in close fellowship with God, can or will deliberately sin. Alas! as long as man is in the flesh he fails of the high ideal of a perfect life.

IV.   THE IMMORTALITY OF MAN.
1.   A Postulate of Religion

The endless existence of man after death is a postulate of religion. Man must be immortal in order to realize the design of his creation. As a child of the eternal God he partakes of His nature and is destined to fuller communion with Him. The Christian belief in immortality is cherished and demanded by faith. An absolute demonstration of immortality is, of course, from the nature of the case, impossible. On the other hand, it is impossible to disprove it. Relying upon the teachings of Scripture and encouraged by the living hope begotten by the resurrection of Jesus Christ from the dead, into an inheritance incorruptible and undefiled and that fadeth not away, reserved in heaven, the Christian looks forward in confidence to an endless future (I Pet. 1: 3).

2.   Scripture Teaching

In the Old Testament the immortality of man is assumed. This must be plain from the fact that at the coming of Christ the Jews, excepting the Sadducees, believed in it. On this point there is no violent transition from the Old

Testament to the New.   Martha, the sister of Lazarus, said of her brother, "I know that he shall rise again in the resurrection at the last day."   This indicates the common faith of the people.

It is true that the nature of the future life is not as clearly set forth in the Old Testament as in the New, but this is to be expected in a preparatory revelation.   Moreover, the somewhat pessimistic utterances of some writers must be explained as the result of temporary despondency. The devout always looked forward to deliverance from the gloom of the grave, and based their hopes upon the love of the everlasting God.

There is nothing in the Old Testament that can be construed as teaching the extinction or annihilation of the soul at death or at the last judgment.   The destruction of the wicked means their punishment and not their extinction.

The positive teaching of immortality in the Old Testament appears on the first pages of the Bible in the assertion that man was made in the image of God, and in the warning that disobedience will bring death.   Man was made to live and not to die.   The frustration of this design through sin is everywhere deplored in the Scriptures and a purpose and a plan are revealed whereby life and immortal joy may be restored to the sinner.

The translations of Enoch, Moses and Elijah are concrete illustrations of Old Testament teaching.   The assurance which Moses gives to the Jews in his farewell address implies immortality.   He says, "The eternal God is thy dwelling place, and underneath are the everlasting arms" (Deut. 33: 27).   The impassioned outburst of Job voices the abiding assurance of the Old Testament saint that he shall surely "see God" in the world beyond the grave (Job 19: 25, 26).   The Psalms abound in expressions of confidence in a future life.   "I shall behold thy face in righteousness" exclaims David (Ps. 17: 15).   In Ps. 49: 15 the writer expresses his faith in saying, "God will redeem my soul from the power of Sheol; for he will receive me."   The same sentiment is expressed in Ps. 16: 10, "Thou wilt not leave my soul in Sheol, neither wilt thou suffer thy holy one to see corruption." "Thou wilt guide me with thy counsel and afterward receive me to glory" (Psalm 73:24).

In the New Testament is the record of the teaching of our Lord "who abolished death and brought life and immortality to light through the Gospel" (II Tim. 1:10). Jesus said to Martha, "He that believeth on me though he die, yet shall he live; and whosoever liveth and believeth on me shall never die" (Jno. 11:25). "Today thou shalt be with me in Paradise" said He to the dying thief (Lk. 23:43). The parable of the rich man and Lazarus (Lk. 16:19-31) sets forth the future life and death. Christ's teaching concerning His return, the resurrection, the intermediate state and final destiny of the good and the evil all imply man's immortality. His own resurrection sheds a flood of light on the subject.

The Epistles and Revelation abound in allusions to immortality and resurrection. Paul expresses a desire to depart and be with Christ, and he writes of the future life in which the saints will be clothed with a new body. The New Testament needs only to be read to convince the reader that it has quite as much to do with the life beyond as with the life here.

3. Rational Arguments for Immortality

1) THE METAPHYSICAL ARGUMENT.

The hope of continued existence has probably always existed among men, and arguments to sustain it have been suggested from time immemorial. Plato based the idea of immortality upon the nature of the soul as a simple, indestructible substance. Of this however we can have no absolute assurance.

2) THE PSYCHOLOGICAL ARGUMENT.

Man as a personality realizes that there is in his being something lasting and indestructible. He shrinks from annihilation; the thought is repugnant. He does not think of himself as going into nothingness. He believes that there is that about him which will survive the wreck of worlds.

3) THE TELEOLOGICAL ARGUMENT.

This is based on the idea that there is an incompleteness about the present life which suggests its continuity beyond. If there be no future life there has been a failure, and the aspirations of the soul are only a delusion. We have a feeling that God has a large plan and purpose for the soul extending into the other world.

4) THE MORAL ARGUMENT.

This contemplates the retribution which the moral order of the universe seems to demand. It is evident that in this life virtue often fails of its reward and wickedness of its deserved punishment. Were there no future these inequalities would seem to reflect upon the ethical nature of God.

5) THE HISTORICAL ARGUMENT.

This is derived from the consensus of the race. In philosopher and peasant, in Christian and pagan there is a well-nigh universal belief that man is immortal! How such a faith could persist without an ineradicable conviction of its reality cannot be explained. There must be that in the nature of man which demands such a belief.

6) CHRISTIAN EXPERIENCE.

The Christian is a Christian because he believes that Christ lived and that he shall live also. His faith takes hold of the unseen, as of that which is more real than that which he sees with mortal eye. That Christ and Moses and Paul and John can have gone into oblivion and annihilation never for a moment enters the Christian mind.

These several arguments together with the Biblical statements may not constitute a mathematical proof of immortality, but they are convincing to the majority of the race and especially to those who believe in Jesus Christ and His precious promise.

4. The Possible Immortality of Adam's Body

The immortality of the soul cannot reasonably be questioned, and the present mortality of the body will not be denied.   Nevertheless, it is not an unreasonable inquiry to ask whether the body of Adam would have died had he not sinned.

1) THE DENIAL OF ITS IMMORTALITY.

(1) Contrary to experience.   Since as far as we know, there is not a single human being on earth who is much above a hundred years old and since the average of life is very brief, it is said to be inconceivable that the body was made to last forever.

(2) Subject to decay.   Composed of purely physical elements, it is said that the body must inevitably pay the debt of nature, which is dissolution.   Worn by age and toil it would under the most favorable circumstances finally break down and return to mother earth.

(3) Over-population.   It is argued further that were the body immortal the earth would soon be over-populated and the race in a frightful dilemma.   Hence it is held that an all-wise Providence has ordained the mortality of the body.   Even under this order it has been feared by economists like Malthus that propagation must finally overtake the production of food.

2) THE AFFIRMATION OF ORIGINAL IMMORTALITY.

(1) The unity of man.   Man consists of soul and body which together form the human person.   Their separation, involving agony, is according to Moses and Paul the result of sin, the wages of which is death.   Hence mortality is not natural, but a punishment, and therefore if Adam had not sinned he would not have died physically or spiritually.

It must be remembered that while man is partially animal he is far above the animal.   That animals should die is natural, but that man should die is not natural.   He is more than natural; he is supernatural.

"We do not assert," says Bernard, "of Adam the *non posse mori* but the *posse non mori* as long as his fellowship with God, the source of life, was unbroken. But sin reduced him to the state of a lower animal and thus man became the prey of death."

(2) The power of the soul.   The beast that perishes is

not controlled by an immortal soul. It has no ambition and cannot be influenced by motives beyond its physical welfare. Man, on the contrary, even in his fallen state, is able by sheer force of will to compel his body to do prodigious work. It may be conjectured therefore that in his unfallen state his body would have been the ready organ of the spirit continuously.

If it be asked how the body could resist decay, it may be said that if the body even now is endowed with remarkable powers of recuperation so that it may endure a century, it is entirely possible that God might have multiplied this power of renewal beyond all possibility of death.

A great scientist, Weismann, has said that "the organism must not be looked upon as a heap of combustible material, which is completely reduced to ashes in a certain time, the length of which is determined by its size and by the rate at which it burns; but it should be compared to a fire, to which fresh fuel can be continually added, and which whether it burns quickly or slowly can be kept burning as long as necessity demands. . . . Death is not an essential attribute of living matter."

(3) Objections considered. Perhaps the foregoing is a sufficient general answer to alleged necessary mortality of the body, yet a specific answer may be given to the argument as to over-population. If in the heavenly state we shall have glorified bodies, and shall neither marry nor be given in marriage, it is probable that in an unfallen world there might have been in due time a cessation of propagation and the transformation of the body into one like the glorified body of the saints. It is also possible that at the good pleasure of God he might have translated His children even as He did Enoch.

B. THE ORIGIN OF MAN

I. THE BIBLICAL ACCOUNT.

The creation of man according to Genesis was a part of the general creation of the universe of which he is the culmination. The account is exceedingly simple but graphic, telling us in short that the body of man was made out of the dust of the earth, that is of earthly elements, and that his life, presumably his higher life, was the special and direct gift of God. His nature transcended that of all other mundane creatures, for he was made in the image of God Himself. He is, therefore, the child of God.

There is no mention whatever of the method of man's creation, whether by a divine fiat or by the process of a divine law. The purpose of the Genesis story is to account for man—his creation, his nature. This is admirably done. We learn that he was made by God and that he was made God-like. This is sufficient for the purpose of the Bible, which tells us whence we came, what our original nature was, how it became depraved, and how it has been redeemed. A technical scientific statement is entirely apart from the purpose.

II.   THE SCIENTIFIC THEORY

It is creditable to man that he should inquire into his origin and suggest theories to explain it. We have already seen that a human person must have his source not in dead matter but in an infinite person, who is God over all. The Christian, therefore, postulates God as the creator of man. This to him is a fixed fact, and he is impatient with any atheistic ideas, as being not only irreverent but scientifically and philosophically untrue.

1.   The Origin of Life

From the purely human standpoint the origin of life is a mystery. All theories have failed to account for it. Spontaneous generation, once proposed as the explanation, has been abandoned. Chemical reaction, though often invoked, has utterly failed. There is no life on earth, as far as we know, without antecedent life. The Christian accepts the Bible explanation that all life comes from God.

2.   The Theory of Evolution

1) ITS SOURCE.

The theory of evolution can be traced at least to Heraclitus (B.C. 500) and in its clearer exposition to Aristotle.

Of course their ideas were comparatively crude. Darwin and Wallace deserve credit for the revival and scientific statement of evolution, about the middle of the last century. They were indefatigable and conscientious investigators and have put the modern world under obligation for their discovery of numerous facts in nature. Their deductions, however, canot be accepted without question.

2) The Alleged Proof of Evolution.

The basis of evolution is paleontology and embryology. A study of the strata of the earth reveals the fact that the simpler forms of life appeared on earth before the more complex. So also biology has discovered that the simpler and earlier form of life is unicellular, and that in higher forms the cells are multiplied but always recapitulate the lower type until its species reaches its final form. For example, it is alleged that the human embryo passes successively through the stages of the lower animals until it reaches its own distinctive character.

In regard to paleontology Sir J. William Dawson denies that it gives evidence of unbroken evolution. "It is not difficult," he says, "to obtain, by selecting series out of known fossil animals of successive periods, chains of forms which may be supposed to have produced each other, but the gaps are enormous in structure, in time, and in place, and there is no evidence of genetic connection, while the apparently abrupt and widespread introduction of new forms of life at certain periods of geological time, and the subsequent gradual decadence, seems to indicate the incoming of new dynasties of animals and plants in successive waves rather than by gradual imperceptible rise."

In reference to embryological evidence Dawson says, "It is not logical to establish an analogy between the evolution of a germ through various stages into an animal, whose parts were potentially present in the germ, and the evolution of an adult animal into an animal of another kind. Nor is it logical to allege an evolution taking place under special conditions of parental origin, incubation, etc., to prove the possibility of an evolution in regard to which all these preparatory conditions and efficient causes are absent" (Johnson's Univ. Ency. Article on Evolution).

3) THE METHOD OF EVOLUTION.

The alleged process of evolution is through variation, heredity and survival.

Variation occurs in every form of life, as can readily be seen in the marked difference in individuals of the same species in shape, size, color and characteristics. This is observed in plants, and animals. A mere glance at even a small number of men verifies the statement. These variations are supposed to be caused by differences in environment, climate, food, habits, etc.

It is further said that these variations are transmitted by heredity and that thus new starting-points of variation and development are reached by the mating of pairs which have reached the most advantageous variation from a lower common type.

According to the principle of survival, or so-called natural selection in the struggle for existence, the stronger and most fitting will survive and propagate the species.

"As a logical result of these factors," says J. S. Kingsley, "a sufficient length of time is alone necessary to people the earth with all its present varied fauna and flora from a single primitive type of life. Further, the apparent gaps between so-called species are but the tombstones of the unfit or less fit which have fallen by the wayside."

Noted scientists like Weismann deny that acquired characteristics can be transmitted, and hence also that there can be so-called transmutation of species.

The late Dr. Orr disagreed with theistic evolutionists who accepted the evolutionary hypothesis as sufficiently accounting for the body. He held that it is impossible that the brain of an anthropoid ape could be a receptacle of the human mind.

Forsyth, in his work on *The Person and Place of Jesus Christ*, has expressed the conviction of many a thoughtful believer. "The evolutionary idea," says he, "is certainly compatible with Christianity; but not so long as it claims to be the supreme idea to which Christianity must be shaped. Evolution is within Christianity, but Christianity is not within evolution. For evolution means the rule of a leveling relativism, which takes from Christ His absolute value and final place, reduces Him to be but a stage of God's revelation, or a phase of it that can be outgrown and makes Him the less of a Creator as it ranges Him vividly in the scale of the creature. There is no such foe to Christianity in thought today as this idea is; and we can make no terms with it so long as it claims the throne. The danger is greater as the theory grows more religious, as it becomes sympathetic with a Christ it does not worship and praises a Christ to whom it does not pray" (Pp. 10, 11).

The Christian view of the origin of man cannot be better expressed than has been expressed in Genesis: "And God created man in his own image, in the image of God created he him."

III.   THE ORIGIN OF SOULS.

The human body is undoubtedly the product of natural generation. But whence comes the soul? Is it produced in like manner as the body, or is it a special creation of God who breathed into Adam the breath of life? Three theories have been advanced to explain its origin.

1. Pre-existence

The theory of the pre-existence of the soul was held by Plato on the ground of its possession of noble conceptions which could not be derived from the body. Origen taught pre-existence as the only explanation of the sinful condition of the soul, which it brought from another world. This was an effort to solve the problem of evil, but it really makes it more difficult. The Mormons have taught pre-existence probably as a cloak for polygamy. They hold that the soul needs an incarnation in order to be liberated from sin. The poets Wordsworth, Browning and others have been tainted with the idea that the soul "cometh from afar."

The objections to the theory are that it has no ground in Scripture or psychology. It accounts for nothing, solves no difficulties and is in fact pure speculation.

2. Creationism

This theory holds that God creates a soul for every body before or at its birth. Its advocates maintain that the generation of souls by parents is materialistic and unworthy. This, of course, misinterprets the traducian theory —(see below)—which does not teach that the soul is begotten by physical generation, but that the whole person is begotten by personalities.

Dr. Charles Hodge, in advocating creationism, claims that it is more consistent with the prevailing representations of Scripture. Among the passages cited is, "The dust returneth to the earth as it was, and the spirit returneth unto God who gave it" (Eccl. 12: 7). The context indicates that this is a poetical expression and not intended as a proof-text on origins. The bodies of men do not come directly from the dust of the earth. Another quotation misses the mark even farther. In Heb. 12: 9 the writer contrasts "the fathers of our flesh" with the "Father of spirits." "The obvious antithesis here presented," says Hodge, "is between those who are the fathers of our bodies and Him who is the Father of our spirits." To us the obvious antithesis is between our earthly father and our heavenly Father. The text does not remotely bear on the subject in hand.

A second argument from the nature of the soul is urged by Hodge. He says that the soul is immaterial, spiritual and indivisible, and that traducianism denies this. But he is mistaken; such a denial, if it exists, is no part of traducianism.

A third argument in favor of creationism is derived from the person of Christ, who it is alleged could not have been sinless if His human soul had been derived from Mary. In reply we would say that he would not have been truly human had not his human soul come from his mother.

The objections to creationism are that it does not account for the mental and moral likeness between parent and child, nor for sin and its transmission. It assumes what is incredible, that sin has its origin in the body. Nor is it possible that God would put a sinless soul into a sinful body or create a soul with a sinful tendency. Creationism fails to account for man as he is.

3. Traducianism

This theory teaches that parents beget children, body and soul. While we have a complex nature, nevertheless man is a unit, in which the natural and spiritual combine. Traducianism accounts most satisfactorily for the resemblance in body and spirit of the child to its parents. It explains the inborn tendencies to sin; and the obvious unity of the race.

This theory no more eliminates God than do the ordinary laws of nature. He is in and over all things which He has made. Nor does it preclude special divine interventions and blessings. It may be said of great men whom God raised up and endowed for particular tasks as it was said of John the Baptist, that he was filled with the Holy Spirit, even from his mother's womb (Lk. 1: 15).

C. THE FALL OF MAN

THE DOCTRINE OF SIN

In considering the freedom of man, we discovered that though man is necessarily a free being his freedom has become seriously impaired. A conflict has been introduced among his powers, so that when he would do good, evil is present. He has lost his sense of nearness and love to God. This abnormal situation is explained in Scripture as the result of man's disobedience to God. The common name for this disobedience is sin, and the first sin is known as the Fall, because therein Adam fell from his state of holiness.

I. THE FACT OF SIN.

Whatever the origin of sin, we shall first examine the evidence of its existence.

1. The Evidence of Consciousness

Man is conscious that he is not doing his best morally. He freely confesses that he falls far short of even his own

standard or conception of right; and that he is, alas! only
too often indifferent to it.   He realizes that he is alienated
from God, whom he may seek to ignore or perchance to
propitiate.   His conscience, or moral judgment, condemns
him and makes him unhappy.   He is not at peace with
himself or with his creator.

This consciousness of sin is not confined to persons who
have come under Biblical influences.   It is more or less
active among the heathen and can be aroused by preaching.
Dr. Thoburn, a veteran missionary to India, says that he
constantly appealed to the sense of sin in the native.   Dr.
George Grenfell found among the Congo tribes the most
revolting cannibalism, which existed uncondemned, yet
upon fuller acquaintance he found that they acknowledged
that the practice was wicked.

So thoroughly convinced are most persons of the reality
and evil of sin in the soul, that denial by an individual will
be regarded as an evidence of hypocrisy or blunted moral
sensibility, which itself is sinful.

2.   The Bible

The Holy Bible, which reveals God and man, assumes sin
as a postulate.   The elimination of the doctrine of sin from
the Scriptures would leave them meaningless.   Their affirmation of universal sinfulness, the legislation for its control or punishment, the provision for sacrifice and the revelation of Jesus Christ who came to put away sin by the
sacrifice of Himself, all center in the idea of sin.   The hold
which the Bible has on mankind and which will never be
relaxed can be explained in large part by its recognition
and diagnosis of the sickness of the soul and the revelation
of the sovereign means of its cure.

3.   Human Government

All statute books and the unwritten laws of uncivilized
peoples bear witness to the reality of sin. To restrain and to
punish evil-doers among men are among the chief functions
of government.   Fines, imprisonment, political disabilities
and even death are inflicted for the violation of righteous

laws. Even the fundamental principle that in law a man must be considered innocent until proved guilty carries the suggestion of possibility, if not the probability, of the guilt of the accused person.

4. Society

The business man has a wholesome distrust of selling on credit to strangers. So universal is the suspicion of evil in men that one must prove himself truthful and honest before he will be recognized as such. The daily record of crime and the reports of medical examiners are appalling. The cruelties of war and the inhumanities of the mob are alike hideous. These facts are not cited to show that there is no good in the world but that sin exists everywhere.

5. History

The centuries are black with sin and crime, with oppression, slavery, war, and vice. The mythologies of the ancients crystalize and illustrate the sins of all the ages. The World War was a culmination of wickedness, wrong, ignorance and unrestrained passion.

To deny the universality and culpability of sin is to be blind to patent facts and to stultify one's better judgment.

II. THE NATURE OF SIN.

The nature of sin may be determined by remembering the Biblical terms employed to describe it.

1. The Biblical Terms

1) THE OLD TESTAMENT TERMS.

The most common name for sin in the Old Testament is *chatath*, which means "missing the mark." It occurs first in connection with Jehovah's warning to Cain (Gen. 4: 7) who in spite of it slew his brother. Cain illustrates the idea that sin causes the doer to miss his true goal, leading him into a terrible mistake and utter failure.

Akin to the foregoing is the word *awon*, used over two hundred times, meaning "crookedness" or "perversity," translated usually "iniquity" (Ps. 51). The sinner follows a crooked instead of a straight road. A characteristic modern description of a dishonest person is to say that he is crooked.

The word *awen,* often translated "iniquity" means vanity or nothingness, indicating that sin is empty and profitless, that it accomplishes nothing and that it is impotent in opposing God. Sin is a sham, a fraud, a delusion, a snare to the soul.

Associated with *chatath* and *awon* in the 51st Psalm and elsewhere is the word *pesha,* usually translated "transgression," and sometimes "trespass" or "rebellion" (Job 34: 37). This carries the idea of deliberate breaking of the law. Sin is looked upon as more than a mere mistake. It becomes personal, involving direct insult to the law or the lawgiver, and consequently guilt and punishment.

Numerous kindred words and passages represent sin as an abominable thing which God hates and which He punishes even with temporal and spiritual death.

2) THE NEW TESTAMENT TERMS.

The most common word for sin in the New Testament is *hamartia,* corresponding to *chatath* in the Old Testament, meaning "missing the mark." *Anomia,* signifying "transgression" or "lawlessness," and *paraptoma,* indicating "disobedience," are among the designations of sin.

The parable of the Prodigal or Lost Son illustrates the nature of sin as wilfulness and departure from God.

The dreadful character of sin is best seen in the tragedy of the Cross, showing on the one hand its heinousness in inflicting inexpressible cruelty upon the innocent and on the other the penalty of its expiation.

In the Pauline Epistles (Romans and Galatians) there are catalogues of sins shocking to contemplate, and revelation of the means whereby deliverance from their curse becomes possible.

2. The Inherent Character of Sin

Sin is looked upon by right thinking persons as something evil, bad, wicked, which is to be condemned and avoided.

It is something that ought not to be done. It is not only offensive to God, but repulsive to a good conscience. It is abnormal, contrary to good order and propriety, defiling and debasing. It is self-will bringing forth evil fruit. Whatever excuses are made for it by evil men, in their hearts they know that their is no excuse, but that it is nothing but evil.

3.   The Guilt of Sin

The commission of sin brings with it guilt, which involves blameworthiness and penalty. The sinner is guilty of sin. He has committed wrong and deserves punishment. His sense of guilt may or may not be poignant, depending upon his moral apprehension and the nature of his sin. But he is guilty whether he feels and acknowledges his sin or not, for guilt and sin go together. Frequently his conscience is alarmed and he becomes unhappy and apprehensive of the consequences of his sin.

In the sight of God the sinner must always be guilty, for he has transgressed divine law. The penitent recognizes this and exclaims with David,

"Against thee, thee only have I sinned
And done that which is evil in thy sight."

II.   THE ORIGIN OF SIN.

1.   The Naturalistic View

To the atheist sin is at best a mere shortcoming of man's imperfect nature, and involves no culpability except in so far as it infringes on acknowledged rights of others.

To the thoroughgoing evolutionist what is ordinarily called sin is only "good in the making." Man is slowly emerging from his animal state with many lapses, but with the goal of perfection in his heart.

2.   The View of Theistic Evolution

A modified and professedly Christian view, allied to that of evolution, is maintained by some theologians (Clarke, Brown) to the effect that sin is the failure of the first man to rise from the state of "animalism and self-will" into the "higher life of the Spirit" when it became possible for him. It does not seem to us that this explanation is as plausible as that offered in Genesis. In fact it seems rather to indicate that man is more to be pitied than to be blamed for not taking the wiser choice.

3. The View of Bodily Infection

Sin has been further explained as an infection conveyed to the soul by the body, which is alleged to be inherently evil. But matter is not sinful; it has of itself no moral character. It may be corrupted and put to evil uses, however, by a carnal mind.

4. The Scripture Teaching

1) THE ACCOUNT IN GENESIS.

The third chapter of Genesis tells the story of man's fall in such a manner as to leave the impression of historicity. The first human pair are placed in a beautiful garden or park to dress it and to keep it. A single restriction is enjoined upon them by way of a test of their obedience to their maker. Some kind of trial seems to have been inevitable to the realization of their fullest freedom. Created pure and holy, with a strong inclination toward the right, they nevertheless possessed the power of contrary choice. Enticed by the wiles and falsehoods of the evil spirit, they yielded to his solicitations, lost their innocence, and fell from God.

2) THE ELEMENTS OF THE FALL.

To what extent the story in Genesis is to be taken literally is a matter of doubt; but whether understood literally or figuratively it presents an adequate explanation of the introduction of sin into the world, as may be seen from the following analysis:

(1) The first sin came through an outward solicitation or suggestion by an evil spirit who himself presumably had fallen from God.

(2) The appeal to the first parents was partly made to

the appetite and to the eye—the external senses. This is the usual approach of evil to the soul.

(3) The appeal came also to ambition under the guise of a desire for knowledge. While this desire was apparently normal and proper, it was influenced by the unholy motive of throwing off allegiance to the Almighty.

(4) The essence of the fall lies in the perversion of the will. It is the assertion of self-will against the will of God, and hence indicates unbelief or lack of faith and implicit trust in the word and character of God. The apparently trivial first transgression held the very essence of all sin. Any act of deliberate disobedience, however small, is an act of defiance or of criminal negligence involving far-reaching and terrible consequences. The unchecked wilfulness of a child tends toward a mean and even criminal life.

The elements of the fall are present in sin today and we must accept the story in Genesis as an adequate explanation of the entrance of sin into the world. This is done through the Bible, in which the contrast between a first and second Adam is conspicuous.

3) THE RESULT OF THE FALL.

The consequences of the first sin were most disastrous to Adam and to his posterity.

(1) It destroyed the original righteousness with which Adam was endowed. His hitherto holy character ceased to exist. He became an enemy to God.

(2) It produced a sense of shame and alienation from God. Adam and Eve became conscious of their physical and moral nakedness and sought to hide themselves from the Lord.

(3) It depraved Adam's moral nature and inclined him to evil. When called to account, he put the blame of his act upon Eve and constructively upon God Himself.

(4) It brought upon the transgressors the threatened consequences of death, spiritual and physical. Death began to work in them the moment they sinned. From the temporal result there was no appeal, but for its spiritual and eternal consequences a remedy was provided.

(5) It entailed upon posterity a depraved nature so that all mankind comes into the world with an enfeebled and sinful nature.

IV. ORIGINAL SIN.

1. Its Nature

1) THE DEFINITION.

The sin which mankind has inherited from Adam is called original sin. By this is meant that all men are born with a sinful nature, which inevitably leads to sins and transgressions involving personal guilt.

2) A CONFESSIONAL STATEMENT.

The Augsburg Confession (Art. II) says: "Since the fall of Adam, all men begotten according to nature are born with sin, that is without the fear of God, and with concupiscence; and . . . . this disease or vice of origin is truly sin, even now condemning and bringing eternal death upon those not born again through baptism and the Holy Ghost."

This article affirms the depravity of human nature and its need of regeneration through water and the Spirit, as is plainly taught by Christ Himself. External baptism is necessary to us, but only relatively in the plan of God. Its omission under certain circumstances may be overlooked by a merciful God; but its deliberate rejection is a great sin and offense in His sight.

In regard to the salvability of those who die unbaptized in infancy there is no doubt, for as in Adam all die so in Christ shall all be made alive. Christ died for all and made atonement for original sin. The infant is in a forgiven state and is regenerated before death by the Holy Spirit. No one is lost through original sin alone.

3) THE BIBLICAL TEACHING.

In the Old Testament the story of the fall and the history of man all imply the natural corruption of the heart since the first transgression. In the 51st Psalm, David voices the conviction of all penitents:

"Behold I was brought forth in iniquity
And in sin did my mother conceive me."

In the New Testament our Lord declares "That which is born of the flesh is flesh" (Jno. 3: 6). The Epistles of Paul abound in affirmations of our natural corruption. "As through one man sin entered into the world, and death through sin; and so death passed unto all men, for that all sinned." "Through one trespass the judgment came unto all men to condemnation" (Rom. 5: 12, 18). "By nature we are the children of wrath" (Eph. 2: 3). "The natural man receiveth not the things of the spirit of God" (I Cor. 2: 14).

2. Its Extent

The foregoing statements and citations indicate that original sin has in a spiritual sense completely disabled man, leaving him in what is called a state of total depravity.

1) IN WHAT SENSE DEPRAVITY IS TOTAL.

(1) It is as universal as the race.

(2) It affects the entire man, body and soul.

(3) It induces deterioration.

(4) It leaves man spiritually helpless; that is, he is unable to save himself.

2) IN WHAT SENSE DEPRAVITY IS RELATIVE.

(1) Man still retains his faculties. He is still a responsible ethical being.

(2) He contains the capacity for redemption.

(3) He is capable of natural virtue. He may be kind, honest, faithful, useful.

(4) He is not in every instance inclined to every form of sin. In short, he is not so depraved that he might not become worse.

3. Its Denial

The doctrine of original sin is not only amply grounded in Scripture but seems also self-evident from experience. Nevertheless, it is denied by Unitarians, who hold that our inborn and natural infirmities are not sinful but mere imitations.

The Pelagians, following Pelagius (370-440), a British monk, deny original sin and ascribe the apparent universality of sin to imitation. Pelagius taught that it was possible for man without the special grace of God to lead a sinless life. The great Augustine effectually answered the false assumptions of Pelagianism as being contrary to Scripture and experience.

4. Its Transmission

1) THE BIBLICAL TEACHING.

The Scriptures plainly affirm that "in Adam all die" (I Cor. 15:22). All his children are partakers of his nature. "Through one man sin entered into the world and death through sin; and so death passed unto all men, for that all sinned" (Rom. 5:12).

2) THE MANNER OF TRANSMISSION.

Sin has been transmitted by natural propagation. Human nature corrupted by sin could not produce human nature uncorrupted. Like produces like. The good tree brings forth good fruit; and the evil tree evil fruit. Adam gave his posterity the kind of nature which he himself had. The race, it is true, is composed of individuals, but these do not stand isolated. They are bound together not only socially and economically but much more racially, even as Paul declared that God "made of one every nation of men" (Acts 17:26). These facts are supported by the laws of heredity as they appear in the study of history, psychology, and physiology.

3) THE THEORIES OF TRANSMISSION.

In the King James Version the word "impute" is used where in the Revised Version we have "reckon." See Romans, fourth chapter. Hence in the older discussions the word "imputation" frequently occurs. The sin of Adam is imputed to the race. The sin of the race is imputed to Christ. The merit of Christ is imputed to the believer. In reference to the first, the imputation of sin, several theories arose, known in America, particularly in Presbyterian theology, as the theories of immediate or antecedent and of mediate or consequent imputation.

The immediate theory was subdivided into the realistic and the federal forms.   According to the realistic form mankind was in Adam, who was incarnate humanity, which is regarded as "a generic spiritual substance." Hence when Adam fell he corrupted this substance.   The federal form of imputation regards Adam as the legal representative of the race, for which he acted and which he therefore involved in his ruin and penalty.

The mediate theory holds that the race inherited a corrupted nature and its consequences.

There seem to be some grounds for the realistic form of immediate imputation, and more ground for the mediate theory.   It is sufficient to hold that as the children of Adam we share his nature and his disability.

V.   THE CLASSIFICATION OF SINS.

1.   Sin a Unit

"For whosoever shall keep the whole law, and yet stumble in one point, he is become guilty of all (Jas. 2: 10).   While the immediate consequences of transgressions are not alike, the character of all transgressions is inherently the same. Disobedience is disobedience, ending in alienation and punishment.   Nevertheless, sin manifests itself in various forms which may be properly considered separately for practical reasons.   While all persons are sinners they are not all guilty of all kinds of sins.   There are besetting sins peculiar to individuals.

2.   Forms of Sin

Sins have been classified as voluntary and involuntary, venial and mortal, of omission and commission, of presumption, secret and public, and the like.

3.   The Unpardonable Sin

One form of sin demands special notice, namely, the sin against the Holy Ghost (Matt. 12: 31, 32; Mk. 3: 28, 29;

Luke 12; 10). Our Lord pronounced this sin unforgivable. Its nature is therefore a matter of deep concern. Misinterpretation of it has been the source of despair to humble souls.

It seems that this sin is committed not by a single act but by the persistent resisting and rejection of the ministry of the Holy Spirit, causing a hardening of the heart so that it cannot repent. As redemption is applied by the Holy Spirit His rejection destroys the sinner. No other way of life is open.

VI.   THE PROBLEM OF EVIL.

1.   God Not the Author of Evil

The fact and the guilt of sin are quite evident. The human spirit sighs for deliverance from its bondage and wonders why a good and omnipotent God allowed it to enter the universe to mar His handiwork. The suggestion is intolerable that God may be charged with the responsibility for the existence of moral evil. Such a thought is forbidden by the nature of an infinite being, whose name is love, as well as by the immeasurable sacrifice which He has made in the gift of Christ for human redemption. We may be sure that God has permitted evil and its possibility for some ultimate wise purpose, however inscrutable this may be to us.

2.   Evil Involved in Finite Freedom

Moral evil has its source in a free being, otherwise it could have no moral character. It seems then that evil is a possibility in a finite free being who passes through the discipline involved in the power of contrary choice. The first man had the ability not to sin, but as a fact he did sin. The responsibility rests with him or the one who tempted him. One naturally inquires why the Omniscient should have created beings entrusted with powers which they are liable to abuse. The answer is difficult, if not altogether impossible. We must rest in the knowledge that what God has done is good and good only. We must wait until it shall please Him to make His way plain.   We have the assurance that He takes no pleasure in the death of the sinner and that He has provided a sovereign remedy for sin in Jesus Christ our Lord.   Surely those who reject Him can have no reasonable excuse if they be lost!

3.   A Remedy Free to All

The study of man as a moral being has led us to see him in ruin.   Traces of his original nature and endowment are not wanting.   There is still beauty, glory and hope in his soul.   There are longings for something better.   He is still capable of redemption, but he is too weak to accomplish this himself.   God in His infinite mercy has provided a mighty Savior.

PART III

CHRISTOLOGY

THE DOCTRINE OF CHRIST

INTRODUCTION. CONCERNING SALVATION.

Sin wrought terrible havoc in man, leaving him not only in deep misery but also without power to restore himself. To be saved from everlasting ruin he needed help from above.

1. The Promise of Salvation

The divine sentence upon the first sinners had scarcely been uttered before the gracious promise of possible salvation was given. The seed of the woman was to bruise the serpent's head. This promise was the rift in the dark cloud of despair. The promise was not an after-thought with God, but the revelation of a plan conceived before the foundation of the world for the redemption of man through Christ.

That the promise might not be forgotten, it pleased God to entrust its conservation to a peculiar people who would cherish it and enshrine it in their hopes and even build their national life upon it. Their prophets would reiterate the promise, connect it with a Messiah to come, and call back the nation when it strayed into forbidden paths.

The fulfillment of the promise, according to human reckoning, was long deferred. Nevertheless, it was valid and valuable through all the centuries. It was a promissory note given by God, who covenanted to pay in full without defalcation. It was an asset upon which Israel could always draw. In the fulness of time God redeemed His promise by sending His Son.

At His coming the ceremonial law with its types and symbols, "having a shadow of the good things to come," passed away. The great Teacher had come, and the pedagogue, the law, the escort of the child, departed, leaving the child with Jesus. With the passing of Judaism, provincialism and nationalism gave way to universalism.   All nations now shared the blessings of a world-redeemer.

2. The Nature of Salvation

In the life of Israel salvation was too often identified with deliverance from earthly ills—from enemies, poverty and sickness.   There was always, however, an inner circle of choice souls who interpreted the promise as a deliverance from sin and as a fellowship with God.   Abraham saw Christ's day and was glad.   Moses foretold the coming of a great leader.   The prophets, moved by the spirit of Christ which was in them, sought and searched diligently concerning the salvation and promise (I Peter 1: 10).

There are, no doubt, many in the churches who think of salvation only as an escape from the consequences of their sins, and as a final and blessed rest in heaven.   But salvation means more than this.   First of all, viewed from the religious side, salvation means the restoration and the personal realization of man's true relation to God as His child.   Access is open; filial love casts out fear; he reposes upon the bosom of God.   The hindrance of sin has been removed.   On its ethical side salvation means transformation of character.   Not only has guilt been removed, but holiness and righteousness are more than imputations; they are actual possessions.   The believer becomes like his Redeemer.   Not only is his status changed, but his life is renewed after the "image of him that created him" (Col. 3: 10).

3. The Mediation of Salvation

Under the old dispensation salvation was mediated through law and symbol, through ceremony and sacrifice, all of which pointed to something better and more real. Holy men were raised up to interpret these preparatory elements until the fulness of time should come.

But finally "God having of old-time spoken unto the fathers in the prophets by divers portions and in divers manners hath at the end of these days spoken unto us in his Son" (Heb. 1: 1, 2).   The mediator of salvation is Jesus Christ, who came into the world to save sinners.   He is the only Savior, the only hope of "forgiveness of our trespasses, according to the riches of his grace" (Eph. 1: 7).

Christian theology centers in Christ.   To understand and to interpret Him is its chief task.   The whole process of salvation is usually expressed by the word soteriology, the doctrine of salvation, which consists of christology or the doctrine of Christ, and pneumatology or the doctrine of the Spirit.   Salvation is obtained through Christ and applied by the Holy Spirit.

We present the doctrine of Christ under the following heads:

    A.   The Gift of Christ.
    B.   The Person of Christ.
    C.   The States of Christ.
    D.   The Work of Christ.

A.   THE GIFT OF CHRIST

I.   THE MOTIVE OF THE GIFT.

"Faithful is the saying and worthy of all acceptation that Christ Jesus came into the world to save sinners" (I Tim. 1: 15).   But what was the secret of His coming, of His infinite sacrifice?

There can be but one answer to the question and it is that given by Christ Himself.   "God so loved the world that he gave his only begotten Son" (Jno. 3: 16).   Divine compassion for His erring and perishing children prompted Him to send His Son.   This is a sufficient reason; no other motive could exist and none could be more powerful.   God is love.

II.   THE UNIVERSALITY OF THE GIFT.

1.   Affirmed in the Scriptures

    1)   CHRIST CAME FOR ALL.
        He came to save the world, to seek and to save
           the lost.   Lk. 19: 10.
    2)   CHRIST INVITES ALL.
        "Come unto me all ye that labor and are heavy
           laden."   Mt. 11: 28.

3) HE DIED FOR ALL.
   "He gave his life a ransom for many." Mt.
   20: 28.
   "He is the propitiation for our sins; and not
   for ours only, but for the sins of the whole
   world." I Jno. 2: 2.
4) HE CONDEMNS THOSE WHO REJECT HIM.
   "This is the condemnation that the light is
   come into the world and men loved the
   darkness rather than the light." Jno. 3: 19.
5) HE SENDS HIS GOSPEL TO ALL.
   "Go ye into all the world, and preach my Gospel to the whole creation." Mk. 16: 15.

2. Limited by Predestinarians

In spite of what seems to be very plain teaching, the
universality of the gift of Christ has been denied by some
who claim that He came only for the elect and that He made
an atonement for them alone. The diversity of views as
to the universality of the gift and the merit of Christ marks
one of the lines of cleavage between the two great parties of
the Reformation—the Lutherans and the Reformed or Calvinists.

1) DEFINITION.

In order to obtain a proper understanding of the matter
at issue it is necessary to have a clear conception of the
meaning of certain terms.

(1) Decrees. The decrees of God are His eternal purposes whereby He has foreordained whatever comes to pass.

(2) Predestination or foreordination is a decree which
relates to rational beings.

(3) Election is a decree of predestination for salvation.

(4) Reprobation denotes a judicial act of condemnation.

(5) Preterition denotes a passing by.

(6) Foreknowledge or prescience expresses God's knowledge of all events before they occur.

(7) Infra-lapsarian or sub-lapsarian refers to the order
of the decrees, viz., creation, fall, election, redemption by
Christ, application of redemption by the Holy Spirit.

(8) *Supra-lapsarian* reverses the order thus: Creation, election, fall, etc.

2) THE CALVINISTIC VIEW OF PREDESTINATION.

Most modern Calvinists hold the *infra* or *sub-lapsarian* doctrine. Following the teachings of Augustine, who held a modified view of predestination, John Calvin developed the doctrine to its logical conclusions and formulated the theory for the Reformed churches. Its salient features are the following:

(1) All things that come to pass are ordered from eternity by the immutable decree of Almighty God.

(2) The decree of predestination precedes foreknowledge, for God determines everything before it comes to pass.

(3) Some individuals have been elected to eternal life, and that solely out of grace, and entirely without reference to their foreseen faith or character.

(4) The elect are redeemed by Christ, irresistibly drawn by the Spirit, and preserved without fail unto the final salvation.

(5) The rest of the human race are either passed by (preterition), and thus left in their lost state, or are judicially condemned (reprobation), the final effect being the same in either case.

3) THE LUTHERAN VIEW.

In the early days of the Reformation, Luther and Melanchthon inclined to the Augustinian view of predestination. Upon a closer investigation they discovered that the logical consequences of the Augustinian view conflicted with the simple Word of God, so they abandoned it. Their view was later (1577) incorporated in the Form. of Concord.

(1) Christ died for all.

(2) It is God's desire that all be saved, and to this end repentance is urged upon all and the Gospel is preached to all.

(3) God has predestined all who accept Christ to be saved. Predestination refers only to the saved and not to the lost.

(4) This predestination is grounded in God's foreknowledge or prescience, but the latter is in no sense causative.

(5) Salvation is purely of grace, without human merit. It is God's gift. Even the faith that accepts salvation is the result of God's ennobling grace. This grace is rejected by the unbelieving, who wilfully harden their hearts. The human will, however impotent to choose good when unaided, possessed the power to resist God.

4) THE ARMINIAN VIEW.

Arminius was a Dutch theologian (1560-1609) who controverted Calvinistic views concerning predestination. After his death his followers, the Remonstrants, expressed their views in five articles, which we condense as follows.

(1) God has decreed to save all who believe in Christ and to condemn the unbelieving.

(2) Christ died for all men, yet the believing only can be saved.

(3) Man cannot save himself, but in order to be saved must be born again of the Spirit.

(4) The grace of God is needful for all good, but is not irresistible.

(5) The question of the perseverance of the saints cannot be dogmatically decided but must be left for further study of the Scriptures.

The view was condemned by the Synod of Dort (1618). While it approximates the Lutheran view, other doctrines of the Arminians must be rejected. In the Reformed churches those who reject Calvinism are known as Arminian in their attitude toward predestination.

5) CONCLUSION.

Calvinism seems untenable because it contradicts some of the plainest passages of Scripture, reflects on the impartiality of God, and ignores man's freedom.

Well has Clark said: "Doubtless our freedom is limited, but surely it is real. Some hold that predestination is the fixed point that must be held, because it is a point reached by necessary *a priori* reasoning, and that our freedom can be only such as is consistent with predestination. But we must affirm, on the contrary, that freedom is the fixed point that must be held, because it is an inalienable certainty of experience, and that predestination can be such only as is consistent with it, else there is no rational and responsible life" (Theology. P. 146).

III. PREPARATION FOR THE GIFT.

1. The Need for Preparation

It is natural to expect that so stupendous an event as the coming of the world's Redeemer would be preceded by preparation commensurate with its greatness. This expectation is more than realized in the history of the world. A profound student, Johann Mueller, has taken as the motto of his Universal History this sentence: "Christ is the key to the history of the world." He is the central figure. Around Him all events revolve. The protevangel of the Garden of Eden has the pledge of God for its fulfilment. As the fall is the greatest catastrophe of history, so the coming of Christ is the crowning blessing. Measured by man's individual life this coming was long-delayed. But in the plan of God, with whom a thousand years are as a watch in the night, events succeed each other in due time. "Providence," as Guizot says, "takes a step and ages roll away."

2. Factors in the Preparation

Many of the actors in the drama of history were, indeed, quite unconscious of the part they were playing in carrying out the divine plan; but none the less was the overruling hand of providence shaping the history of the race. Little, · for instance, did the Roman emperor dream that he was fulfilling prophecy when he issued an edict that brought Joseph and Mary to their ancestral village where Christ was born.

The time arrived when it pleased God to separate from the mass of mankind a people whom He called peculiarly His own. While not ignoring the rest of the race, He manifested Himself in a marked way to Abraham and his descendents. From the time of Abraham to Christ's coming, mankind is divided into two classes, the Jews and the Gentiles. Through the former God proposed to save mankind, and through the latter He prepared mankind for salvation. The former preparation was positive, the latter, mostly negative.

1) PREPARATION THROUGH THE GENTILES IN GENERAL.

(1) The Universality of Religion.

Among the heathen there remained everywhere some traces of the primeval faith, however distorted. Moreover, the innate longing of the soul for God was not utterly destroyed by sin. Hence we find religion in some form, gross or refined, among all the ancient peoples. This fundamental fact must be reckoned with in the evolution of faith until its climax is reached in Christianity.

(2) Insufficiency of Heathen Religions.

The misbelief of the heathen did not and could not keep the people from sinking deeper in corruption. This is true not simply of the grosser forms of idolatry, for the most refined of ancient races fell into the most atrocious licentiousness. In spite of the boast of its philosophy, Athens expressed its lack of confidence in its deities by erecting an altar to an unknown God. The gods of the heathen were after all but the fantastic enlargements of men's minds, and were controlled by passions like our own. The heathen had their religious cravings, and no god to satisfy them.

2) PREPARATION THROUGH THE GREEKS.

(1) Conquest.

The two nations which came into closest touch with Christianity at its entrance into the world were the Greek and Roman. In them were centered the culture and force of the ancient world. The former, especially through Philip and Alexander, dreamed of universal empire. While this dream was not realized the conquests of Greece carried with them the fuller light of the invader and prepared the way for the true light.

(2) Philosophy.

The Greek philosophy approached the truth more nearly than any other effort of the human mind. Socrates and Plato undermined polytheism through their belief in a supreme being, and thus prepared the way for the acceptance of monotheism. Moreover, philosophy so stimulated the mind as to make it more susceptible to the truth of the Gospel. It also furnished the dialect for the apologetics and polemics of the early Church. Even the Stoic philosophy founded by Zeno (380 B. C.) and later developed by the Romans, contributed materially to the acceptance of the Gospel. Its sentiments of self-denial and charity and its cosmopolitan character were no doubt elements in the transition.

(3) Culture.

The greatest service rendered by the Greeks came through their broad culture and especially through the language in which that culture was expressed. Science and art and literature reached their climax in Greece. Thence the Church brought them and consecrated them to the use of religion. "It was not an accident that the New Testament was written in Greek, the language which can best express the highest thoughts and worthiest feelings of the intellect and heart; and which is adapted to be the instrument of education for all nations; nor was it an accident that the composition of these books and the promulgation of the Gospel were delayed till the instruction of our Lord and the writings of the apostles could be expressed in the dialect of Alexandria" (Conybeare and Howson's Life of St. Paul. V. I; p. 10).

The military and commercial conquests of Greece made its language the medium of intercourse among all known nations. When Rome conquered Greece, the language of Greece conquered Rome. Pilate's inscription on the cross, in Hebrew, in Greek, and in Latin, suggests the union of the three powerful elements for the promulgation of the meaning of the Cross.

3) PREPARATION THROUGH THE ROMANS.

(1) The Extent of the Empire.

The most potent Gentile influence for the spread of Christianity was, without doubt, the Roman Empire. With a population of one hundred millions it embraced practically all known civilized nations. Its territory covered nearly all modern Europe, the north of Africa, and western Asia to the Euphrates. Its splendid highways opened its lands to speedy communication, while its ships connected the ports of the Mediterranean and adjoining seas.

(2) Its Code of Laws.

Wherever the empire extended, there, in the main, justice was fairly administered. Travel could be pursued with safety under the protection of the strong arm of the law. The rights of citizenship were everywhere respected.

(3) Its Spirit of Tolerance.

While there were outbreaks of persecution, the general spirit of the Roman Empire was that of toleration, which allowed undisturbed missionary effort over a large territory for long periods of time.

(4) Its Unifying Influence.

The commingling of the nations, the spread of a common language, the centralization of authority, the intellectual activities and commercial enterprise all combined to make the inhabitants of a vast realm a homogeneous people, thus rendering them more accessible to Christianity.

4) PREPARATION THROUGH THE JEWS.

Of all the factors in the preparation for the kingdom, the Jews were, no doubt, the most positive and influential.

(1) Their Deep Religious Character.

The Jews were pre-eminently a religious people. Religion was dominant in their national life. Their prosperity and their decay were measured by its fervor and its decline. Monotheism had its complete triumph in Israel.

(2) Their Miraculous History.

The Jews are the miracle of history; in them the supernatural finds its fullest manifestation. Their history and

literature become inexplicable if the idea of divine inter-
ference is eliminated.

(3) Their Aspirations and Hopes.

At the advent, the golden age of Greece and Rome was
in the past. Among the Hebrews it was in the future.
Abraham's seed was to be a blessing to all nations. Moses
predicted the coming of a great prophet like himself. The
Messiah, "the one who was to come," was the hope of
Israel, which sustained them through centuries of waiting.

(4) The Geographical Position.

Palestine was located on the highway of the nations.
Egypt and Babylon sent their merchants and their soldiers
through her domain. She has also been the battleground
of empires. She has been providentially so situated that
her gospel could easily be carried east and west.

(5) The Dispersion of the People.

The Jews were practically everywhere in ancient times.
Attracted by commerce or driven by political upheavals
they settled in Babylon, Alexandria, Athens, Rome, and
lesser cities. The apostles found synagogues wherever
they went. Consequently, there was a knowledge of the
true God among the Gentiles. On the day of Pentecost
there were present devout Jews from every nation.

(6) Proselytes of the Gate.

The Jews were not given to proselyting, yet many noble
heathen accepted their faith in God without organically
uniting with them. These converts formed a fruitful soil
for the new seed of the Gospel and gave Christianity a
hold upon the upper classes.

All these factors and influences, here hastily sketched,
constituted a providential preparation for the coming of
the Son of Man. (On the whole section see: The Beginning of Christianity, Fisher; Life of St. Paul, Conybeare
& Howson; History of the Christian Church. Vol. I. Schaff.)

B. THE PERSON OF CHRIST

I. THE TESTIMONY CONCERNING CHRIST.

Before entering upon a dogmatic construction of the person of Christ we should aim to picture to ourselves Christ as He really was as He walked among men. We should study Him as we would any other great character of history.

The sources of our information must be primarily the four Gospels. The first three tell the story of His life from a purely historic standpoint. The fourth regards it more subjectively. The combination of the features delineated by the four gives us a clear view of the historic Christ. We may confidently regard these sources as authentic, not simply from a critical standpoint, but as the only adequate explanation of Jesus Christ, who is undeniably a great historic person. Besides these primary sources we have also incidental references in the rest of the New Testament.

The relation of this literary and ethical study of Christ to theology is obvious. Upon the background of historic fact must appear the complete picture of our Lord. The doctrine of His person must be drawn from the facts of His life. The study of His life suggests the great problems with which theology deals. If this study reveals to us an exceptional character, differing from great and good men only in degree, there is no problem. But if we discover a character which cannot be classed, a person whose relation to God and man is absolutely unique, then we have a problem, the solution of which calls for theological discussion. Such a treatment of the problem will present Christ not as a mere theme but as a living person.

1. His Birth and Early Years

1) THE MIRACULOUS CONCEPTION.

At the very threshold of our study we are met by the assertion of the miraculous conception of Christ. Whatever explanation theology has to offer, the record is very plain. Were this miracle the exception in His life we might dismiss it as a myth, but as it harmonizes with His subsequent development, and His influence in the history of the world, we must accept it as it stands. Nor should one who believes in the personality of God and in God as the infinite creator of all things stagger at the story of Christ's supernatural birth.

2) THE HOME.

The mother and foster-father of Jesus belonged to the inner circle of the Jewish people who anxiously shared the hopes of Israel. Mary especially appears as a noble, pious woman. The story practically passes Joseph by, and deals rather with the relation of the mother and the Son. We find that under her instruction and influence Christ grew up in her faith and developed noble traits of manhood.

3) TRAINING.

Apart from the home, Christ received His training in the synagogue and the school connected with it. The chief, perhaps the only, text-book which He studied was the Old Testament. He never quotes from any other book. He came into contact with thoughtful people both at home and in His later annual visits to Jerusalem. When we are asked how His teachers, who must have been narrow in their views, could have produced so broad-minded a pupil, we are constrained to repeat the saying of His hearers, "Man never spoke like this man." We are at a loss to account for this extraordinary character on the basis of His opportunities for intellectual training.

4) GROWTH.

With a single astonishing glimpse into His boyhood, the record tells us of His subjection to His parents and of His growth in stature, and in favor with God and man. In these few words are contained the suggestion of personal growth through self-control, love and communion with God, yet these alone could not have prepared a mere man to accomplish what He did.

2. His Relations With Men

1) HIS FAMILY.

Christ lived a natural life at home. He was obedient and loving. For years He seems to have supported His mother's family.   His mother carried the secret of His birth in her heart, but does not seem always properly to have interpreted it.   His brothers did not understand Him.

2) HIS DISCIPLES.

In due time Christ chose special disciples, whom He called His friends.   To these He was bound by the closest ties, opening His heart to them, yearning for their sympathy, and chiding them for their faults, patient with them in their failures, but never resentful nor angry.

3) MANKIND.

His relation to men was most extraordinary.   On the one hand He manifested the most unaffected lowliness of mind, not shrinking from the humblest service, while on the other He maintained a dignity which forbade any undue familiarity.   His compassion for the lowly and unfortunate was a distinguishing trait of His character.   But more wonderful than all was the fact that He pronounced over the penitent the forgiveness of their sins, as though He were God's representative or even a divine person Himself. This paradox furnishes another problem for theology.

3.   His Relations With God

To Christ, God is His Father.   There is an evident closeness of relation which distinguishes Him from other men. He loves the Father with supreme affection, which expressed itself in absolute obedience, even unto death.   This obedience is unmarred by any distrust.   He is possessed literally by that perfect love which casteth out fear.   He is unconscious of any lack even in God's sight.   He never confesses any sin and never prays for forgiveness.   He claims to be perfect.   He declares, "I and the Father are one."   He puts Himself on an equality with God.   How to reconcile these assumptions with a purely human life suggests still another problem.

4. His Ministry

The life purpose of Christ was evidently to fulfill the Old Testament promise of a redeemer of the world. He proclaimed that He came to usher in the kingdom of heaven. To this He consecrated His life. He accomplished His mission in a threefold manner: by teaching, by working miracles, and by suffering. In each of these His extraordinary character appears. His teaching combines all the truth and excellency of the law, the prophets and the sages; and at the same time He gives a new interpretation to life. His miracles were not mere wonders, but much more, signs. His sufferings, which He might have avoided, were, as He claims, both vicarious and atoning.

His clear spiritual vision which knew no mystery; His holiness which was without stain; His love toward men which was without alloy; His sacrifice of Himself which He sought not to hinder; together with His whole bearing and temper justify the claim of being in a unique sense *the* Son of God.

5. His End

That Christ really died on the Cross cannot be denied. But His sufferings were more mental than physical. He died because His mission demanded it. "He saved others; himself he could not save." A Roman centurion who witnessed Christ's behavior in His supreme trial and who beheld the sorrowful scene and all its phenomena exclaimed, "Truly this was the Son of God!"

On the third day Christ rose from the grave. This is a fact confirmed by the most indisputable testimony. He was seen alive for forty days by numerous witnesses, and then in the presence of a large company ascended into heaven.

6. Summary

Christ stands alone. "Man though He be, He is distinguished from all men by unique moral and spiritual excellence. Between Him and God there is a relationship to which there is no parallel in the case of any other man. The absolute distinctness of the character of Christ is not a dogma, constructed under philosophical or theological influences. It is a fact to which every line of the portrait bears unanswerable evidence. Stated as a fact, however, it at once becomes a problem which cannot be evaded. 'Whence hath this man these things?' How the answer shall be framed, whether the Nicene formula is adequate, or if not, how it is to be corrected and supplemented, is the task laid upon the intellect and conscience of the Church of today." (Kilpatrick's article, "Character of Christ," in Dict. of Christ and the Gospels).

II. THE INCARNATION.

The solution of the problem suggested by the unique historic Christ must be sought in the doctrine of the incarnation. There is no other explanation of His supernatural life and work.

1. The Meaning of the Incarnation

The word incarnation is derived from the Latin *in* and *caro* signifying *in the flesh,* or an embodiment. "The word became flesh and dwelt among us," says John. In short, it is another way of saying that the Son of God became man. In theological language, the Son united with His divine and everlasting person a human nature, consisting of body and soul, thus forming the God-man. This is the simple teaching of the apostles which was later formulated in the Nicene Creed. After confessing the deity of Christ, it says of Him, "Who, for us men, and for our salvation came down from heaven and was incarnate by the Holy Ghost of the Virgin Mary."

2. The Scripture Basis of the Incarnation

In the Old Testament there was at best a dim foreshadowing of the incarnation. The thought of it is suggested by such a passage as "The Lord himself will give you a sign; behold a virgin shall conceive and bear a son and shall call his name Immanuel" (Is. 7:14; Matt. 1:23). More striking is another prophecy by Isaiah, "For unto us a child is born, unto us a son is given; and the government shall be upon his shoulders; and his name shall be called

Wonderful, Counsellor, Mighty God, Everlasting Father, Prince of Peace" (Is. 9: 6).

1) THE STORY OF THE NATIVITY.

The incarnation is taught in the New Testament in unequivocal language. It is said in the Gospel of Luke that at a certain time the angel Gabriel was sent from God to the virgin Mary to announce to her, "The Holy Spirit shall come upon thee and the power of the Most High shall overshadow thee: wherefore the holy thing which is begotten shall be called the Son of God." Luke and Matthew relate in most explicit terms the story of the birth with the accompanying beautiful incidents of the angelic messengers, the worship of the shepherds and the adoration of the wise men.

2) THE DOCTRINE OF CHRIST'S PRE-EXISTENCE.

(1) Affirmed by Himself.

In His interview with Nicodemus, Jesus says, "No one hath ascended into heaven, but he that descended out of heaven, even the Son of man who is in heaven." "God sent not the Son into the world to judge the world" (Jno. 3: 13-17).

In His discourse in the synagogue at Capernaum, Jesus declared, "I am come down from heaven, not to do mine own will, but the will of him that sent me." "I am the living bread which came down from heaven." "What then if ye should behold the Son of man ascending where he was before?" (Jno. 6: 38, 51, 62).

In His teaching in the temple, vindicating Himself and reproving the unbelieving Jews, Jesus cried out, "I know him; because I am from him and he sent me" (Jno. 7: 29). A little later he said, "Before Abraham was born, I am" (Jno. 8: 58).

In His last discourse He said to the disciples, "I came out from the Father and am come into the world: again I leave the world and go unto my Father" (Jno. 16: 28).

In His high-priestly prayer He beseeches the Father, saying, "I glorified thee on earth, having accomplished the work thou hast given me to do, and now, Father, glorify thou me with thine own self with the glory which I had with thee before the world was." In interceding for the disciples He says, "The words which thou gavest me I have given unto them; and they received them, and knew of a truth that I came from thee, and they believed that thou didst send me." "Father, I desire also that they whom thou hast given me be with me where I am, that they may behold my glory which thou hast given me: for thou lovedst me before the foundation of the world" (Jno. 17:4, 5, 8, 24).

(2) Taught by the Apostles.

In the prologue to his gospel the apostle John proclaims in the most striking language the eternal pre-existence of the Logos. "In the beginning was the Word, and the Word was God." Christ is the Logos, or Word, the expression of God, the revelation of God. In one of his Epistles John says concerning Christ, "The Word of life," "We have seen, and bear witness, and declare unto you the life, the eternal life which was with the Father, and was manifested unto us" (I Jno. 1:1, 2).

The learned Paul recognizes the pre-existence of our Lord, when in contrasting the first and the second Adam he says, "The first man is of the earth earthy; the second man is of heaven" (I Cor. 15:47). He alludes to Christ's state before He became man in that beautiful saying, "Though he was rich, yet for your sakes he became poor" (II Cor. 8:9). In the classic passage in Phil. 2:5-11, he represents Christ as existing in the form of God and through His love for man relinquishing His glory to take "the form of a servant, being made in the likeness of men." In Colossians he glorifies Christ as the image of the invisible God, the creator of all things (Col. 1:15-17).

3) ITS ACCEPTANCE BY THE APOSTOLIC CHURCH.

The incarnation was accepted by the apostles and their successors as a fact. The man Christ Jesus was with them but they saw in Him more than man. They "beheld his glory, glory as of the only begotten of the Father" (Jno. 1:14).

3. The Possibility of the Incarnation

So stupendous a fact as the incarnation naturally challenges rational investigation. If it is unthinkable and inherently impossible, it is vain to press its acceptance by faith.

1) ACKNOWLEDGED UNIVERSALLY.

(1) Ethnic Beliefs.

That an incarnation is not unthinkable must be evident from the fact that the doctrine is the common property not only of all Christians, but of practically all religions. Paul and Barnabas, when they cured the lame man at Lystra, were hailed as gods incarnate. Paul was supposed to be Mercury and Barnabas, Jupiter. At the present day the Oriental religions, especially those in India, include incarnations and reincarnations without end.

(2) Philosophical Intimations.

Philosophy, whatever its protests against any specific form of religion, is essentially religious in its endeavor to relate man to the absolute. The ancient Stoic philosophy, which once dominated the best thinking, postulated the divine immanence as an omnipresent and permeating principle dwelling in the world and in the soul. There is nothing repugnant to the philosophical mind in the idea of a union of God and man. Pantheism is the extreme expression of this idea. Among the Hindus the incarnation or indwelling of their gods in men and the final absorption of the soul in God are but perversions and exaggerations of a universal longing for union with God.

(3) In Old Testament Teaching.

The pre-Christian ideas of incarnation find their clearest and most rational expression among the Hebrews. Having the light of divine revelation, they were prevented from indulging in the vain and grotesque fancies of the heathen. The possibility of an incarnation is a corollary of the doctrine that man was made in the divine image. The various theophanies recorded in the Old Testament where God or the angels appear in human form are a direct testimony to Hebrew belief that God may condescend to appear as man. Illustrations of these supernatural manifestations are found in the life of Abraham, Lot, Hagar, Joshua, Gideon, Manoah, David, Elijah, Daniel and others.

The anthropomorphisms of the Old Testament are not mere accommodations to the limited intelligence of the people, but are fundamental to the thought that God and man are closely related.

2) BASED UPON AFFINITY.

At first thought man and God seem antithetical, essentially and totally different, separated by an impassable gulf. But a little reflection shows that they are more alike than unlike, that they have much in common, and that the vague dread often felt by the human heart is an intrusion which may be removed.

In fact there is a real and necessary affinity between God and man, because they are both personalities. God made man in His own image. Though sin entered into the world and marred the soul of man, it did not utterly destroy the image of God. The capacity for restoration remained.

It might, indeed, have been impossible for man to approach God and have fellowship with Him; but it was not impossible for infinite love and power to reach down and to draw man to itself. That God has actually done this is affirmed by Jesus Christ, who claimed oneness with the Father and declared, "He that hath seen me hath seen the Father."

The incarnation shows the capacity and the power of the infinite God for manifestation and expression in any manner consistent with deity. We may not limit Him to any one mode of showing Himself, and surely we should not exclude Him, in our thought, from manifesting Himself in human form—the only way in which He could come near. Let us not imagine that it is derogatory to the glory and dignity of the Godhead to appear as a man upon earth. To do so is, of course, condescending, but infinite love is capable of infinite condescension. Even human love prompts heroic sacrifices. To save a son a mother will leave a palace for a hovel; to save a soul a missionary will dwell among lepers. But the love of Christ transcends this, for it is a love that passeth knowledge (Eph. 3: 19).

4. The Purpose of the Incarnation

1) THE POSITIVE TEACHINGS OF SCRIPTURES.

The redemptive purpose of the incarnation is evident throughout the Bible from the promise in the garden recorded in Genesis to the vision of the blood-washed throng described in Revelation. Jesus declared that God gave His Son that whosoever should believe on Him should not perish but have eternal life. He also declares that He came to give "his life a ransom for many" (Matt. 20: 28). "To seek and to save that which was lost." John the Baptist designated Christ as the "Lamb of God that taketh away the sin of the world" (John 1: 29). The apostle John declared that God loved us and "sent his Son to be the propitiation for our sins" (I Jno. 4: 10). Paul's conception agrees with that of John when he says "that Christ Jesus came into the world to save sinners" (I Tim. 1: 15). The Epistle to the Hebrews represents Christ as coming into the world for the express purpose of saving men. "Wherefore, it behooved him in all things to be made like unto his brethren, that he might be a merciful and faithful highpriest in things pertaining to God, to make propitiation for the sins of the people" (Heb. 2: 14-19).

2) AN UNTENABLE THEORY.

That the purpose of the incarnation is solely redemptive is controverted by a few eminent Christian scholars who maintain that the incarnation would have taken place even if man had not sinned. Sin, it is said, is a mere incident in history, and not the occasion of the incarnation. "Are we to suppose," says Martenson, "that that which is most glorious in the world could only be reached through the medium of sin; that there would have been no place in the human race for the glory of the only begotten one, but for sin?"

This theory holds to the idea that the first man was

imperfect and incapable of perfection without the incarnation. It claims for its support two brief passages of Scripture, Eph. 1: 9-12, 22, and Col. 1: 15-17.

The objections to the theory are (a) that it really has no Scripture basis. The passages quoted do not seem to have any bearing upon the subject and can be better explained in accordance with the current belief. (b) It rests upon a misconception of the state of the first man. (c) It underestimates the evil power of sin. (d) It is purely speculative and cannot be fairly deduced from any known facts, or from any necessary conclusions of reason.

5. The Mode of the Incarnation (The Virgin Birth)

1) THE DOCTRINE OF THE CHURCH.

(1) Derived from the Scriptures.

The doctrine of the Church concerning Christ includes the virgin birth. It is plainly taught in the Gospel of Matthew (1: 18-25) and in the Gospel of Luke (1: 26-38; 2: 1-10). That these are genuine and authentic Gospels cannot be denied even on critical grounds. All the ingenuity of hostile critics has not sufficed to discredit them. The sources whence the evangelists received their information are obscure. It seems, however, that Matthew writes from the viewpoint of Joseph, and Luke from that of Mary. Luke evidently must have carefully investigated the whole matter and reported it in good faith to his friend Theophilus. There is no evidence that the virgin birth was ever denied in the Apostolic Church.

(2) Confessed in the Creeds.

The faith of the Church concerning the virgin birth is confessed in the ecumenical as well as in the modern creeds. The Apostle's Creed, which is derived from the baptismal formula, has the sentence concerning the virgin birth in its most ancient form, going as far back as the beginning of the second century. The doctrine, therefore, has come down from the days of the apostles, and is confessed in the liturgy of thousands of churches every Sunday.

2) THE DENIAL OF ITS AUTHENTICITY.

(1) By Whom.

As early as A.D. 100, Cerinthus, a Gnostic teacher of Asia Minor, impugned the virgin birth, holding that Jesus was the natural son of Joseph and Mary, possessing great wisdom, and that at His baptism He received supernatural power. Celsus, a pagan philosopher, living toward the close of the second century, also wrote against the credibility of the virgin birth. These cases show that the doctrine of the Church was already established in their day.

Besides pagans, Jews, agnostics, rationalists and Unitarians, some professed Christians in these latter days have expressed doubts concerning the authenticity of the virgin birth accounts, and have held that a belief in it is not essential to faith and to salvation.

(2) On What Grounds.

a. The objection urged against the virgin birth is first of all that it is highly improbable, if not impossible; that at best it is a myth, perhaps derived from heathen sources, intended to glorify the great teacher. But the same might be said against the resurrection, whose authenticity is well established. These both belong to the realm of miracle—the coming of God into human life in an extraordinary way. The affinity of man and God has already been mentioned.

b. Interpolations. Upon purely *a priori* and dogmatic grounds the Matthew and Luke accounts are alleged to be interpolations in spite of the fact that they are found in all great and most ancient manuscripts, the Sinaitic, the Alexandrian, the Vatican, and in all the ancient versions, the Syriac, Latin and Coptic. Textual criticism fails confessedly in the attempt to discredit the story. "There never were forms of Matthew and Luke without the Infancy narratives" (Virgin Birth. Orr, p. 52). Higher criticism, reasoning from style, context and the like, fares no better. It is evident even to the casual reader that the story is an integral part of the Gospel and that its omission would seriously disintegrate the narrative.

c. The silence of other New Testament writers. Objection is also made against the virgin birth that its mention is too brief and that it is confined to only two books. Why should only two of the four evangelists record so important a matter, it is asked? For the evident reason that two independent, complementary accounts are ample for the purpose. What more needs to be said than is reported by the two in the most beautiful, delicate and appropriate language?

In regard to the Gospel of Mark it may be said that he had no occasion to mention the nativity, since he begins his account with the ministry of Christ.

The Gospel of John was written by the apostle with a full knowledge of Matthew and Luke. Mary was a member of his household after the crucifixion. He must have known the story of the virgin birth and must have given his assent thereto, otherwise he would have contradicted it. His declarations, "the Word became flesh" (John 1: 14) and "every spirit that confesseth that Jesus Christ is come in the flesh is of God" (I John 4: 2) seem to harmonize with the infancy stories.

In reference to Paul it is incredible that he should not have known anything of the virgin birth. So profound a philosopher could not have rested without inquiring how Christ came into the world. His valued traveling companion was Luke, with whom he must have conferred on the subject and who evidently was well acquainted with the traditions. Nor can we agree that Paul is silent concerning the incarnation through Mary, for in several striking passages he evidently has it in mind. He speaks of God's "Son who was born of the seed of David according to the flesh, who was declared to be the son of God with power, according to the spirit of holiness by the resurrection from the dead" (Rom. 1: 3, 4). "God sending his own Son in the likeness of sinful flesh" (Rom. 8: 3). In Galatians 4: 4 he writes that "God sent forth his Son, born of a woman, born under the law." In that striking passage in Philippians 2: 5-8 he speaks of Christ as for a period renouncing His glory, "taking the form of a servant, being made in the likeness of man."

6. The Importance of the Doctrine

The question is not whether one may be saved without the knowledge or acceptance of the doctrine of the virgin birth. All faith is more or less imperfect and so a want of it in reference to the virgin birth is not necessarily fatal to salvation. No doubt millions have died not knowing or comprehending it, and have been saved because they accepted Christ as their Savior.

Nevertheless, there are weighty considerations which make the acceptance of the virgin birth vital to intelligent faith and to the theological construction of Christian doctrine.

1) THE TRUSTWORTHINESS OF THE GOSPELS.

The elimination of the infancy narratives without the authority of textual criticism and after their universal acceptance by the Church from the beginning, would sadly discredit the Gospels and thus destroy their authority. It is of special importance in these days when the tendency is strong to make the Bible a purely human book not to yield anything which faith and reason have always cherished.

2) THE HONOR OF OUR LORD'S MOTHER.

The discrediting of the virgin birth exposes Mary to the most dreadful imputation of her character for purity. This very charge was made against her by the vulgar critics of the early centuries and has been repeated ever since by the evil-minded. It is unthinkable that so divine a life as our Lord's should flow from a tainted source.

3) THE DOCTRINE OF THE PERSON OF CHRIST.

A rational construction of the doctrine of the person of Christ, as the God-man, and the Savior of the world, is impossible without the virgin birth. Without it there is no narrative or explanation at all of His birth and His early life is left open to conjecture and grotesque invention. Without it there is no adequate background to account for His sinlessness, for His extraordinary claims and for His influence. Much of His language would become vague and the story of His life be left in confusion. The Christian view of Christ, as pre-existent, as incarnate by the Holy Ghost and Mary, as leading a perfect life, as a sin-offering on the Cross, as a victor over death in a triumphant resurrection, satisfies the mind with its completeness and its consistency and establishes a firm ground upon which the hope of salvation may securely rest.

The writer heartily agrees with the paragraph with which Dr. Orr closes his treatise: "I cannot acquiesce in the opinion that the article of the virgin birth is one doctrinally indifferent, or that can be legitimately dropped from the public creed of the Church. The rejection of this article would, in my judgment, be a mutilation of the Scripture, a contradiction of the continuous testimony of the Church from apostolic times, a weakening of doctrine of the incarnation, and a practical surrender of the Christian position into the hands of a non-miraculous, purely humanitarian Christ—all on insufficient grounds."

III. THE CONSTITUTION OF CHRIST'S PERSON.

The Scriptures clearly state that Jesus was both man and God. Sometimes the divine side is emphasized; sometimes the human. The relation of the two is nowhere discussed in the Bible. This must be discovered from the nature of the case, through rational deduction.

The need of a well-defined doctrine of Christ's person must be self-evident, and is apparent from the history of doctrine. The early Church found it necessary, in order to exclude manifest error, to formulate its faith in the various great creeds which are still extant and received as authoritative by the Catholic and Protestant Churches. The great mass of Christian believers does not deem it necessary to revise them on the doctrine concerning Christ.

1. The Deity of Christ

1) THE PROOF (See Trinity).

(1) He is mentioned on an equality with the Father and the Spirit in the Trinitarian passages.

(2) He is spoken of as equal and identical with God.

a. Divine titles are given Him.

  b. Divine worship was offered Him.
  c. Divine works are attributed to Him.
  d. Divine attributes are ascribed to Him.
  e. Deity is claimed by Him.
(3) Other facts.
  a. His supernatural birth.
  b. His sinless life.
  c. His resurrection.
  d. His influence on men and nations.

2) THE DENIAL OF CHRIST'S DEITY.

(1) In the post-apostolic age the Ebionites, who were more Jewish than Christian, denied the divine nature and virgin birth of Christ, holding that He was simply a man elevated at His baptism to a state of perfection by the Holy Spirit.

(2) The Arians and the Semi-Arians in the fourth century disputed Christ's deity. The former held that He was a mere creature, through whom God created the universe. The Semi-Arians held that He was not a creature, yet subordinate to God. He was *homoiousios,* of like essence with the Father, but not *homoousios,* of the same essence.

(3) The Socinians of the 16th century and the Unitarians of our day also deny the deity of Christ, making Him merely a model man.

2. The Humanity of Christ

1) PROOF OF HIS HUMANITY.
(1) His Natural Body.
  a. His birth.
  b. His growth.
  c. His natural wants.
(2) His Human Soul.
  a. His intellectual operations.
  b. His sensibilities, love, anger, etc.
  c. His will.

2) NECESSITY FOR HIS HUMANITY.
(1) To furnish a medium between God and man.
(2) To become a model.

(3) To experience sympathy as a brother.

(4) To become a sacrifice.

(5) To be fitted to be a Judge.

3) DENIAL OF HIS HUMANITY.

The humanity of Christ is not often denied in modern times, though under-estimated. From the third to the sixth century various sects like the Docetæ taught that Christ's body was not real, and the Monophysites and the Monotheletes held that He had only one nature and one will, thus practically denying a normal body and soul.

3. The Relations of the Two Natures

1) THEIR UNION IN ONE PERSON.

(1) The Fact.

Though Christ possessed both a divine and human nature He was but one person. This is everywhere evident in His life. He always speaks and acts as a person. In speaking of Himself He uses the personal pronoun "I" in the singular number. When He is spoken of, the pronouns "he," "his" and "him" are used.

The possibility of a union of Christ's two natures is illustrated by our own constitution, in which body and soul form a human being. Christ possesses the divine essence, as well as soul and body. He is a theanthropic person. We have also several forms of consciousness, the physical and the psychical, and yet every man is a unit. We may therefore not limit the God-man in His attributes and powers.

(2) The Method of Union.

Christ, the eternal Logos, has always been a person, was a person before He became a man, and did not renounce His personality when He became incarnate. To His eternal personality He united not a human person but a human nature. A dual personality in a normal being is probably unthinkable. Let us hold distinctly and clearly to the fact that Christ was a person before He came into the flesh.

Nevertheless, Christ possessed all the elements of humanity, a real body and a rational soul, otherwise He would not have been a real man. But it was not needful for His humanity to exercise the peculiar functions of personality, self-consciousness and self-determination, apart from the person already existing. His human soul, being incorporated with the heavenly personality, developed under its gracious influence, and blended or submitted in its desires and decisions to the divine. The human nature of Christ was, therefore, not impersonal. "It is the privilege of minds to penetrate each other, without confusion with one another. In communion with God we are one with Him and yet we maintain our personality. The very surrender of the finite will to the infinite is itself an act of will" (*Ethical Principles.* Seth, p. 442).

2) THEIR DISTINCTNESS FROM EACH OTHER.

(1) The Confessional Statement.

It is the teaching of the Church that the human nature of Christ was not deified and absorbed in the divine. The divine nature is, of course, immutable.

Three forms of error arose in the Church concerning the nature of Christ. Apollinaris of Laodicea taught that the Logos took the place of the human soul. Nestorius separated the two natures so widely that they became two persons. Utyches so closely identified the two natures as to make them one. Various councils from 374 to 448 condemned these aberrations. The Fourth Ecumenical Council held at Chalcedon in 451 expresses most nearly the belief of the Church. It declares that Christ is to be acknowledged in two natures, "inconfusedly, unchangeably, indivisibly, inseparably; the distinction of natures being by no means taken away by the union, but rather the property of each nature being preserved and concurring in one subsistence."

With this representation the Form. of Concord agrees, saying, "We believe, teach and confess that now in this one undivided person of Christ, there are two distinct natures; the divine which is from eternity, and the human which in time was assumed in the unity of the Son of God. And these two natures in the person of Christ are never either separated or commingled with each other, nor is the one changed into the other; but each one remains in its nature and essence in the person of Christ to all eternity."

(2) The Perpetual Humanity of Christ.

As a corollary from the above the Christian faith has always been that Jesus retains His humanity forever, that inseparably united with His divine Person is the nature which He took when He became incarnate. He is still the "man Christ Jesus," "who is over all, God blessed forever" (I Tim. 2: 5; Rom. 9: 5).

a. The Rational Argument.

(a) The affinity of the two natures has not been changed by Christ's ascension. They are still congruous and there is nothing in mere change of plans that needs to affect this affinity. God is Father, and man is His child.

(b) The need of Christ's humanity for the peace and consolation of the human mind still remains. We think of Him as He was when on earth. We invest Him with human attributes. He seems more approachable thus. We want an advocate who knows our frame, who shares our lot and tasted of our sorrows.

b. The Scripture Argument.

(a) He retains His earthly name Christ Jesus. Christians are raised up with Him and made to sit in fellowship with Him (Phil. 2: 4-10).

(b) He has a body though glorified. This is apparent from the meaning of Christ's resurrection and His subsequent appearances. Paul says "there is a spiritual body" (I Cor. 15: 4) and that Christ "shall fashion anew the body of our humiliation, that it may be conformed to the body of his glory" (Phil. 3: 21).

(c) He ascended in visible bodily form. Not only did He ascend in His glorified body which He assumed at His resurrection, but He shall return in like manner (Acts 1: 9).

(d) He is mediator as man in heaven. "There is one God and one mediator also between God and men, himself man (*anthropos*) Christ Jesus" (I Tim. 2: 5). As mediator Christ is also the high priest who is touched with the feeling of our infirmities having been tempted in all points like as we are (Heb. 4: 14, 15).

(e) He shall judge the world as man. Paul declared at Athens that God "hath appointed a day, in which he will judge the world in righteousness by the man (*aner*) whom he hath ordained; whereof he hath given assurance unto all men, in that he hath raised him from the dead" (Acts 17: 31). He will return to judge the world as "the Son of man" (Mark 8: 38).

3) THEIR COMMUNION WITH EACH OTHER.

As we have seen, the two natures of Christ are united in one person and yet are forever distinct and unmingled. Nevertheless, there is necessarily between them a very close relation and fellowship which has been expressed as the *cummunicatio idiomatum,* or the communion of properties peculiar to each nature. There are three aspects of communion: *genus idiomaticum, genus apotelesmaticum,* and *genus majestaticum.*

(1) The *Genus Idiomaticum.*

This is the most generic form and affirms that the properties of both natures are ascribed to the one person. Illustrations: "Before Abraham was, I am" is strictly predicable of the divine nature only, yet it is said of the person. "I thirst" is strictly true of His humanity, yet Christ says it of Himself. This form is not disputed by any school of theology.

(2) The *Genus Apotelesmaticum* (from *apotelesma,* an official act).

This refers to the redemptive office of Christ and is a particular application of the first form. Thus it is said by Christ, "I came that they may have life" and "I lay down my life" (Jno. 10: 10 and 17). Here the divine and human acts are ascribed to the one person.

(3) The *Genus Majestaticum.*

This genus is peculiar to Lutheran theology and closely   .
related to the doctrine of the real presence of the divine-
human Christ in the Lord's Supper.   It is intended to set
forth the thought that the human nature, in virtue of its
abiding union with the divine, "has received over and above
its natural essential and permanent human properties, also
special high, great, supernatural, inscrutable, ineffable
heavenly prerogatives and pre-eminence in majesty, glory,
power and might above all that can be named, not only in
this world but also in that which is to come" (Form. of
Concord, II, viii, 685).

In virtue of its eternal union with deity, the accidental
and earthly limitations of the human nature have been
modified to conform with its new and exalted relations.

"To say that the divine nature of Christ is personally
present without His humanity is to deny that this humanity
is a part of that personality, and the doctrine of the incarnation falls to the dust.   If the Evangelical Lutheran be
asked, How can Christ's human nature be with us? he
can reply, After the manner in which an infinite spirit renders present a human nature which it has taken to be an
inseparable constituent of its own person, a manner most ·
real, but utterly incomprehensible to us" (Krauth, Con-
servative Reformation.   P. 349, f.).

4. The Impeccability of Christ

1) HIS SINLESSNESS.

Jesus Christ, as far as we can tell, lived a sinless life
on earth.   There is no record of any transgression, no
well-founded charge of any irregularity.   On the contrary,
He challenges His enemies to convict Him of sin.   His disciples saw in Him marvelous beauty of character, He appeared to them as one who was "holy," "harmless, undefiled,
separated from sinners."   He was never known to pray for
pardon or to express regret for anything He had said or
done.   His recorded utterances have stood the test of centuries and none of His followers see any reason to revise

them. The principles which He announced are still the noblest and most ideal conceivable.

The acknowledgment of His sinlessness is practically universal even by those who deny His deity. A few critics have, indeed, quibbled over His cursing a fig-tree of which He was not the owner, and of causing the destruction of a herd of swine, but such criticisms are too trifling to require answer. The pessimists have condemned His so-called pacifism and lack of courage, neither charge having any real basis. He stands supreme and alone in history, without a flaw, above criticism.

No explanation short of an acknowledgment of His deity can account for His exemption from sin. Postulating the incarnation and the virgin birth His sinless life becomes a possibility.

2) His Impeccability.

(1) A Corollary of His Perfect Life.

Christ's sinless life is a very strong presumption in favor of His impeccability. He lived in a sinful environment. He had to face the temptations common to His fellows, as well as those which arose from His possession of extraordinary gifts. He was, moreover, the special target of the evil spirit, who, we may well presume, left no method of attack untried. As a matter of fact, neither Satan nor man did in the least weaken our Lord's character. All that sin could do was done to overthrow Him, but without avail. It is hardly conceivable that any new form of temptation could have been concocted, that any greater foe could have confronted Him, or that any weakness could have developed in His character to lead to His downfall. We are warranted, therefore, to believe on the basis of actual testing that He was impeccable.

(2) The Ground of His Impeccability.

a. His Nearness to God.

Our Lord lived in conscious fellowship with God, whom He addressed as Father in the most confidential manner. Not for a moment did He seem to lose the sense of the divine presence. Moreover, besides the beatific vision He drew strength from God, whose angels ministered unto Him. How could He have sinned with God ever before Him, and His heart attuned to the love of God?

This state of Christ may be illustrated by the life of the ordinary Christian. His freedom from sin and His power to overcome temptation are in direct proportion to the nearness of His fellowship with God. The life that is hid with Christ in God, that is characterized by watching and praying, is a holy life. Could that fellowship and watchfulness be perfect we hesitate not to affirm that they would produce a perfect life. Our Lord lived in such pure light that darkness had no power over Him.

b. His Divine Nature.

The fundamental ground of Christ's impeccability must be sought in the fact that He was God. To hold that He could have sinned is equivalent to denying His deity. Christ could no more sin than the Father in heaven. No earthly environment could destroy His divine nature.

It may be urged however that He had a human nature also, and that therefore, this element in Him was inherently liable to sin. But what kind of human nature did He assume? It was an uncorrupted nature as Adam's was before the transgression. He therefore, had no original sin, but entered the fight against the old enemy unhampered by depravity.

Moreover, His divine and His human natures were united in one person. Hence it is impossible to conceive that the human or weaker nature should have deceived or overcome the divine or omnipotent nature. It is true that He had two wills, but His human will was always ready to blend with the divine.

If it be said that Christ Himself confessed ignorance of some things and that therefore He might have been deceived by a crafty tempter, the answer would be that the limitations of His knowledge were not in the realm of morals or religion, but of events. He never betrayed any moral obtuseness or lack of knowledge of the inner man, or of the real nature of sin. His discernment touched the thoughts and intents of the heart.

"Christ's victory over sin is not something merely which happened; it is something which was bound to happen. Faith cannot acquiesce in the thought that conceivably the divine redeeming plan might have been frustrated; yet frustrated it would have been had Jesus yielded to temptation even once. . . . There was that in Him from the first which offered a completely effective disturbance of His perfect spiritual growth, and secured the inner fount of subsequent feeling and will from all defilement" (MacIntosh, Doct. of The Person of Christ. P. 412 f.).

3) HIS TEMPTABILITY.

It may be said that an impeccable person is incapable of being tempted; and that therefore Christ must have been peccable because He was sorely tempted. But the fixed point in this case is the deity and, hence, the impeccability of Christ. Therefore those who have thought that impeccability and temptation could not be reconciled will have to revise their conception of temptation.

(1) The Reality of Christ's Temptation.

The sacred record is most explicit in its affirmation of Christ's temptation. It depicts Him engaged in deep spiritual struggle with the adversary in the wilderness, the garden and elsewhere. He was oppressed and afflicted, despised and rejected. "He suffered being tempted." "He was tempted in all points like as we are, yet without sin" (Mt. 4; Lk. 4: 2-13; Heb. 2: 18; 4: 15).

(2) The Nature of Temptation.
a. The Meaning of the Word.

The word temptation in the New Testament, in Greek and in English, means to try or to test. The motive of the one who tries may be good or evil. God tries His children to prove them and to improve them. Satan tries men to mislead and to destroy them. There is nothing, however, in the word or in the fact of temptation which implies any necessity to sin. Liability to temptation, which may be useful for the development of character by no means indicates yielding to evil. Every Christian is liable to be tempted and frequently is sorely distressed by temptation, but certainly he does not yield in every instance; and when he does he reproaches himself for not having resisted. He is conscious that had he watched and prayed, thus keeping open communication with heaven, he would not have sinned.

b. Relation to Freedom.

The relation of temptation to free-will is sometimes defined as the power of contrary choice. If this is interpreted to mean that a person may deliberately choose evil and yet remain free, there must be an error in the conception, for when he yields to sin he becomes the bondservant of sin. Freedom of choice is not synonymous with personal freedom. The freest man will not and cannot deliberately choose evil or yield to it, for should he do so he would at once sacrifice his real freedom. God is the freest of all beings, but it is inconceivable that He should choose evil. It is an idle boast when men say that they can do evil or not, just as they wish. No man can do anything essentially evil without weakening his power of resisting evil.

c. The Source of Christ's Temptation.

Christ's liability to temptation arose from His human nature and its limitations as well as from an imperfect environment and the active opposition of the evil one. He was a man, the second Adam, and subjected Himself to our human lot. He was solicited to use unlawfully His appetites and powers. "He felt the pressure of moral evil; He experienced the pain of resistance to it."·

He passed through countless trials which have brought men to despair. Toil, unkindness, depression of spirit, disappointment, poverty, sickness, bereavement, mental anguish, physical pain, indifference of friends, hostility of friends, slander, injustice and unspeakable cruelty — all these and kindred trials must have weighed upon the pure heart of the Master and formed a part of the moral conflict in which He learned obedience by what He suffered. This conflict was terribly real to Jesus, for He resisted it with strong crying and tears.

There was in all Christ's temptations no inward response such as arises in man from a disordered nature. Though He was tempted in all points like as we are, yet it was "without sin" (Heb. 4:15). This does not mean without sinning but without any propensity to sin. He entered life as Adam did without contamination. He had no illicit desires, no discord between the flesh and the spirit, sin could have no enticing or illusive power in His case (Jas. 1:14). He had no affinity for sin, no experimental knowledge of it (I Jno. 3:5; II Cor. 5:21).

d. Christ's Sympathy for the Tempted.

It might be thought that because Christ had no sinful nature and "did no sin" that therefore He could not have any real sympathy for the sinners in their daily trials. But it must be remembered that He had a most intimate knowledge of sin; He felts its power; He suffered from its assaults; He saw the frightful havoc which it wrought, with its disease, disgrace and death; He knew the malice and craft of the tempter; He experienced its bitterness upon the cross. To His infinitely pure spirit sin must have been inexpressibly horrible, and His heart went out to its victims as ours might go out to a poor child in the toils of a slimy serpent.

It is not necessary personally to experience every form of temptation in order to know its power or to sympathize with the weak. A pure mother has the deepest pity and love for her boy who may be the victim of temptation, at the very moment when his companions in sin are making sport of him, and are utterly without sympathy for him.

To hold that an impeccable Christ can have no sympathy for the sinner is to deny that God, who so loved the world that He gave His Son for its redemption, can have such sympathy.

Whatever mystery may exist in reference to Christ's impeccability, it should not deprive us of the consolation of which we are assured. "Wherefore it behooved him in all things to be made like unto his brethren that he might become a merciful and faithful high priest in things pertaining to God, to make propitiation for the sins of the people. For in that he himself hath suffered being tempted, he is able to succor them that are tempted" (Heb. 2: 17, 18).

C. THE STATES OF CHRIST

Our Lord Jesus, being God and being possessed of infinity and perfection, cannot be fully comprehended and described. We regard Him now in this and now in that aspect, and from various viewpoints. His person has already been briefly considered and contemplation of His work is to follow. A survey of His person and work seems to demand a summary or connecting link, which theology finds in a discussion of His states from the time of His incarnation to His ascension and session at the right hand of God. These states comprehend His humiliation and His triumph as the redeemer. They are known as the state of humiliation and the state of exaltation.

I. THE STATE OF HUMILIATION.

1. Its Duration

The state of humiliation may be said to begin with Christ's conception and end with the revivification after death, embracing His life on earth with its labor and suffering.

2. Its Nature (Kenosis)

Subjectively considered, the humiliation of Christ consisted in self-limitation and temporary renunciation of the exercise of certain divine powers and prerogatives. No humiliation of any kind could have been forced upon Him. He deliberately allowed it for the sake of poor sinners. He was willing to expose Himself to all conditions and impositions incident to the redemption of men.

This is powerfully set forth by Paul when he declares that Christ Jesus, "existing in the form of God, counted not the being equal with God a thing to be grasped, but emptied himself (*ekenose*), taking the form of a servant, being made in the likeness of men; and being obedient even unto death, yea the death of the cross" (Phil. 2: 5-8).

It indicates profound condescension on the part of the Son of God, that He was willing to forego for a time some of the glory which He possessed, "being on equality with God," by becoming incarnate of a human mother and by "taking the form of a servant." The incarnation in itself was not a humiliation, for Christ might have become incarnate apart from sin without any violence to His divine nature, for man was made in His image. His humility and humiliation, however, were incident to a human life in a sinful world. Of course, in our Lord's humiliation there was no impairment of His deity, which is immutable. But there is no occasion to distinguish too sharply between His human and divine natures in this matter.

In what Christ's emptying or *kenosis* consisted has been much discussed. Some have held that He entirely renounced certain divine prerogatives while on earth. Others have more properly held that in order to be a real man He held in abeyance the exercise of some divine attributes. He declares that He was ignorant when the judgment would occur, thus limiting His omniscience (Mt. 24: 36). He told His disciples that He was glad that He was not there when Lazarus died, thus foregoing omnipresence (Jno. 11: 15). He yielded to force, thus surrendering omnipotence. That these limitations were voluntary is evident when He says that He had power to lay down His life and power to take it again and also when He declares that He could summon legions of angels.

"The *Kenosis* did not obscure His moral insight and spiritual discernment, did not involve any moral defect or failure or any religious mistrust, did not weaken or narrow His love, mercy or grace, did not lower His authority or lessen His efficiency as revealer of God and redeemer of men; but, on the contrary, it was necessary, for only under such human conditions and limitations could He fulfill His mission, deliver His message, present His sacrifice, and effect salvation. That He might receive the name of Savior and Lord, which is above every other name, He must empty Himself" (Garvie Dict. of Christ and the Gospels, I. 928).

3. Its Expression

The humiliation of Christ may be seen throughout His entire earthly life. A birth of the creator from a creature, the humble birthplace, a peasant home in a poor village, the limitations of an artisan's life, the constant unremunerative labor, and the prejudices of the teachers all combine to make the environment of the youth and early manhood of Jesus singularly unattractive.

His ministry, so beautiful and noble, stands out from the background of opposition, persecution and rejection. He came to His own and they received Him not. The leaders in Israel scorned Him and caused His arrest upon false charges and clamored for His blood. The people who once heard Him gladly joined in the cry, Crucify Him! Betrayed by one of the Twelve, forsaken by the rest, His life sworn away by perjurers, scourged, mocked, spat upon, thorn-crowned, He finally expires upon the cruel Cross where He cries in bitter agony, "My God, my God, why hast thou forsaken me!"

The terrible sufferings of our Lord must have been far worse for Him than they would have been for a mere man. A being of infinite holiness with a soul sensitive to evil and a body sensitive to pain in an unusual degree must have endured agony of soul and body far beyond our comprehension. "He was despised and rejected of men, a man of sorrows and acquainted with grief." But He willingly endured all this humiliation for us and for our redemption.

II. THE STATE OF EXALTATION.

The humiliation, the suffering, the agony, has its reward. "Wherefore also did God highly exalt him, and gave unto him the name which is above every name, that in the name of Jesus every knee should bow of things in heaven and things on earth and things under the earth, and that every tongue should confess that Jesus Christ is Lord, to the glory of God the Father" (Phil. 2: 9-11).

1. Revivification

Our Lord was crucified under Pontius Pilate, was dead and buried. His body hung upon the Cross and was later laid in the tomb. On the third day His body was no longer there, as testified to by His friends. But on the same day He appeared to His disciples in a glorified form. It is not so important to know the exact moment when death and the grave were conquered and the soul of our Lord was united with His new body. His triumph began with that event. His victory was complete over death and him that had the power of death even the devil (Heb. 2:14).

2. Descent Into Hell

1) THE CREEDAL STATEMENT.

The Nicene Creed, 325, makes no reference to the descensus.

The Apostles' Creed as far back as 390 contains the expression, "descended into hell." In the Greek the word hell is *hades;* in the Latin *ad inferos* or *ad inferna.*

The Athanasian Creed, traceable in its Latin form to 500, follows the language of the Apostles' Creed and uses the word *ad inferos.*

The Augsburg Confession uses the same terms in the Latin edition, and *Hölle* in the German.

The Heidleberg Catechism adopts the language of the Apostles' Creed, using in the German the word *Hölle.*

The Thirty-nine Articles of the Church of England say that it is "to be believed that he went down into hell," *ad inferos.*

Of modern liturgies the Roman Catholic, Lutheran, Episcopal, Presbyterian, and Reformed retain the article, using the word "hell," except the Reformed which uses *hades.* The Congregational churches generally omit the article. In the margin of the American Book of Common Prayer, permission is given to substitute for the word "hell" the phrase "the place of departed spirits." For a period this phrase was used in the liturgy of the General Synod of the Lutheran Church.

2) INTERPRETATIONS.

(1) The Greek Catholic Church, though not confessing the Athanasian and Apostles' Creed, nevertheless accepts the doctrine of the descensus. Its theologians teach that the soul of Christ (not in His glorified body) descended into Hades in order to triumph over it and to deliver the Old Testament saints, who looked for a Messiah.

(2) The Roman Catholic Church received the three ecumenical creeds and hence confesses its belief in the descensus. Its theologians teach that Christ in His spirit descended in order to manifest His power and glory in the underworld and to deliver the souls of the just held captive there and to take them to heaven.

(3) The Reformed churches in general refer the descensus to Christ's state of humiliation and regard it as figurative, setting forth His suffering and death. Such an interpretation leaves the article without any rational context, and is, therefore, logically omitted by some of the churches.

(4) The Lutheran Church, following the ancient belief based upon certain Scripture passages, accepts the explanation suggested by a sermon of Luther's given in the Formula of Concord. "We simply believe that the entire person, God and man, after the burial descended into hell, conquered the devil, destroyed the power of hell, and took from the devil all his might. We should not, however, trouble ourselves with the sublime and acute thoughts as to how this occurred. (Chap. IX.) The doctrine is to be accepted not because it is plain to the five senses but because it is revealed in Scriptures as a blessed consolation that neither hell nor the devil can take captive or injure us and all who believe in Christ."

a. The Rational Ground.

The age-long belief of the Church in the descensus must be grounded not only in Scriptures but also in reason. By this we mean that there is propriety in ascribing complete victory to our Lord, extending to every part of the universe. No lurking, unconquered foe can be tolerated. He must be brought into subjection whoever he may be and wherever he may reside. That old serpent, the devil, who brought sorrow and ruin to the first Adam, met his complete defeat when the God-man proclaimed His victory in the prison house.

b. The Scriptural Basis.

(a) The principal passage concerning the descent into hell is found in I Peter 3: 18-20: "Because Christ also suffered for sins once, the righteous for the unrighteous, that he might bring us to God; being put to death in the flesh, but made alive in the spirit, in which also he went and preached unto the spirits in prison, that aforetime were disobedient, when the long-suffering of God waited in the days of Noah, while the ark was preparing."

(b) An exegesis of the foregoing passage seems to yield the following result:

The *time* of the descensus was after Christ was "made alive in the spirit," that is, after His revivification in the tomb.

The *place* whither He went was the "prison," the abode of the devil and his angels (Rev. 20: 7) and of those who obey him.

The *persons visited* were the "disobedient," of whom a particular class is mentioned—those who rejected the preaching of Noah.

The *message* was not evangelical, for the word preached (*kerusso*) used in this connection is the general word for proclaiming any fact or truth. Moreover, the context indicates that the preaching was evidently a vindication of Noah and a condemnation of the disobedient.

(c) The descensus does not deny that Christ also went to paradise, as promised to the denying thief. We may well believe that no condition, place or state excluded our triumphant Lord.

c. The Meaning of Hades.

The meaning of the word *hades* in the creeds has a bearing on the descensus. The interpretation of it as "the place of departed spirits," including both the good and the evil, is not justified by New Testament usage.

The word occurs in ten passages and always has an unpleasant meaning. Capernaum was condemned to go down into Hades—destruction and oblivion (Mt. 11:23; Lk. 10:15). Christ declared that "the gates of Hades" should not prevail against the Church, that is, it would not be destroyed, buried or forgotten (Mt. 16:18). The rich man was in Hades, "being in torment" (Lk. 16:23). Christ was not "left unto Hades" or the grave (Acts 2:27, 31). Death and Hades are associated in Rev. 1:18; 6:8; 20:13. Finally death and Hades are cast into "the lake of fire" (Rev. 20:15).

The conclusion is inevitable that Hades does not embrace paradise, which certainly will not be consigned to hell or the lake of fire. Paradise and Hades are plainly antithetical. The former is a good place, the portal of heaven; the latter an evil place, the portal of hell or *gehenna*.

It seems plausible, therefore, that the word *hades* in the creed is equivalent to hell. In the English version the word hell should be retained because it conveys the idea which it was intended to convey, namely, that Christ visited the "prison" to vindicate the faith of true believers and to proclaim His victory over the opposition of devils and of his followers.

3.   The Resurrection

The next step in our Lord's triumph was His resurrection, which indicates His complete victory over death and the grave.

1)   THE FACT OF THE RESURRECTION.

The resurrection of Christ is an outstanding and undeniable fact. No event of ancient history is more surely fixed. The actions of the apostles and the survival of the early Church can be explained only on the basis of the resurrection. Upon it were founded their hopes and it was the theme of their preaching. The resurrection has great apologetic value. With it accepted as a fact, the miracle of Christ's birth and life is established.

2) THE RESURRECTION ITSELF.

By Christ's resurrection is meant that He brought forth from the sepulchre His body in a glorified form. His divine personality and His human soul did not die, but were separated from His body in death. In the resurrection His body was glorified.

3) THE SOURCE OF THE RESURRECTION.

In Eph. 1: 20 it is said that the Father raised Christ from the dead. Jesus declared, "I lay down my life that I may take it again" (John 10: 17). The Spirit also participates in the resurrection (Rom. 8: 11). It was, therefore, the act of the triune God.

4) THE RESURRECTION BODY.

The body of Christ was a real body, which was somehow related to the body which died on the Cross. It retained in a miraculous manner, for the sake of identification, the print of the nails and the mark of the spear. The resurrection body is described as a body of glory and also as spiritual body. There is a natural, "psychical" or soul-body, and a "spiritual" or "pneumatic" body. The former is suited to the present life, the latter to the future life. But they are both material, the one of grosser and the other of more refined nature.

5) THE LESSON OF CHRIST'S RESURRECTION.

Christ's resurrection indicates His victory over the devil, death and the grave. It is the assurance of His deity, and the promise of our resurrection and immortality.

4. The Ascension

1) THE FACT.

Forty days after His resurrection, Christ led His disciples out toward Bethany and "as they were looking he was taken up; and a cloud received him out of their sight" (Acts 1:9). "And was carried up into heaven" (Lk. 24:51). It would be difficult to make the account more simple and explicit. The ascension was Christ's departure into the invisible. The action belongs to the realm of miracle.

2) THE PURPOSE.

The withdrawal of Christ's visible presence was a part of His triumph. "When he ascended on high, he led captivity captive, and gave gifts unto men" (Eph. 4:8). His purpose in departing was to present his sacrifice in heaven and "to appear before the face of God for us" (Heb. 9: 12, 24). His departure was expedient because the Comforter could not come until Jesus returned to heaven to send him to apply the work done by Jesus (Jno. 16:7). Moreover, He consoles His disciples by telling them that He went away to prepare a place for them (Jno. 14:2). Let us not conclude, however, that our Lord has personally withdrawn from His people on earth, for He declared before His departure, "Lo, I am with you always, even unto the end of the world" (Mt. 28:20). Nor should we imagine that His visible absence destroys His reality to Christian experience. It is as true with the Christian now as it was when Peter wrote, "Whom not having seen, ye love; on whom though now ye see him not, yet believing ye rejoice greatly with joy unspeakable and full of glory" (I Peter 1:8).

5. The Session at God's Right Hand

"He ascended into heaven, that He might be on the right hand of the Father and forever reign, and have dominion over all creatures, and sanctify them that believe in Him, by sending the Holy Ghost into their hearts, to rule, comfort and quicken them, and to defend them against the power of sin" (Art. III. Augsburg Confession).

"The right hand of God" means the position of highest authority and influence. The writer to the Hebrews says of Jesus that for the joy that was before Him He "endured the cross, despising the shame, and hath sat down at the right hand of the throne of God" (Heb. 12:2; 8:13). The God-man has been exalted to the place of universal dominion. He has received the name which is above every name.

D. THE WORK OF CHRIST

The consideration of the gift, the person, and the states of Christ has prepared the way for the discussion of His work as the saviour of men. His person and His work, however, must not be separated, for that which gives value to what He has done and is doing is what He is. The acts of a divine being naturally transcend those of a mere man.

The work of Christ has generally been thought of as threefold, namely; that of prophet, of priest, and of king. This division is justified by the Scriptures, by reason, and by the functions performed.

1. Scripture

Moses proclaimed the coming of a prophet whom the people should hear (Dt. 18: 15). The psalmist calls the Messiah a priest after the order of Melchizedek (Ps. 110: 4) ; and the Epistle to the Hebrews shows how Jesus is our great high priest. Zechariah (6: 13; 9: 9) foresees His coming as a king, and the Gospels record the fulfillment of this prophecy.

2. Reason

The division is also in harmony with the Scripture and functions of the human mind. As a prophet and teacher Jesus addresses the intellect; as priest and sacrifice He appeals to the emotions; as king He claims the surrender of our wills to His will.

3. Functions

The threefold division is justified by the functions of the God-man in three striking aspects. It presents Him as the revealer, who knows past, present, and future, who reveals God and interprets man; as the priest who offers the infinite sacrifice and who awakens repentance, faith and love in the soul; as sovereign who conquers all our foes and is able to help to the uttermost.

These offices must not be mechanically separated, but should be regarded as the several aspects of the person and work of our blessed Lord, who teaches, loves and rules for the salvation of men. His teaching comes to us not simply through the word but also through the act. His Kingdom is realized through the reign of truth and love.

I. THE WORK OF CHRIST AS PROPHET.

Under the old dispensation, God revealed His will through prophets, who spoke as they were moved by the Holy Spirit. The chief content of the Old Testament message is the promise of a Messiah. For four hundred years before His coming there was no prophecy, but the expectation of it was earnestly cherished by the devout. As was fitting, just before the advent the voice of prophecy is again heard in the utterances of Zacharias, Elizabeth, the Virgin Mary, Simeon, Anna, and John the Baptist.

Finally when Christ appears it is a prophet to shed light on the past, to illuminate the future and especially to make God known to His generation and to all men. His role as prophet is unique in that He is not only a prophet, but also the subject of prophecy.

In the order of His office, prophecy stands first, because through it in its teaching aspects the appeal is made to the intellect in order to establish a rational ground for the acceptance of Christ as the object of adoration and as the Sovereign and Lord of all. We shall consider the office first as that of foretelling, and secondly, as that of teaching.

1. The Prophet

1) HIS CLAIMS.

Jesus claimed to be a prophet not simply in a general way but in specific utterances. In His sermon at Nazareth, He applied to Himself the words of the prophet Isaiah, "The Spirit of the Lord is upon me." He also frequently predicted the destruction of Jerusalem and the end of the world. In foretelling His own death He classes Himself as a prophet when He says, "It cannot be that a prophet perish out of Jerusalem" (Lk. 13: 33). He clearly foresaw how He would be betrayed, delivered into the hands of the Gentiles, mocked and crucified, and the third day raised from the dead. He reveals what would befall His disciples, and how His kingdom would triumph.

2) His Recognition.

He was recognized as a prophet by His contemporaries, some of whom identified Him with the Old Testament prophets. At Nain the multitude, who witnessed the raising of the young man, exclaimed, "A great prophet is risen among us; and God hath visited His people." At the triumphal entry He was acclaimed as "The prophet Jesus, from Nazareth of Galilee (Mt. 21: 11).

3) His Qualities.

Jesus possessed the marks of a prophet in a superlative degree. (1) He was holy, without the taint of sin. (2) He was conscious of the divine call, for He said, "As the Father taught me, I speak these things" (Jno. 8: 28). His Father testified out of the opened heavens, "This is my beloved Son, hear ye him." (3) His messages were not only of the highest ethical import but also of the most profound spiritual significance. (4) He had the comprehensive vision of a prophet embracing not only the destiny of the Jews but of the Gentiles also. It was world-wide and eternal.

2. The Teacher

The prophet of the Old Testament was both a foreteller and a forth-teller, or preacher or teacher. He reminded and admonished the Jews in reference to blessings and duties. In the exercise of His prophetic office our Lord was rather a teacher than a foreteller. He was called rabbi or teacher and His followers were disciples or learners. His teachings have become the doctrines of Christianity and He is recognized as the world's foremost teacher.

1) His Qualifications.

Our Lord possessed in a pre-eminent degree the qualities which characterize the real teacher. The qualities may be defined as personality, skill and knowledge.

(1) By personality in this connection is meant the possession of a clear, strong mind, moral earnestness, and the consciousness of being right. To these may be joined a pleasing manner and a prepossessing appearance. Our

Lord was apparently gifted with the power which draws men and stimulates thought and action.

(2) Skill indicates aptness to teach. Jesus knew how to make truth plain and interesting. The common people heard Him gladly because they understood what He said. He could gain and hold the attention of His hearers.

(3) Knowledge means acquaintance with the subject taught. Jesus was a master of knowledge. He knew God and so could reveal Him as He was; and He knew men and needed not that anyone should tell Him. He knew how to help man in his infirmity, for He is the way, the truth and the life.

2) His Relation to the Disciples.

We can here only indicate some of the points of contact which Jesus had with those especially who for three years sat at His feet. (1) He was approachable, (2) appreciative of their real worth, (3) sympathetic with them in their shortcomings, (4) patient with their slowness to learn, (5) hopeful of their growth, (6) sacrificial in laboring, suffering and dying for them.

3) His Manner of Teaching.

Christ's teaching was characterized by (1) sympathy, (2) tact, (3) freshness, (4) adaptation, (5) authority, (6) finality.

4) His Originality.

It has been said by unfriendly critics that much of Christ's teaching can be gleaned from the writings of the Jewish prophets and of the Gentile sages. With the latter He certainly could have had no acquaintance; and He gladly gave the more striking sayings of the former a new and richer setting. Before His advent the light of truth came to men in broken rays through clouds of ignorance; but He brought life and immortality to light. As the light of the world He flooded the sky with radiance. No other teacher is comparable with Him in the understanding and interpretation of life.

5) THE SCOPE OF HIS TEACHING.

The entire realm of religion and morals is comprehended in the teaching of Jesus. Nothing is wanting in the way of instruction in spiritual and ethical principles. His teachings reveal the creator as Father, and man as the child of God.

(1) The Revelation of God.

Jesus came into the world to make God known to men, to clarify and to enlarge their conception of Him, and to reveal Him as love. The Jew too often thought of God as peculiarly his own, and of himself as the favorite of God. Jesus proclaims the Fatherhood of God, before whom there is neither Jew nor Gentile.

(2) The Revelation of Man.

Man often over-estimates himself and often under-estimates himself. The few are apt to lord it over the many. Our Lord knew the value of a soul as greater than a material world. He understood and taught the worth of the individual. The least man is no mere chattel, or puppet, or infinitesimal atom in the mass of mankind. He is a child of God whom Jesus came to seek and to save. Jesus also teaches that mankind is a brotherhood, a social body composed of immortal units, each of whom owes something to his fellows. To the strong He commends the weak, and commissions them to bear the gospel of light and love to all who sit in darkness.

(3) The Interpretation of Life.

Jesus gives mankind a new view of life as something desirable and worth while when rightly lived. It is not mere existence, burdened with trial and terminating in the grave. It is an opportunity and an education. Its inevitable crosses may be blessed and glorious. In no case need it be a failure. Men are shown how to live and for what to live.

(4) The Way of Salvation.

Jesus came above all for the purpose of saving men. "And in none other is there salvation; for neither is there any other name under heaven that is given among men, wherein we must be saved" (Acts 4 : 12). He teaches us the destructive power of sin, the need of a new heart, the necessity of reconciliation with God through an atonement by the blood of the cross. He reveals Himself as the hope of the sinner, who through faith is united to Him and becomes the heir of heaven.

6) THE PERPETUATION OF CHRIST'S TEACHING.

The teaching of Christ as the eternal Logos, in its early stages came through patriarch and prophet, in divers manners, by symbol and ceremony, by type and shadow. When the fulness of time was come He appears on earth to fulfill the ancient promises, and in a new and living way to proclaim salvation. At His departure He promised His disciples the presence and guidance of the Holy Spirit, who should lead them into all truth, and who did inspire them to make a record of His life and teaching. And finally "the ministry of reconciliation" was committed to the Apostolic Church and thus to the Church of all the ages.

II.   THE WORK OF CHRIST AS PRIEST.

In His office as priest our Lord reaches the climax of His redemptive work. In it is involved the exhibition of the most stupendous love and sacrifice of which we can have any conception. The office may be regarded from the standpoint of fact and of purpose.

1.   The Fact of Christ's Priesthood

1) ITS REALITY.

Since Jesus was not a descendant of the priestly tribe of Levi and hence never ministered at a Jewish altar, it might be inferred that He was not a priest at all, except in a figurative sense. The fact, however, as we shall see, is the very reverse, for He is the only true priest and the Jewish priests merely prefigured Him in their temporary and imperfect ministry. Their offerings were only types, "having a shadow of the good things to come" (Heb. 10: 1). Their office really ceased when Jesus became the offering on the Cross.

2) A COMPARISON.

The Jewish priesthood, however, furnishes us with a most interesting ground upon which may be construed the doctrine of the priesthood of Jesus, which was both similar and superior to it, as may be seen by comparison and contrast. (See Hebrews.)

(1) The Similarity.

a. Appointment. Not assumed. "No man taketh the honor unto himself." Heb. 5, 4.

b. Call. Called of God, "even as was Aaron. So Christ glorified not himself."

c. Qualifications. a) Human. "Taken from among men." b) Sympathetic. "Touched with a feeling of our infirmities." c) Perfect. "Without blemish."

d. Induction. a) By washing. Lev. 8: 6. Baptism. b) By anointing. Lev. 8: 12. Anointed by the Holy Spirit.

e. Function. a) Sacrifice. b) Intercession.

f. Purpose. Reconciliation.

(2) The Superiority.

a. In personal character. Christ was sinless. He made no offering for Himself.

b. In office. a) Independent. Like Melchizedek, without predecessor or successor. b) Alone. Over against the many Jewish priests. c) Perpetual. "A priest forever."

c. In offering. a) Himself. b) Once for all.

d. In the place of ministry. "Heaven."

e. In the effect. "Eternal Redemption."

2. The Purpose of Christ's Priesthood

RECONCILIATION.

Jesus Christ came into the world to reconcile God and men. He came to be a mediator between God and men. He came to put away sin by the sacrifice of Himself and to restore the moral order which was broken by man's transgression.

1) THE MEANING OF RECONCILIATION.

In the comprehensive word reconciliation (*katallage*) may be summed up the Lord's work for our salvation—His incarnation, life, death, resurrection, ascension and intercession. His work for man is a unit. His life was redemptive, as well as His death. Nevertheless, it is true, as Paul says, that in Christ "it was the good pleasure of the Father that in him should all the fullness dwell, and through him to reconcile all things unto himself, having made peace through the blood of his cross" (Col. 1: 19, 20). Reconciliation, therefore, is generally thought of as finding its fullest expression in the supreme sacrifice made on Calvary.

The Greek word *katallage* is well translated and defined by the English word reconciliation, which means "to restore to friendship" or "to harmonize." In theology it refers to the restoration of "peace with God through our Lord Jesus Christ."

2) THE NEED OF RECONCILIATION.

(1) The Manward Side.

That man is a sinner against God needs little more than affirmation. He is without God and without hope. He is an alien and an enemy. Until restored by grace, he does not love God. If he fears Him at all, it is with the apprehension of His just wrath and merited punishment. Such is the representation of Scripture and the fact as realized in history and experience. He is conscious of the need of reconciliation with God. "My soul thirsteth for God, for the living God," cries the psalmist. In his estrangement man does not know that God loves him and he needs, therefore, to be assured of this, and even to be entreated to become reconciled to God.

(2) The Divine Side.

Granted that man needs to be reconciled to God, on the other hand does God need to be reconciled to man? Does the work of Christ in bringing man to God involve also some satisfaction rendered to God? No question of the soul is more vital than this. Upon its answer depends the assurance of his hope for forgiveness. Around this question revolves endless discussion and theorizing. In the discussion of this problem we assume as postulates the deity of Jesus Christ, the authenticity of the Gospels and the inspiration of the Epistles. We accept the testimony of the apostles as interpretive of the work and teaching of Christ.

(a) The Teaching of the Church.

It has always been the teaching of the Protestant Church that God needs to be reconciled. This is evident from the following creedal statements.

The Augsburg Confession (1530) declares that "the Son of God did take man's nature—truly suffered, was crucified dead and buried that he might reconcile the Father unto us" (Art. III). The Belgic Confession (1561) confessed Christ as the everlasting High Priest, "who hath presented Himself in our behalf before His Father, to appease His wrath by His full satisfaction."

The Scotch Confession of 1560 says Christ "suffered not onlie the cruell death of the Crosse, quhilk was accursed to be the sentence of God; but also that he suffered for a season the wrath of his Father, quhilk sinners had deserved."

The Thirty-nine Articles of the Church of England (1563) use practically the language of the Augsburg Confession.

The Westminster Confession (1647) declares that the Lord Jesus "Fully satisfied the justice of His Father, and purchased not only reconciliation, but an everlasting inheritance in the kingdom of Heaven, for all those whom the Father hath given to Him."

(b) The Nature of God.

God is a person. Whatever belongs to a normal personality must be ascribed to Him. Holiness and love are His pre-eminent attributes. Wrath, anger and indignation are terms which express the reaction of the holiness and love of God against sin. A being incapable of indignation is incapable of love. A father who fails to correct a disobedient child on the plea of pity and love destroys his own authority and spoils the child. Surely no one will for a moment imagine that God is a weakling, that He can regard sin with indifference or allow it to go unpunished! God is our heavenly Father and also our ruler and law-giver. His laws are not the arbitrary decrees of a tyrant, but the very expression of His character. A wilful disregard of them, therefore, is an insult to a perfect being, and cannot be passed by, but must inevitably meet with disapproval.

(c) The Teaching of Scripture.

Numerous passages may be quoted from the Old Testament showing that God is angry with the sinner and that His wrath abideth on the children of disobedience. He appears as righteously indignant with transgressors. In the New Testament He is spoken of as a "consuming fire," and it is declared to be "a fearful thing to fall into the hands of the living God" (Heb. 10:31). "The wrath of God is revealed from heaven against all ungodliness and unrighteousness of men" (Rom. 1:18). "The day of wrath and revelation of the righteous judgment of God" is sure to come (Romans 2:5).

Those who would deny the reality of the wrath of God will have to explain away the words and deeds of our Lord. He repelled Satan with anger in the great temptation in the wilderness. He "looked round about on them with anger" in the synagogue when He healed the man with the withered hand. He was "moved with indignation" when the disciples tried to prevent the bringing of little children to Him. He cleansed the temple in indignation against those who profaned the house of God. He vehemently denounced the Sadducees for denying the resurrection and the future life. He broke forth in terrible resentment against the Pharisees for their hypocrisy and cruelty; and pronounced the most frightful judgments upon the cities of Palestine. He declares that the wicked will at last be sentenced to depart into hell prepared for the devil and his angels.

(d) The Meaning of the Word Reconcile.

It is important to know the exact meaning of the word *katallasso* in order to determine whether reconciliation in its beginning refers to something that has been effected in

God or in man. In the New Testament as well as in classic usage, the word in the passive voice always signifies that "One ceases to be angry with another and receives him into favor." This is apparent in the passage (Mt. 5: 24) which commands a man about to make an offering who remembers that his brother has aught against him, to go and "first be reconciled" to his brother. He is to go to his brother and conciliate him. To reconcile, therefore, means to render favorable.

There are three distinct passages which bear directly on the subject, namely, Romans 5: 10, 11; 11: 5, and II Cor. 5: 18, 19. Paul declares, "For if while we were enemies we were reconciled to God by the death of his Son, much more being reconciled shall we be saved by his life; and not only so, but we also rejoice in God through our Lord Jesus Christ; through whom we have now received the reconciliation" (Rom. 5: 10, 11). In commenting on this passage in The Expositors' Greek Testament, Dr. James Denny says, "We were in a real sense objects of the divine hostility. As sinners we lay under the condemnation of God, and His wrath hung over us. This was the situation which had to be faced: Was there love in God equal to it? Yes, when we were enemies we were reconciled to God by the death of His Son. *Katallagamen* is a real passive. 'We' are the objects, not the subjects, of the reconciliation; the subject is God. To represent *katallagamen* by an active form, *e.g.*, 'we laid aside our hostility to God,' or 'we were wont to lay aside our hostility' is to miss the point of the whole passage. Paul is demonstrating the love of God, and he can only do it by pointing to what God has done and not to what we have done. That we on our part are hostile to God before the reconciliation, and that afterward we lay aside our enmity is no doubt true, but here it is entirely irrelevant. . . . The subjective side is here complete and intentionally left out of sight. The laying aside of our hostility adds nothing to God's love, throws no light upon it; hence in an exposition of the love of God it can be ignored. To say that the reconciliation is mutual is true in point of fact, also to all the suggestions of the English word, but it is not true to the meaning of *katallagamen*, nor to the argument of this passage, which does not prove anything about the Christian, but exhibits the love of God at its height on the Cross, and argues from that the comparatively smaller demonstration of that love."

With this exposition agree practically all the great commentators; and it is the only one that the text allows. We may remark in addition that the eleventh verse makes it perfectly plain that "the reconciliation" is something outside of ourselves and offered to us for our acceptance. "Through whom (Christ) we have now received (*elabomen*, appropriated) the reconciliation." This objective work and offer comes to us through Christ, and as Christians we have accepted it.

In Romans 11: 15, Paul says, "For if the casting away of them is the reconciling of the world, what shall the receiving of them be, but life from the dead?" The evident meaning of this passage is that the rejection of the Jews on account of unbelief admitted the Gentiles to a participation in the reconciliation. The gospel came to the Jews first, then to the Gentiles, whose acceptance of the gospel would be a veritable spiritual resurrection.

In II Cor. 5: 19, Paul says, "that God was in Christ reconciling the world unto himself, not reckoning unto them their trespasses, and having committed unto us the word of reconciliation." This can only mean exactly that which Paul declared to the Romans. Through Christ the offense of the world was removed, and their trespasses were not reckoned against them. God occupied a new attitude, in consequence of which the Gospel—the word of reconciliation, the good news of God's reconciliation, His favorable attitude—was committed to the apostles to be proclaimed.

And now the ambassadors (II Cor. 5: 20) come with the word of reconciliation, already complete in Christ, and offer it to sinners, beseeching them in turn to be reconciled to God. The divine, objective reconciliation is to be accepted on certain conditions by the Corinthians and all others, and thus they would be subjectively reconciled. They are asked to lay down their enmity and accept the offered pardon and thus experience a personal reconciliation.

The foregoing interpretation of the meaning of the word *katallassein*, to reconcile, is supported by the leading lexicographers and commentators. Thayer defines the word to mean "to receive into favor," "to be restored to the favor of God." Grimm gives the same definition. Cremer defines reconciliation as "the new moulding of the relation in which the world stands to God, so far as it now no longer remains the object of God's wrath." Meyer: "God through Christ causes that sin should cease to be an occasion of wrath against the sinner." Lipsius: "The change indicated by *katallage* is primarily and essentially accomplished in God." Liddon: "The reconciliation must be taken passively, not merely or chiefly actively. The reconciliation is accomplished not only in the hearts of men, but in the heart of God." Marvin Vincent: "We were made subjects of God's reconciling act" (Rom. 5: 10). H. E. Jacobs in *Lutheran Commentary*: "We were reconciled. Rendered pleasing to God."

3) THE MODE OF RECONCILIATION.

It appears from the foregoing that God Himself cannot condone sin without some kind of reparation, so that He may be just and yet the justifier of the believing. His yearning Father heart desires to forgive the offender. In what way this can be done without impairing the divine majesty the Christian Scriptures alone reveal.

(1) Through Atonement.

The usual representation is that the reconciliation both of God and man took place through an atonement made by Christ. The word atonement is indeed not found in the Revised Version, but the idea of it is prominent. The thought of Christ dying for us as a ransom for sin is fundamental. The Cross of Jesus and the Lamb slain for us stand out above all else. In the Old Testament the word atonement, *kaphar*, occurs about seventy times. The Hebrew word literally means "to cover," hence to pardon, to expiate, to appease.

(1) The Elements of the Atonement.

When the Old Testament priest made atonement for sin, especially on the great annual day of atonement, it was through a vicarious or substitutionary sacrifice. These two ideas, substitution and sacrifice, must be kept in mind.

3. The Atonement by Substitution

1) THE TESTIMONY OF THE OLD TESTAMENT.

Did our Lord take the sinner's place in any rational sense? Did He suffer in our stead? This seems to be implied in the very idea of sacrifice, but it seems also to be explicitly asserted. It will hardly be denied that Christ did not suffer for any sins of His own, for as Isaiah 53 declares, "Surely he hath borne our griefs and carried our sorrows; . . . . . he was wounded for our transgressions, he was bruised for our iniquities; the chastisement of our peace was upon him; and with his stripes we are healed; he bare the sin of many and made intercession for the transgressors."

2) THE TESTIMONY OF CHRIST.

It is alleged that the idea of substitution and sacrifice is not apparent from our Lord's own words. This is not true, as we shall show. Nevertheless, it is to be expected that the application and explanation of His death should be made by the apostles in their preaching and epistles rather than by Christ.

Jesus, however, when He urges upon His disciples a life of sacrifice and service, says, "The Son of man came not to be ministered unto but to minister, and to give His life a ransom for many" (Mt. 20:28). Now a ransom is a price paid for the release of a captive. Jesus in using words "a ransom for many," *lutron anti pollon*, clearly affirms that He gave Himself and His life instead of another. It is not needful to construe the language as that of commercial barter, but one cannot escape the idea that our Lord did something for the sinner which was equivalent to purchasing his release. This is confirmed by apostolic language. Paul says, "Ye were bought with a price" (I Cor. 6:20). Peter says, "Ye were redeemed not with corruptible things, with silver and gold, but with the blood of Christ" (I Pet. 1: 18, 19).

At the institution of the Lord's Supper Jesus speaks of the bread given and broken "for you" and "for many" and likewise He speaks of the cup as containing His blood shed for the remission of sins. He speaks of Himself as the good shepherd who lays down His life for the sheep (Jno. 10: 14). "I lay down my life," said he. "No man taketh it from me, but I will lay it down of myself" (Jno. 10: 17, 18).

In His conversation with Nicodemus He declares that the Son of Man must be lifted up that whosoever believeth in Him should not perish but have eternal life (Jno. 3: 14-16). All the above passages indicate the vicarious character of our Lord's death. He died instead of and in behalf of sinners.

3) THE TESTIMONY OF THE APOSTLES.

Paul says of Christ, "Him who knew no sin he made to be sin on our behalf, that we might become the righteousness of God in him" (II Cor. 5: 21). In Galatians 3: 13 it is written, "Christ redeemed us from the curse of the law, having become a curse for us." These passages can mean only that Christ took the sinner's place and endured the curse in his stead. Some have supposed that such passages are a relic of Paul's so-called legalism. As a fact Paul became emancipated from the law when he obtained pardon in Christ. He affirms boldly that men are justified by faith without the deeds of the law, because Christ became the end of the law for righteousness to everyone that believeth. He warns the Galatians against the folly of returning to the bondage of the law.

The vicariousness of Christ's work is affirmed when Paul says, "When we were yet without strength Christ died for the ungodly" (Rom. 5: 6). "He spared not His own Son, but delivered him up for us all" (Rom. 8: 32). "The Son of God who loved me and gave himself for me" (Gal. 2: 20). "Christ loved the Church and gave himself for it" (Eph. 5: 2, 25). "God hath not appointed us to wrath but to obtain salvation by our Lord Jesus Christ, who died for us" (I Thess. 5: 9, 10).

With the declarations of Paul concerning the death of Christ for us agree these of the other New Testament writers. Peter says, "Christ also suffered for sins once, the righteous for the unrighteous" (I Pet. 3: 18). "Who his own self bare our sins in his body on the tree" (I Pet. 2: 24). "Ye were redeemed not with corruptible things, with silver and gold, but with the precious blood as of a lamb without blemish and without spot, even the blood of Christ" (I Pet. 1: 18, 19).

"God commendeth his love toward us," says Paul, "in that while we were yet sinners Christ died for us" (Rom. 5: 8). "He laid down his life for us" (I Jno. 3: 16). "He is the propitiation for our sins, and not for ours only, but also for the whole world" (I Jno. 2: 2, 4; 9, 10).

The Epistle to the Hebrews makes frequent mention of the doctrine of vicariousness. Jesus "tastes of death for every man," "makes propitiation for the sins of His people" (Heb. 2: 9, 17). He was "once offered to bear the sins of many" (Heb. 9: 28).

4) OBJECTIONS TO SUBSTITUTION.

It is objected by some that the doctrine of substitution is absurd and immoral, that the substitution is impossible or if not impossible then unjust. The fallacy of such an objection is apparent; for vicarious suffering is the law of life. In the family the parents bear the burdens of the children. In the state, the patriot dies on the field of battle that others may live. In society the noble and far-seeing endure for the public good. The injustice of substitution can be urged only when it is compulsory, which in the case of Christ is not a fact. He freely gave His life. He had power to lay it down and power to take it up. His matchless love prompted Him to die for sinners.

4. The Atonement by Sacrifice

Christ is our substitute and as such makes the sacrifice; He is the vicarious sacrifice for sin.

1) THE UNIVERSALITY OF SACRIFICE.

The practice or the idea of sacrifice is universal because of a universal sense of the need of a medium through which to approach God. It originated like prayer from an inner necessity. The underlying motive is usually the propitiation of an offended deity. Crude and terrible has been the expression of fear or gratitude among pagans who have offered human sacrifices. But this perversion by no means destroys the validity of sacrifice in general.

2) THE OLD TESTAMENT SYSTEM.

The prominence of altars and offerings in Jewish worship is significant. It must not be regarded as a mere survival of some heathenish primitive cult, but as approved by God. Unless this be granted there can be no special divine purpose concerning Israel; and there remains but a faint trace of supernatural guidance in its history. But how would the elimination of Old Testament sacrifices as divinely ordained affect the New Testament, which represents Christ as the great high priest offering Himself? It would leave Christianity in a dilemma and make it merely an ethical and not a religious system.

The Old Testament sacrifices were never meant to be final, but symbolical and preparatory. Nor was their objective observance intended to take the place of heart worship. They had a real place, however, in temporarily satisfying a need in that they contained the promise of something better.

3) THE NEW TESTAMENT FULFILMENT.

It has been claimed that our Lord never directly sanctioned the sacrificial practices of the Jews and that He passed them by in silence. In reply to this claim, if a refutation be needed, Dale has pertinently asked, "If these ideas were false, how was it that our Lord did not protest against them? If the Jewish people had misinterpreted their national institutions, if God never intended to train them to the recognition of a direct relation between the offering of sacrifices and the remission of sin, how can His silence be explained? . . . His silence! It is no ordinary silence which has to be accounted for. At the very commencement of His ministry He received without a protest the testimony of John the Baptist—'Behold the Lamb of God that taketh away the sin of the world.' His silence was a definite acceptance of the testimony; it was an acknowledgment that he had come to fulfill the idea of the sin-offering of the Jewish law, and to secure for men the remission of their sins" (The Atonement, pp. 87-88).

"The Old Testament sacrifices expressed a need which Christ satisfies, and embodies a faith which Christ justifies. The need to which they gave utterance was that felt by the human heart for some ground of religious confidence external to itself; and this which the animal sacrifice only seemed to supply is fully met in Christian conviction that sin is forgiven in some real deep sense for Christ's sake."

4) THE FACT OF CHRIST'S SACRIFICE.

The interpretation of Christ's death as a sacrifice for the remission of sin is embedded in every part of the New Testament teaching.

He is the Lamb of God which taketh away the sin of the world. He is "the propitiation through faith in his blood" (Rom. 3: 25). "He made peace through the blood of the Cross" (Col. 1: 20). "He gave himself for us an offering and a sacrifice to God" (Eph. 5: 2). "Who is he that condemneth; it is Christ that died" (Rom. 8: 34). "He tasted death for every man" (Heb. 2: 9). "The blood of Christ, who through the eternal Spirit offered himself, purges the conscience of dead works" (Heb. 9: 14). "He gave himself for us that he might redeem us from all iniquities" (Tit. 2: 14). These several passages and those quoted before leave no doubt that the Scriptures teach that Christ died for us to redeem us from destruction. He has done something which God accepts and which accrues to our benefit.

5) THE VALUE OF CHRIST'S SACRIFICE TO GOD.

The righteousness of God demanded obedience. "If God does not assert the principle that sin deserves punishment by punishing it, He must assert that principle in some other way. Some divine act is required which shall have all the moral worth and significance of the act by which the penalties of sin would have been inflicted on the sinner." Dale.

The sufferings of Christ both physical and mental were terribly real. He agonized in the Garden and on the Cross. His Father's face was hidden from Him. He felt forsaken of God. It was certainly not because of any personal sin that He suffered; it must have been for the sin of others. Had there not been some necessity in the divine plan for this suffering it could have been averted, for Jesus would have remained away from Jerusalem and evaded the malignity of His enemies. He undoubtedly became a willing victim.

The death of Christ can be adequately explained only in the language of Scripture. It was a ransom, a propitiation, an atonement, provided by God Himself. "For what the law could not do, in that it was weak through the flesh, God sending his own Son in the likeness of sinful flesh and for sin condemned sin in the flesh" (Rom. 8: 3).

The law gave a knowledge of sin, showing man his wickedness and his helplessness. It became also the schoolmaster to lead him to Christ.

God sent His Son into the flesh. He became incarnate. He was a man, identified with the race. He was the new sinless leader and head of humanity, the second Adam. He is man's representative before God, takes man's punishment and thus atones for man's sin.

Man's failure to become righteous through the law which he could not keep left him exposed to death. "But now apart from the law a righteousness of God hath been manifested being witnessed by the law and the prophets, even the righteousness of God through faith in Jesus Christ unto all them that believe; for there is no distinction, for all have sinned and fallen short of the glory of God, being justified fully by His grace through the redemption that is in Christ Jesus, whom God set forth to be a propitiation through faith in his blood, to show his righteousness because of the passing over of the sins done aforetime in the forebearance of God, for the showing of his righteousness at this present season, that he might be just and the justifier of him that hath faith in Jesus" (Rom. 3: 21-28).

In the foregoing passage Paul clearly and powerfully sets forth that Jesus supplied the means of justification for the sinner's pardon, a righteousness of God apart from the law having been manifest in Him. On the Cross He offered up His life to restore to divine favor all who by faith appropriate that offering. In the death of Christ is seen God's judgment against sin and the vindication of God's holiness. And now satisfaction having been made by the blood of the Son of God, a sinless being, God can be just, His righteousness having been vindicated, and at the same time accept as righteous all that believe in Jesus. Believing in Jesus means accepting Him, becoming one with Him, entering into a holy partnership with Him.

6) OBJECTIONS TO THE PAULINE DOCTRINE.

It is alleged that the foregoing interpretation of the doctrine of the atonement makes God propitiate Himself, which it is said is absurd. This objection ignores the most sublime act of God in giving His Son in the incarnation through which He became so identified with men that He became the God-man, and as such died for humanity. By His infinite love God maintained His infinite honor. We need not understand how God could do this, for "without controversy great is the mystery of godliness."

The atonement "is only the supreme example of a universal spiritual law. Thus *e.g.*, God both requires and gives repentance or power to repent, for of course He does not repent for us. And so with every grace as the word implies. The grace is in us but is of God. God worketh within us both to will and to do His good pleasure. He neither wills nor acts for us, but enables us so to will and to act in the time of His own good pleasure. So in the work of reconciliation: God made it possible to humanity by the gift of Christ, but Christ as the head and representative of the race actually accomplished it. The principle underlying it is identified with the principles which underlie our whole religious life, and finds instinctive expression in the language of prayer, wherein we virtually ask God to fulfil His own law in us, to fulfil in us all the good pleasure of

His goodness and the work of faith with power.   If this is a paradox, it is a paradox inherent in our very existence as finite creatures who have yet a certain moral independence over against God; and on its religious side it has never been better expressed than in Augustine's words: *Da quod jubes, et jube quod vis"* (A. Adamson.   Art. on Reconciliation, Hastings D.B.).

5.   Theories of the Atonement

The formulation of Biblical teaching took place not in the apostolic age, but later as the need of scientific statement became apparent, usually because of perversion of the simple belief of Christians.   The first complete formulation of the doctrine of reconciliation or atonement was made in the eleventh century by Anselm, the Archbishop of Canterbury, in a little treatise called *Cur Deus Homo*.   Anselm's theory has met with wide acceptance, and of all ancient theories it comes nearest to the "orthodox" view.

1) THE SATISFACTION THEORY OF ANSELM.

(1) Every creature owes obedience to God as a debt of honor to His sovereign.

(2) Sin is a withholding of this debt.

(3) Justice demands payment of this debt by rendering some kind of satisfaction.

(4) Punishment would be satisfaction, but also destruction.   Hence if punishment be remitted some other satisfaction must be made.

(5) Man is powerless to render any satisfaction, except death.

(6) But man must make this satisfaction, and yet is not able.   Hence there must be a God-man.

(7) This God-man renders satisfaction by His life of perfect obedience which He owed; but He also gave in addition His life which He did not owe.

(8) His life surpassed in worth all the world, and

is more valuable than sin is heinous. It is therefore more than equivalent for sin.

(9) The gift of Christ's life merits a reward which He personally does not need, and hence He allows it to accrue to the benefit of those for whom He died.

2) THE MORAL INFLUENCE THEORY OF ABELARD.

Abelard (1097-1142) disputes the theory of Anselm. He taught that:

(1) God sent His Son into the world as a revelation of His love.

(2) Christ assumed our nature and became our teacher and example, remaining faithful to His mission unto death.

(3) The love of God awakens our love toward Him.

(4) Our faith in God's love manifested in Christ unites us to Christ in a social bond of love.

(5) Our responsive love becomes the ground of God's forgiveness.

Abelard attaches no redeeming merit to the death of Christ. This theory is the root of many of the popular and "liberal" theories of modern times, held by Sabatier, Bushnell, W. N. Clark, G. B. Stevens, McLeod, Campbell, Haering and others.

3) THE ACCEPTILATION THEORY OF DUNS SCOTUS.

Duns Scotus (1265-1308) denied the need of any satisfaction. Sin is not as heinous as some have taught and Christ's merit is not infinite. The so-called atonement is altogether an arrangement of God's will. God determined that He would ordain a certain plan and accept its execution as sufficient, regardless of the demerit of sin and the merit of Christ.

4) THE GOVERNMENTAL THEORY OF GROTIUS.

Grotius (1583-1645), a distinguished Dutch theologian and jurist, regarded the relation of God to man as that of ruler to subject. His theory is that a ruler has the right to remit a penalty, provided the end for which the penalty is ordained is otherwise attained. The end of punishment is the preservation of order and the prevention of future transgressions. The death of Christ effected this in becoming "a penal example." It shows the nature and desert of sin, but the death of Christ is not punishment but a symbol of it. Pardon is dependent upon what God may deem proper.

This is the theory of the Arminians and of the Methodist Episcopal Church, advocated by Dr. Miley.

5) THE MYSTICAL THEORY.

This theory makes the atonement consist in the identification of Christ with humanity which took place especially in incarnation. We share the blessings of His divine life and are delivered from sin through a living mystical union with Him.

6) A COMPARISON OF THESE VIEWS.

(1) In the acceptilation theory there seems to be no truth at all. Its low view of sin, its underestimate of the merit of Christ, and its perverted idea of the righteousness of God, all of which are unscriptural, leave it without any reliable foundation.

(2) In the moral influence, the governmental, and the mystical theories there is some truth. The first represents the manward side of the atonement, the reconciliation of man; but it totally neglects the Godward side. Hence it really denies all atonement. The governmental theory sets forth the truth of the righteousness and the mercy of God, but it fails much as the former theory does. The third has elements of truth, but really is not a theory of atonement at all.

(3) The satisfaction theory of Anselm seems to us the most Scriptural and reasonable of all; yet in its original form it contains some objectional features. (a) Its terms are too commercial. (b) The connection between the active life and the suffering of Christ is not made clear. (c)

The transfer of the merits of Christ is not intelligibly set forth.

The Anselmic theory has undergone various modifications from the time of the Reformation until now, but its central substitutionary idea is still held in orthodox theology, as set forth in these lectures.

6. The Extent of the Atonement

The universality of the gift of Christ has already been affirmed. The same argument applies to the benefits of the atonement. They are intended for all men, on the simple condition of receiving them in repentance and faith. Moreover, it is plain from the Scriptures that all men who have ever lived or shall live are included.

1) SCRIPTURAL PROOF OF ITS UNIVERSALITY.

The Bible declares that:

(1) Provision has been made for all. Christ is said to take away the sin of the world (Jno. 1: 29). He Himself declares that God so loved the world, etc. (Jno. 3: 16). Paul teaches that the free gift came unto all men (Rom. 5: 18) ; that Christ was delivered up for us all (II Cor. 5: 14-15) ; that He is the Saviour of all men, especially of those that believe (I Tim. 4: 10; 2: 4). John rejoices in a propitiation that was made not for himself alone but for the whole world (I Jno. 2: 2).

(2) Salvation is to be offered to all. The ends of the earth and those that thirst for God are invited (Isa. 45: 22; 55: 1-3). Christ invites all those who labor and are heavy laden (Matt. 11: 28) ; and commands His apostles to go into all the world and preach His gospel to every creature (Matt. 28: 19). He stands at the door of the heart and says if any man will open, etc. (Rev. 3: 20).

(3) The rejection of salvation involves guilt. Christ weeps over Jerusalem and condemns Capernaum for rejecting Him. He affirms the condemnation of men who love darkness rather than light (Jno. 3: 19). We are asked, "How shall we escape if we neglect so great salvation?" (Heb. 2: 3; 10: 28, 29).

(4) God is no respecter of persons. Peter so declares to Cornelius (Acts 10: 34), and Paul also affirms the same thing (Rom. 2: 11). Moreover, this is in accordance with God's nature and is illustrated by His dealings with men. A limited atonement would seem to reflect upon His infinite love, and to contradict our inherent idea of benevolence.

2) OBJECTIONS TO THE UNIVERSALITY OF THE ATONEMENT.

There are those who hold that the merits of Christ are sufficient for all, yet that, nevertheless, they were not intended for all. This is expressed thus: "Christ died sufficiently but not efficiently for all" (Lombard). This statement seems to be contradicted by the passages quoted above. Moreover, the efficiency of the atonement is not disproved even in the case of those who are not saved. The inherent virtue of a remedy is not destroyed by those who refuse to take it.

(1) Argument from the Design of God.

It is alleged that "the design of Christ in dying was not to effect what he actually does effect in the results" (Hodge's Outlines, 417). It has also been held that a general atonement represents God as making provisions beyond the limits of necessity, knowing that the non-elect would not be saved. In regard to the design of God it may be said that His design never included the ultimate salvation of those who wilfully rejected Christ.

His design plainly comprehended certain conditions. It would be denying the veracity of God to impugn His universal call to repentance. In reference to the provision made beyond actual necessity, it may be said that the salvation of even a single sinner demanded the whole work of Christ as much as the salvation of all men.

(2) Argument from the Absoluteness of God.

It is alleged that to make the effect of atonement conditional upon the act of man is to limit the will of God by something outside of Himself. We reply that in the plan of redemption the divine will ordained that salvation should be offered to men to be received or rejected.   Hence there is no subversion of His will, even when men reject salvation.

7.   The Intercession of Christ

1) THE FACT.

The first function of the priest as before stated is sacrifice and the second intercession.   This function is clearly affirmed in the Bible.   Isaiah declares of Him who was wounded for our transgressions that He "maketh intercession for the transgressors."   This our Lord did in His high-priestly prayer (Jno. 17) and upon the Cross.   This function is still discharged by Him in heaven, whither He went "to appear in the presence of God for us" (Heb. 9: 24) and "where he liveth to make intercession" (Heb. 7: 25). John comforts us by saying "we have an advocate (*parakleton*) with the Father, Jesus Christ, the righteous" (I Jno. 2: 1).

2) THE NECESSITY.

The necessity for intercession is represented by the Epistle to the Hebrews as arising from the nature of Christ's priestly office.   The earthly high priest presented his sacrifice in the holy of holies, the type of the true sanctuary of heaven.   Hence the divine high priest must present His sacrifice before the Father in heaven.,   The work was not completed until the sacrifice was- offered.   This sacrifice became the ground of His intercession for us.

3) THE POSSIBILITY.

Exception has been taken to the doctrine of the intercession of Christ on the ground that it is inconceivable that God should intercede with Himself.   This objection proceeds on the error that Christ is not man, not our representative, and that He is God alone.   Whatever difficulty exists in this matter holds also against the incarnation and atonement.

4) THE NATURE.

(1) Definition.

Intercession is the mediation of Christ with the Father in heaven for the salvation of men. It is the consummation and the culmination of His work begun on earth.

(2) Exclusive.

There is one mediator between God and men (I Tim. 2:5), Himself man, Christ Jesus. This excludes the Romish idea of the intercession of the saints in heaven for the Church on earth, a false doctrine which has wrought untold mischief in misleading souls and in augmenting the temporal power of the Church. One divine infinite mediator is sufficient in view of His own merit and of the love of God. It is derogatory to the character of Christ to hold otherwise.

(3) Perpetual.

The priesthood of Christ never ceases. He is a "priest forever" (Heb. 7: 17-24; Ps. 110: 4) and "ever liveth to make intercession" (Heb. 7: 25). His relation to His redeemed people will never change, and He will ever remain the God-man.

(4) The Manner.

There is no explicit revelation as to the manner of Christ's intercession. We may presume, however, that His presence as the priest and the offering in the heavenly sanctuary constitutes the fact that we have an advocate with the Father. He is called the "righteous" (I Jno. 2: 1), indicating that His righteousness or moral perfection constitutes the basis of His intercession.

Yet, humanly speaking, the Scriptures seem to assert a pleading for us, after the manner of Christ's prayer in Jno. 17. It is not necessary, however, to suppose that human language is used, for we do not know the manner of the divine intercourse. "If not like our speech, it is because it is better and truer, if not in mortal tones, it is with immortal meaning, if not articulate in the air, it is articulate in the very plan of God; if it is not expressed in sentences, it is wrought into the counsels of the Father of all" (H. B. Smith, 486).

(5) The Objects.

Judging Christ's heavenly intercession by that on earth, we conclude that it embraces all men, and we would not limit it to the so-called great things of life, for He cares for birds and counts the hairs of our head.

(6) The Result.

a. The general result of Christ's mediation is that of a new covenant relation between God and man.   Redemption assumes a new and distinct phase.   Man is again permitted in a special sense to come directly to God as his right through Christ.   Every true believer is a royal priest.

b. Some special blessings are mentioned in Scriptures as accruing from Christ's intercession.

Justification.   Rom. 8: 33, 34.

Boldness in coming to the throne of grace.   Heb. 4: 16.

Hope.   Heb. 6: 18-20.

An abiding priest.   Heb. 7:17, 24, 25.

III.   THE WORK OF CHRIST AS KING.

1.   The Fact

The third office of Christ as redeemer is that of king. Through it He makes the work and office of prophet and priest effective.   The three offices of our Lord are not to be separated or too sharply differentiated.   He is a royal prophet and priest.   Long before He became our teacher and priest He was a king enthroned in majesty.

The Scripture references to Christ as a king and to His kingdom are very numerous.   There are about a hundred and fifty passages in the New Testament referring to the king and kingdom.   Jesus Himself claimed to be a king, and this His enemies recognized with derision.   The fact of His kingship is apparent.

2. The Ground

The kingship of Christ is not merely a symbolical or poetic conception. It rests upon ample and rational grounds.

1) His Birth.

Christ was born a king in a double sense. As the Son of God He is the Lord of heaven and earth. His kingdom is everlasting. As a descendant of David He has claims also on earthly sovereignty.

2) His Person.

Not only has Christ hereditary claims to royalty, but still more has He personal claims. His relation to the race as the second Adam makes Him its proper head and ruler. As the perfect ideal man He has inherent and indisputable claims to be regarded as Lord.

3) Add to the foregoing the work which He has done, the victories which He has achieved and the deliverance which He has accomplished for the race. These constitute the claims and the fact of His kingship. On His head are many crowns.

3. The Necessity

The conception of Christ's kingship comes to us through the Bible. As God and God's representative, He must necessarily rule all things. The dominant earthly form of government in the ancient times was the monarchical. The idea of such a rule may be repugnant to those brought up under democratic institutions; nevertheless, divine kingship still underlies all government. The will of God must be supreme. For the very reason that human kings are too weak or too wicked to maintain moral order, it became necessary that this should be restored by a perfect king. As sin is not only of the body but also of the soul, and as it is universal among men, it became necessary that one should arise whose character should be spiritual and whose dominion should be universal.

4. A Definition

The word "kingdom" is used in such a variety of ways and with so many different shades of meaning that an accurate definition seems impossible. The thought suggested is too great to be comprehended in one sentence. The paraphrase in the Lord's Prayer sheds much light on it: "Thy kingdom come, Thy will be done as in heaven so on earth" (Mt. 6:10). The meaning must be that the kingdom is that realm or condition in which the will of God is supreme, not only by power but also by free choice.

5. The Characteristics

1) SPIRITUAL.

The kingdom of Christ is not of this world, that is, it is not after the manner of an ordinary kingdom. Efforts to give it a complete, concrete, visible form have always failed and always must. Its origin, form, methods, agencies, administration and object are far above those of earthly kingdoms. It has, indeed, much to do with the ordinary efforts of men but it is rather in the way of elevating and ennobling than by directly controlling them. It is both an inner and an outward kingdom. It is both a personal experience and a social condition.

2) UNIVERSAL.

The scope of the kingdom of Christ is unlimited. It has sometimes been divided into three realms—the kingdom of power, of grace, and of glory. Such divisions are arbitrary, though they may be suggestive. By "power" is meant God's universal dominion, His administration by way of providence and of judgment. His kingdom is irresistible; before Him every knee shall bow. By "grace" is meant the exercise of the divine sovereignty for the salvation of men, especially through the Church. By "glory" is meant the realm of the triumphant Lord, when all His enemies shall have been put under His feet, and when His Church shall be glorified with Him in heaven.

6. Its Relation to the Church

The kingdom of God and the Church of God are closely related, but not synonymous. The latter is only a part of the former. All efforts to identify them have resulted in oppression and disaster. The Romish hierarchical idea, which makes the Church and the kingdom one, has been the bane of the Church. There is a true sense in which the kingdom finds its highest expression in the Church. Here God is acknowledged to be supreme and man's worth is recognized and his inherent rights are conserved. Here the higher things are cultivated and sin is avoided and denounced. But the kingdom of God includes all things, temporal and eternal, human and angelic. The Church is but one phase of it.

7. Its Relation to the State

The state as well as the Church is a divine institution. It also is a part or phase of the kingdom of God. "The powers that be are ordained of God . . . rulers are not a terror to the good work but to the evil" (Rom. 13: 1, 3). Law, government and authority are divine appointments without which society cannot exist. The express form of government is not designated; this is flexible and adapted to conditions. Tyranny is not sanctioned and must be regarded as an abuse of authority. It is evidently the divine purpose that government shall be just and beneficent. To this end God has revealed great principles and endows men with high spiritual qualities. The best form of government is that which obtains under the influence of Christianity.

8. The Relation of the Church and State

It is obvious that the parts of a great kingdom must have certain relations to each other; they cannot be absolutely independent. As both have been ordained of God, and as members of the Church must necessarily belong to the state, the two must touch. Are they equal, or is one superior, or how otherwise are they related? Theories vary and practice has varied.

1) The theory that the Church is supreme has been held by the Roman Catholic Church. The state exists

by virtue of the appointment through the Church. The pope is Christ's vicar in temporal as well as in spiritual things. He is to sanction and even to crown kings. The state is the secular arm of the Church and is to execute its mandates. This theory is repudiated by all states. The pope has lost even the small territory called the States of the Church, formerly held by him.

2) The theory that the state is supreme is held by practically all monarchical governments. It is also maintained by the Greek Catholic Church. The state regulates the Church and supports it out of the public treasury.

3) The theory that both are independent receives its best illustration in the United States, where Church and State are separate. This does not imply an absence of community interest. They support each other morally in their respective spheres and neither can thrive without the other.

Several questions originate in this connection:

(1) Should a Christian state recognize Christ in its constitution?
(2) Should the Bible be taught in its public schools?
(3) Should any property of the Church be exempt from taxation?

In regard to the first it is our opinion that there would be no practical gain in pressing the matter. In regard to the second we hold that the Bible ought not to be excluded from the schools. It is not sectarian and is the standard of ethics and morals in every Christian state. In reference to the last the practice of exempting the Church edifices from taxation may be defended on the same ground as the exemption of schools and other benevolent enterprises.

9. The Consummation of the Kingdom

The restoration of a theocratic government is not probable. Providence teaches that the kingdom of God may come and exist in the world under any just form of government. There can be no doubt however, that the influence of true religion always tends to produce a constitution which recognizes civil and political equality. How fully the idea of the kingdom of God in all its aspects will be realized on earth is of secondary importance. That it will grow and bless mankind is surely the burden of prophecy and is in accordance with its own nature. That there will be a personal reign of Christ on earth, as held by the premillenarians, is without the support of Scripture.

The final consummation of our Lord's kingship will take place at the judgment "when he shall deliver up the kingdom to the Father, when he shall have abolished all rule, authority and power."

PART IV

PNEUMATOLOGY

THE DOCTRINE OF THE SPIRIT

We have considered the doctrine of God, the doctrine of man, and the doctrine of Christ. We have learned that God is the Father Almighty, the maker of heaven and the earth; that man, made in the divine image, has become alienated from God, is without strength to save himself, and needs a more than human Savior; and that the Son of God became man in order to effect reconciliation between God and man. The doctrine of the Spirit treats of the application of redemption to man through the Holy Spirit.

The doctrine of the Spirit may be considered under four heads: The person, the office, the work and the means.

A. THE PERSON OF THE SPIRIT

I. HIS NATURE.

The word "spirit" is broad in its significance. It sometimes means *wind* or *breath;* again it signifies an influence, emanating from a person; and again it means a person. We have already seen in our study of the Trinity that the Holy Spirit is a divine person, co-equal and co-eternal with the Father and the Son, with whom He is worshiped and glorified.

II. HIS MANIFESTATION.

The full revelation of the Trinity came gradually and does not appear clearly in the Old Testament though there are intimations of the doctrine. We learn in the New Testament that the prophets were men who "spoke from God, being moved by the Holy Spirit" (II Pet. 1: 21). This indicated the interest and activity of the Holy Spirit in human redemption. However, John 7: 39 says that at the advent of Christ "the Holy Spirit was not yet given, because Jesus was not yet glorified." These statements are not contradictory. They assert on the one hand that the Holy Spirit is eternal and on the other hand that His distinct revelation to man and His dispensation in the matter of redemption did not take place until after the death of our Lord. Our knowledge of Jesus comes through His historical manifestation in the Incarnation and His human life. Likewise our knowledge of the Spirit comes through His historical manifestation on the day of Pentecost and since that day in the life of believers and in the progress of the Church.

III.   HIS RELATION TO CHRIST.

There is a holy fellowship not only of personality but of service between the Spirit and Jesus. 1) At Christ's birth the Spirit is active filling the hearts of Zacharias and Elizabeth and John the Baptist. He overshadows the Virgin Mary at her conception. 2) In His childhood Jesus was filled with the Spirit, the grace of God being upon Him. 3) At His baptism the Spirit descended upon Him and thus anointed Him for His work. 4) In His ministry the Spirit of God was upon Him, leading Him into the wilderness, filling Him with power as He returns to Galilee, enabling Him to cast out demons and do many mighty works. 5) At His resurrection the Spirit bears witness to the truth.

B.   THE OFFICE OF THE SPIRIT

I.   WITNESSING.

The Holy Spirit bears witness to Christ that He is the Son of God and the Savior of men (Jno. 15:26). "The Spirit himself beareth witness with our spirit that we are the children of God" (Rom. 8:16). He is the Spirit of truth illuminating the minds of men. He inspires Christians to know the things of Christ. He is our teacher.

II.   CONVICTING.

"And he, when he is come will convict the world in respect of sin, and of righteousness, and of judgment" (John

16: 8-11). The Spirit convicts men of their sinful nature and state, especially of their unbelief in rejecting Christ. He convicts the world in respect to righteousness in showing it the insufficiency of all merely human righteousness on the one hand, and on the other the perfect righteousness of Christ which is imputed to the believer. Lastly, He convicts the world "of judgment, because the prince of this world has been judged." Christ has conquered Satan—a blessed truth which the Holy Spirit shows in the application of the power of Christ's blood to the heart. This threefold conviction is wrought in men not so much by the process of reason as by the illumination of the Holy Spirit.

III.   COMFORTING.

Jesus calls the Spirit "another Comforter," the Paraclete —advocate, adviser, friend in need. To those who yield to His call, the Spirit becomes an indwelling presence, a regenerating and sanctifying power. He is the source of the blessed gifts of love, joy, peace, long-suffering, kindness, goodness, faithfulness, meekness, and self-control. He is also the transformer of character.

C.   THE WORK OF THE SPIRIT

We are now to consider the actual application of redemption by the Holy Spirit to the individual. As the process is chiefly spiritual and internal, it is not easy to make an exact analysis. The transformation of the soul into the divine image implies such a radical change in thinking, feeling and willing that we find it difficult to trace the various steps involved. These, however, may be set forth in the following *ordo salutis*: The call, repentance and faith, justification, regeneration and conversion, sanctification.

I.   THE CALL.

1.   The Definition

By "the call" is meant the invitation of the Gospel to the sinner to accept salvation in Christ. As the Holy Spirit is the inspirer of the Word and the one who applies the work of Christ it is proper to ascribe the call to the Spirit. Luther in his Catechism says, "I believe that I cannot by my own reason or strength believe in Jesus Christ my Lord, or come to Him; but the Holy Ghost has called me through the Gospel, enlightened me by His gifts and sanctified and preserved me in the truth of faith."

2. The Subjects

The call of the Spirit is intended for all, for God desires all to be saved (I Tim. 2: 4; II Pet. 3: 9), and Jesus commanded that His Gospel be preached to all. Any limitation of the so-called predestination is not warranted by Scripture and reason.

3. The Method

We may not limit the call of God to any particular method. The Spirit is not bound. He works variously, whence His work has been described as follows:

1) IMMEDIATE.

The Spirit in extraordinary cases may call a person directly without external medium or instrument. Such cases are rare.

2) MEDIATE.

Usually the Spirit calls men through the Word of God— its perusal or its preaching. To this end He has ordained the Christian ministry; but there are many other channels through which the truth reaches men.

3) EXTERNAL.

When the objective presentation of the call is contemplated, it is described as external. It comes to a person from without, through the senses, much as any other appeal. This takes place whenever the Gospel is preached.

4) INTERNAL.

The call to salvation, however, is always accomplished by the power of the Holy Spirit, who is immanent in the Word. The Word of God is as much the Word of the Spirit today as it was when He moved holy men to record it. The mere accident of time, distance or dialect does not affect the integrity of the divine call.   Hence, when the Gospel is properly preached the Spirit strives to awaken saving faith in the person who is attentive.   As truly as the heart of Lydia was opened by the Lord, so the Spirit strives to open men's hearts today.

5) RESISTIBLE.

The gracious advances of the Holy Spirit are by no means irresistible.   He does not compel attention or obedience. Though the human will has been so perverted that it cannot deliberately and unaided choose good, it still possesses the power of rejecting and resisting truth and salvation. Jesus chided the Jews by saying, "Ye will not come to me that ye may have life" (Jno. 5: 40), and He declared that "he that believeth not hath been judged already" (3: 18).   Stephen charged the Jews with resisting the Holy Spirit (Acts 7: 51), and Paul turned from them to the Gentiles because they had thrust away the Word of God (13: 46).   The Epistle to the Hebrews (2: 3; 10: 29) lays the guilt of rejecting salvation at the door of the lost themselves.

The sin against the Holy Spirit is nothing less than the deliberate and persistent rejection of His ministry, without which there is no salvation.   Hence we are warned not to quench or grieve the Spirit (I Thess. 5: 19; Eph. 4: 30).

Calvinistic theology makes the call irresistible in the sense that it carries with it the will and the affections. God having predestinated the elect to salvation they cannot and will not resist the Spirit.   This seems to be in conflict with the nature of the human will as well as with the direct assertions of the Bible.

4. The Effect

Various positive effects follow the call when it is heeded, issuing in the full salvation of the believer.

1) ILLUMINATION.

The natural unregenerate heart and mind of man are not alive to the true nature of sin.   He is apt to believe himself to be much better than he really is.   He is in the condition of a sick man who is unconscious of his malady though he may be at the very point of death. The Holy Spirit comes to the sinner through the word and enlightens him not simply by the ordinary power of truth but by a special quickening of his soul so that he fully apprehends his danger. This is in accordance with the promise of our Lord, Jno. 16, and with experience. "The natural man receiveth not the things of the Spirit of God" (I Cor. 2:14). But when the Spirit calls and a man heeds, there comes to him the light of God showing him his true state.

2) CONVICTION.

Following illumination comes conviction. The sinner not only sees himself in a measure as he is, but he realizes his utter helplessness, acknowledges his just condemnation, and is sorely distressed over his attitude toward a loving God. This conviction is wrought in man by the Spirit, "who convicts the world of sin, of righteousness and of judgment (Jno. 16:8).

If we have properly interpreted the call, we see that it has brought the soul into the vestibule of the temple of salvation. It is being saved. If the process be unhindered by the wilful resistance of man, it will inevitably eventuate in his justification and full salvation.

II.   REPENTANCE AND FAITH.

The call being heeded, the sinner is next brought to repentance.

1. Definition

Repentance denotes godly sorrow for sin. It indicates "a change of mind," as the word *metanoia*, the Greek equivalent, signifies. It is used in this sense in the New Testament over fifty times. The Augsburg Confession (Art. XII) says very truly, "Repentance consists of two parts. The one is contrition or terror of conscience on account of sin. The other is faith." It implies a turning away from sin and a turning to Christ. Where either of these elements is lacking there is no true repentance.

2. Contrition

1) ITS ELEMENTS.

It is important to analyze more minutely the several elements which make up contrition.

(1) Fear. The soul, seeing itself a culprit, is afflicted with the fear of the wrath of God. It realizes that it has broken God's law and trampled upon His love.

(2) Self-condemnation. The penitent further realizes that his plight is of his own making. His language is "I have sinned." He does not blame God or his fellow man. He alone is responsible. He ought not to have sinned. Often there is a sense of self-loathing and always a hatred of sin.

(3) Confession is usually accompanied by prayer and pardon. He is ready to make confession of his transgressions. While ashamed of himself he is not ashamed or afraid to acknowledge his sin. It is not uncommon for great criminals, goaded by remorse, voluntarily to confess their crimes and surrender to justice. This is the experience of the penitent in relation to God.

Confession is usually accompanied by prayer for pardon. "God have mercy" is the instinctive cry of the convicted in all ages. It is the universal language of humanity expressed in sacrifices, in tears, as well as in audible language.

2) ITS DEGREE.

The degree of contrition depends upon many circumstances, such as the clearness of the spiritual apprehension, the intelligence, the temperament, as well as upon the degree of guilt. There are also degrees of the manifestation of contrition, from almost imperceptible emotion to violent outbreaks. The depth and the sincerity of contrition are not to be measured by the degree of visible demonstration, but rather by its fruit. Nevertheless, it is not improper nor unusual for genuine sorrow for sin to make itself manifest in emotion.

3) ITS VALUE.

(1) Contrition has no saving merit or value. It does not justify the sinner, for there is nothing in it to re-

concile God or to atone for sin. It may afford relief to a burdened soul to confess its sins, but confession cannot annul guilt. No "works of righteousness" or so-called penance can in the least mitigate our offenses.

(2) Contrition shows receptivity. Though without saving merit, contrition is the indication that the grace of God is having its effect in softening the heart and making it receptive to the cleansing power of Christ's blood. It is a sign that the sinner is yielding, that his stubborn will is breaking, and that he is passive in the hand of God. But he deserves no more credit than does a drowning man who ceases his struggles and lies helpless in the arms of his rescuer.

(3) Contrition becomes deterrent. Contrition also remains in the memory of the Christian and in times of temptation may be a deterrent against lapsing into sin. Its very memory is bitter.

3. Faith

1) ITS DEFINITION.

The generic word in the New Testament for faith is *pisteuein*, from which comes the noun *pistis*. These words are used about five hundred times. The meaning of *pisteuein* is "to believe," "to be persuaded of," "to place confidence in," and "to trust." The nearest formal definition of faith is "assurance of things hoped for, a conviction of things not seen."

A study of the passages in which "to believe" occurs shows that faith is a technical term expressing reliance on Christ for salvation, an attitude of mind wrought by the Spirit of God. Faith is not an entity, but something that exists apart from a person. It may be thought of as an act in which the whole soul participates.

2) ITS ELEMENTS.

(1) Knowledge. Faith must have a rational basis. The mind can accept only things of which it has knowledge which is imparted and obtained in various ways. Paul says, "Faith cometh by hearing." "How shall they

believe in him whom they have not heard? And how shall they hear without a preacher?" (Rom. 10: 14-17). "That we may attain this faith, the office of teaching the gospel and administering the sacraments was instituted" (Augs. Con. V).

(2) Assent. Mere knowledge cannot save. In the spiritual realm a man to be profited must not merely know; he must give deliberate assent; he dare not be neutral. The truth must mean something to him. He must embrace it and seek to realize it and to affirm it as his own.

(3) Confidence. Intellectual assent is not of the essence of faith. Even the devils believe and tremble. The Roman Catholic definition of faith as "the assent of the intellect to a truth which is beyond its comprehension but which it accepts under the influence of the will moved by Grace" is only a partial definition. True faith means reliance, confidence and trust. Knowledge and assent are but the preliminaries that lead to it. Faith is self-surrender to Christ, who is our life and the well-spring of new life in the soul. It is a joyful experience of freedom in God.

3) Its Origin.

From what has been said it is evident that the source of faith is not in us but in God. Of course God does not believe for us, but gives us the power to believe. Hence Paul says, "For by grace have ye been saved through faith; and that not of yourselves, it is the gift of God; not of works, that no man should glory" (Eph. 2: 8, 9). In this passage "and that" refers to faith and not to grace; for grace is the gift of God as a matter of course. To make "and that" refer to grace would be tautological. Faith and works are contrasted.

Paul expresses the same thought when he says, "To you it hath been granted in the behalf of Christ not only to believe in him, but also to suffer" (Phil. 1: 29). "It is God who worketh in you both to will and to work for his pleasure" (Phil. 2: 13).

"So little indeed is faith conceived as containing in itself the energy or ground of salvation, that it is consistently represented as in its origin, itself a gratuity from God in the prosecution of His saving work.   It comes not of one's own strength or virtue, ... it is His gift through Christ, ... a gift which God lays in the lap of the soul . . . . a benefaction out of heaven" (Dr. Warfield in Hastings B.D. 1: 837).

Man's part in faith is to exercise it.   Though man be dead in trespasses and sins, he is not physically or psychologically dead.   When he is touched by the gracious hand of God, he is lifted up and given power to believe.

4) ITS EFFECT.

The effect of the exercise of faith, of the sinner's new attitude, is that of bringing him into a new relation to God in which he is restored to sonship through Christ.

III.   JUSTIFICATION.

1.   The Biblical Teaching

The Holy Spirit having awakened, illuminated and called the sinner and having wrought in him repentance and faith, forgiveness is granted.   The Biblical term for this is justification by faith.   A proper understanding of this doctrine is most important and not difficult.   Its restoration through the experience and work of Luther is the source and explanation of the Reformation.   Luther calls it the doctrine of a standing or falling Church.   He means that the character and perpetuity of the Church is measured by it.   He called it also the most important article of the Christian faith.   It is "the material principle of the Reformation" as the Word of God is its "formal principle."

1) ITS NATURE.

Its nature must be determined chiefly upon exegetical grounds.   The Old Testament word translated "to justify" is *tsadak*.   Its New Testament equivalent is *dikaio* and its derivations.   The all but universal explanation of these terms is that they are used in a legal or forensic sense; that is, they are declarative of a legal status.   A person is declared to be righteous, or reckoned to be righteous.   The penalty has been lifted. The righteousness with which he is credited is an imputed one. It is ascribed to him. It has no reference to his ethical character. It only indicates that somehow the demands of the law have been fulfilled in his case. That this is true will appear from the examination of a few passages from the Pauline Epistles in which we have the fullest exposition of the doctrine.

In Romans it is declared that "by the works of the law shall no flesh be justified" (3: 20), that "a man is justified by faith apart from works of the law" (3: 28), that "Abraham believed in God, and it was reckoned unto him for righteousness" (4: 3), and that man is blessed "unto whom God reckoneth righteousness apart from works" (4: 6). In Gal. 2: 16 we read that we are not justified by deeds of the law and that "if righteousness is through the law then Christ died for naught" (Gal. 2: 21).

Justification, being a forensic and objective act, is *for* the sinner rather than *in* the sinner. It does not effect a change of character. It does not impart aught to the sinner. The Romanists and other errorists have confounded justification with regeneration, thus ascribing to it a subjective character. Augustine thought of it as an infusion of grace, which brought life and strength. Its true meaning is that the righteousness of Christ is reckoned to the sinner on certain conditions.

2) Its Source (*causa efficiens*).

Since justification is a work *for* man, its motive must be sought outside of man, viz., in the love of God (Jno. 3: 16). We are said to be "justified freely by his grace through redemption that is in Christ Jesus" (Rom. 3: 24). The grace of God has sometimes been understood as a quality wrought within us, but it is God's favor toward us. It is His love and beneficence that seeks to save. The entire Trinity is deeply concerned in our justification. "It is God that justifies" (Rom. 8: 33). "Ye were justified in the name of our Lord Jesus Christ, and in the Spirit of our God" (I Cor. 6: 11). The baptismal formula and the apostolic benediction also indicate the co-operation of the Father, the Son and the Spirit in our justification.

3) ITS GROUND (*causa meritoria*).

The ground upon which God can justify man is the fact that Christ took the sinner's place in all things; in becoming man, in fulfilling the law, and in being a propitiation for the sins of the whole world. Hence, it is said that God can "be just and the justifier of him that hath faith in Jesus Christ" (Rom. 3:26). The second Adam becomes the new head and representative of the race, the perfect divine man whose merit far exceeds His debt as man. This truth has been set forth in the consideration of the atonement.

If the old question be revived, whether Christ saved us according to His human or His divine nature, and whether it was done by His active or passive obedience, we would answer that we should not separate His natures and His work. It is the Lord Jesus Christ who saves us through His perfect obedience in life and death. It is true that His sufferings and His death are especially magnified, because they were the culmination of His obedience and particularly emphasize His love. The Spirit well knew that scoffers would arise to deride the idea of a bloody sacrifice, and therefore inspired the sacred writers to make it clear that "we have our redemption through his blood, the forgiveness of our trespasses, according to the riches of his grace" (Eph. 1:7).

The righteousness of Christ — His righteousness with God—is imputed to or reckoned to the account of the sinner who accepts Him, "for Christ is the end of the law unto righteousness to everyone who believeth" (Rom. 10:4).

4) ITS INSTRUMENT (*causa instrumentalis*).

The means of apprehending justification or of obtaining forgiveness is faith. "Being therefore justified by faith we have peace with God through our Lord Jesus Christ." (Rom. 5:1). "A man is justified by faith without the works of the law" (Rom. 3:20-28).

We have already considered the nature of faith. Let us remember that it is an attitude rather than an entity. It has no merit at all and does not justify the sinner by virtue of anything that it is. Its saving efficacy arises from what it embraces.   The characteristics of saving or justifying faith are *"receiving"* (Jno. 3: 14-15) ; *"coming to Christ"* (Mt. 11: 28) ; "fleeing for refuge" (Heb. 6: 10), and the like.   These terms indicate no inherent value in faith itself. This lies in its object, that which it receives, looks to, flees to, and trusts in.   This object is Christ.   Hence justification is the result of receiving Christ.   Our faith, not in itself, but as embracing Him, justifies us.

5) ITS DEFINITION.

We are now prepared for a definition of justification. Justification is that act of God's free grace whereby, for the sake of Jesus Christ, He pardons the believing sinner, receives him into favor and accepts him as righteous.

The Augsburg Confession (Art. IV) says, "They in like manner teach that men cannot be justified before God by their own strength, merits or works; but that they are justified gratuitously for Christ's sake, through faith; when they believe that they are received into favor, and that their sins are remitted for the sake of Christ, who made satisfaction for our transgressions by His death. This faith God imputes for righteousness before Him."

2.   False Views of Justification

1) PELAGIANISM.

Very early in the history of the post-apostolic Church a destructive error appeared regarding the value of good works as the means of meriting God's favor.   This error was formulated by Pelagius, a British monk, at the close of the third century and the beginning of the fourth.   He regarded sin not as inherited, but as an act.   He did not deny the existence of divine grace, but exalted man's ability as being sufficient to save himself.   He was ably refuted by the great Augustine, who vindicated the Biblical doctrine of man's depravity and inability to save himself; and hence he exalted the grace of God as the source of salvation.   The rich fruit of this controversy was Luther's doctrine of justification.

2) Semi-Pelagianism.

Semi-Pelagianism or Semi-Augustinianism teaches that grace is indeed necessary to salvation but that the human will is so weakened that it cannot begin or take the initiative in salvation.

3) Romanism.

The Roman Catholic Church does not formally teach Pelagianism, but the common belief of the people is practically Pelagian. It holds that grace must begin salvation, but that man cooperates through good works after grace has been operative. It teaches synergism, which must always leave the sinner in a state of uncertainty. It mingles true justification with sanctification, holding that the former as well as the latter is progressive. Augustine wrongly taught that there is an infusion of grace in justification.

The folly of the foregoing views is apparent from Scripture, reason and experience. We are saved by grace through faith and that not of ourselves, it is the gift of God. Obedience is not possible to the weakened sinner.

IV. REGENERATION AND CONVERSION.

Justification, as we have seen, is an objective forensic act. The call and repentance, while affecting the soul directly have brought light to it but no life. This last is the work done in regeneration.

1. Definition

Regeneration is synonymous with "the new birth," or "born from above," or "born of the spirit" (Jno. 3: 3-7). It is a quickening of man's moral nature by the power of God. It may be defined as follows: Regeneration is the work of God in us by which the Holy Spirit makes us new creatures in Christ Jesus. Another definition: "Regeneration is the action of grace by which the Holy Spirit, in and through faith, bestows the power by which the soul is quickened and made capable of a new and holy life, in love to God and spiritual things."

2. Nature

It is self-evident that a dead man cannot make himself alive; he cannot resuscitate himself. This is true physically and spiritually. Yet we need to remember that in the so-called spiritual death man's faculties have not gone into dissolution and are not incapable of rational acts. Hence we draw the following conclusions:

1) Regeneration is the act of God. Life comes from Him. The initiative is His. Without Him there can be neither beginning nor progression in salvation. In this sense man has absolutely nothing to do with his quickening. He is saved by grace.

2) Faith accepts the grace. Man being psychologically alive is not unconscious of God's movement toward him and in him. He as a free agent had power to resist and repel the Holy Spirit, though through sin he has been so disabled that he cannot of himself accept. But faith has already been aroused in him as we have seen in the matter of repentance and justification. He is, therefore, enabled to cease opposition, yield to the ministry of the Spirit, and accept His gracious power.

3) Regeneration is resistible. To make regeneration a divine act regardless of man's personality would be the simplest determinism. He would be carried into the kingdom *nolens volens*. This would seem to contradict our very nature and also the plain teachings of the Scriptures in which we are admonished to hearken to the Holy Spirit and to yield ourselves to God.

4) Regeneration makes the subject a child of God. The nature of regeneration may be judged from its effects. It makes the sinner a child of God. It brings him into the kingdom of heaven. His faculties are restored and quickened so as to perform their normal functions. No substance is added or subtracted. It is a matter of a new attitude brought about by a new life.

5) Regeneration is the beginning of the Christian life. A regenerated soul only begins the divine life. Starting with it the soul normally goes on unto perfection

through the process of sanctification, which is never complete in this life.

6) Regeneration is both instantaneous and gradual. Whether regeneration is an instantaneous act or a gradual process depends upon the point of view taken. Regarded as a transition from death to life it must be instantaneous. Regarded as a transformation or motive and faculty, realized by the consciousness and expressed in holy living, it must be gradual.

3. The Means

The divinely ordained means through which the Spirit ordinarily works are the Word and the Sacraments. Of course, the Spirit works when and where He pleases and is not bound to means. An unbaptized heathen infant, entirely removed from the influence of Christianity, dying in infancy, is surely saved apart from the application of any external means. Yet ordinarily it pleases the Spirit to work through appointed means. We must be born of water and the Spirit. Baptism is represented as a washing of regeneration. "Of his own will he brought us forth by the word of truth" (Jas. 1: 18). Christians are spoken of as "having been begotten again, not of corruptible seed but of incorruptible, through the word of God which liveth and abideth" (I Pet. 1: 23). Paul represents the great transformation as dependent upon the preaching of the Gospel (Rom. 10: 14-17). The effect of the application of the means will be considered later, yet we may here say that the effect is not magical in any sense and that it does not follow *ex operato*. God acts upon man as a moral personality and not as a dead body.

4. The Relation of Regeneration and Justification

There has been much discussion as to the order of salvation, some holding that justification precedes regeneration, and others the reverse. The difference seems to arise, partly at least, from confounding the first motions of grace within us with the fuller work of God which we call regeneration. The awakening of the soul in the call and repentance, it seems to us, is precedent to the impartation of life. It will be urged that it is impossible for the soul to believe unless it is regenerated. This misconception arises from a false psychology and from limiting the grace of God in the call and illumination. Moreover, it would seem to be in accordance with the nature of the soul that God should first do His work for the soul as in justification, before working in it as in regeneration.

The two acts are not widely separated in time; they may be synchronous. Those whom God justifies He also regenerates, for when forgiveness takes place the soul naturally becomes the subject for regeneration. On this matter we may profitably quote from Luthardt. "It may be asked how are regeneration and justification related to each other in point of time. They must not be temporarily separated, for it is true here of the great master weaver, in the sphere of the inner life, that one stroke effects a thousand combinations. The internal and not the temporal relations of the two may be determined. In general it may be said that while the present prevailing teaching in our Church, influenced by the combination of regeneration with infant baptism, places the former at the beginning of the order of salvation and hence also before conversion and justification. Luther and the earlier teaching in general, on the other hand, place justification (that is, the forgiveness of sin) before regeneration or else call justification right out regeneration, as Melanchthon in particular does. For before God makes a temple of our souls for His indwelling, He purifies it by the pardon of sin. We may also with later theologians like Quenstedt, who have more thoroughly investigated the precedent psychological conditions, distinguish between the working of the Spirit on us and His indwelling in us" (*Glaubenslehre*, p. 477).

5. Conversion

The word conversion is used with a wide latitude of meaning. Sometimes it is made to stand for the whole process of salvation. Thus we speak of a man's conversion. The word has today, however, a technical meaning and is defined as the act by which the sinner turns to God. The

Catechism says, "Conversion is the work of the Holy Spirit by which through faith in Christ we turn from darkness to light and from the power of Satan to God." In short, conversion is man's response to God's work of salvation. Enabled by grace he turns to God. An exegetical study of the passages bearing on conversion shows that the word translated "conversion" means in nearly all cases a "turning" on man's part. The words are used intransitively. Conversion takes place chiefly in repentance, which is almost synonymous with it. The subject is introduced at this point, however, because a man's conversion is not complete until after his regeneration.

V. SANCTIFICATION.

1. Definition

Sanctification is the continuous growth in the new life begun in regeneration, producing a change of character from sinfulness to holiness. It is related to regeneration as growth is related to birth. It differs from justification in that the latter is a judicial act for us while it is a process within us. It differs from both in being a work in which man is enabled by the Holy Spirit through the new life to cooperate in producing a life in conformity with that of Christ. "The religious experience of acceptance with God is not the same as the ethical experience of the moral ideal; nor is it necessary for the latter to enjoy the former. The true relationship is rather the reverse. It is the religious experience of acceptance and forgiveness which makes possible the realization of the ethical ideal" (W. A. Brown, p. 315).

2. Nature

Sanctification has two aspects, negative and positive. The new-born soul has still the motions and the habits of the natural man. It may shrink from them, but, alas, it finds that it is yet somewhat under their dominion. Hence arises the struggle between the old and the new life. The Canaanite is still in the land and must be expelled. On the one hand sanctification implies the putting away of sin. Paul

(Eph. 4 : 22), exhorts the Ephesians to "put away, as concerning your former manner of life the old man." The vestiges of sin must be destroyed. The self-will of the sinner must decrease, and Christ must increase in the thought and life of the regenerated. On the other hand sanctification demands the "putting on" of new, clean, holy ideas and activities. "Be renewed in the spirit of your minds and put on the new man" (Eph. 4 : 23-24). "Put on the Lord Jesus Christ" (Rom. 13 : 14). The Christian lives by dying and dies by living.

3. Method

The process of sanctification corresponds with the negative and the positive aspects of its nature. It consists on the one hand in putting away the filth of the flesh, the crucifixion of the old man and separation from the corrupting influences of wicked and worldly-minded persons. On the other hand it consists of fostering the spiritual life especially through the "mystical union" with Christ who is our life. He says, "If a man love me he will keep my word; and my Father will love him, and we will come unto him and make our abode with him" (Jno. 14 : 23). "Abide in me and I in you" (15 : 4). The Spirit also dwells in the earnest believer, making his heart a veritable temple (I Cor. 3 : 16).

The means are pre-eminently the word and the sacraments on the objective side, and prayer and the exercise of acquired Christian virtues on the subjective. In all this is distinctly implied the quickening power of the Spirit and the deliberate response of the soul in Christian activity in the suppression of evil and the practice of good. Every Christian knows what is meant by growing in the divine life and what struggles it involves to substitute "the outgoing for the self-centered life."

4. Degree

While the aim of the Christian is perfection, its attainment can only be measurable in this life. This is implied in the Lord's Prayer and in numerous other passages. John says, "If we say that we have no sin we deceive ourselves"

(I John 1:8). Paul warns the over-confident, saying, "Let him that thinketh he standeth take heed lest he fall" (I Cor. 10:12). Eminent saint though Paul himself was, he says, "Not that I have already attained or am already made perfect, but I press on" (Phil. 3:12). History records only one perfect life. Nevertheless, there are great possibilities within the reach of the Christian. It is a reproach that we are too easily content with low attainment in spiritual life.

The following table shows the several elements and experiences involved in the Christian life.

Justification	*Regeneration*	*Sanctification*
An act	An act	A process
Of God alone	Of God alone	Of God and man
External	Internal	External & internal
Instantaneous	Instantaneous	Gradual
Equal	Equal	Unequal
Perfect	Perfect	Partial
Free from guilt	From death	From defilement
Imputed	Imparted	Attained

D.   MEANS OF GRACE

In the accomplishment of the salvation of men the Holy Spirit employs certain instruments by which and through which He works. In the divine ordination there is always wisdom; and hence objective means are evidently needed for the application of redemption.

The technical term for the means through which the Holy Spirit works is "Means of Grace." They are the media through which grace operates and imparts itself. The term is used with some latitude of meaning. Strictly, only the word and the sacraments are the true means of grace, because they are objective and come directly from God to man. To these some have added the spiritual exercises of prayer, of alms-giving, of any service that expresses and promotes the Christian life. But these experiences, however helpful and even necessary, are subjective and the result rather than the means of the Spirit's workings.

It is not unusual or improper to add to the word and the sacraments, or true means of grace, the Church, because Christ has committed the ministry of the means to His Church.

I. THE WORD.

1. The Fitness of the Word

The Bible has been inspired by the Holy Spirit. He is immanent in it and it is His medium still for the communication of the divine message and power. "It is the power of God unto salvation to everyone that believeth" (Rom. 1: 16; I Cor. 1: 18). "It was God's good pleasure through the foolishness of preaching to save them that believe" (I Cor. 1: 21). Christians are said to be "begotten again, not of corruptible seed but of incorruptible, through the word of God which liveth and abideth" (I Pet. 1: 23). That the word is quick and powerful is the testimony of all who have believed it.

It is not at all strange that the Holy Spirit should use the Bible as His medium, for language is the vehicle of thought, the expression of promise and the means of conferring power and authority. The permanency of the written word makes it possible to investigate its meaning and to transmit it without change from language to language and from age to age.

2. The Form of the Word

The word comes to us in a twofold form, law and gospel.

1) THE LAW.

Broadly speaking, the Old Testament is said to contain the law. Nevertheless, there is also much gospel. With the stern requirements come also the offers of pardon and mercy. By the law is not meant so much the ceremonial and civil ordinances of the Jews as the ethical and religious duties of mankind as summed up in the decalogue. Law is needed for the regulation of conduct and the welfare of society; but the ultimate purpose of law in the Old Testament is to reveal sin and to arouse the fears of men and to awaken repentance. The law wounds, but it cannot heal; yet it may lead to the omnipotent healer.

2) THE GOSPEL.

The New Testament contains the fullest expression of "Good Tidings," yet it is not without its law. Even good Christians need directing. Nevertheless the regenerated are no longer in bondage to law, but are under grace. They seek, however, to keep the moral law in the spirit of the "new obedience." The New Testament is as the words signify, a new covenant, wider and fuller and richer than the Old Testament. In it are the record of the historical fulfilment of the gracious promises of the Old Testament and the clearer revelation of God and His plans for mankind.

Through these two forms, law and gospel, the Holy Spirit works for the accomplishment of salvation. The Bible is, therefore, of incalculable importance, if one would know the mind and the message of the Spirit.

II.   THE SACRAMENTS.
1.   The General Doctrine
1) THE WORD SACRAMENT.

The word sacrament is derived from the Latin *sacramentum*, signifying something set apart. The Romans applied the word to money deposited as a pledge in law suits, also to a military oath. Tertullian was the first Christian writer to use the term as a translation of the Greek word *mysterion* or mystery, which described the rites and ceremonies of the Greek Church. Hence, it is apparent how it assumed its present use as including Baptism and the Lord's Supper.

2) THE DEFINITION.

A sacrament is a religious rite instituted by God in which, by the union of the divine word and a visible element, grace is signified, offered and conveyed.

3) THE NUMBER.

If a free use of the word sacrament be allowed, the number of sacraments may be large. The Roman and the Greek churches hold to seven: baptism, confirmation, the eucharist, penance, marriage, ordination, and extreme unction. These mark important times and experiences in life and convey, it is alleged, special grace. The Reformers were at first undecided in regard to the number. For a while "absolution," signifying pardon, was added to the two recognized sacraments, Baptism and the Lord's Supper, which are generally observed by all the larger Christian churches. The Friends do not observe any sacraments, holding that their intent is covered by the spiritual experiences of inward cleansing and communion. A few small sects practice foot-washing as a sacrament. Baptism and the Lord's Supper, however, alone have the sanction of general usage and of divine command.

4) THE RELATION TO THE WORD.

The connection of the sacraments with the word is very intimate. They receive their divine character through the word of divine appointment; and the word of promise connected with them alone gives them validity and efficacy. Augustine defined a sacrament as a "visible word"—the word seen, symbolized, and set forth in an external tangible form. The sacraments effect nothing in man different from that effected by the word. They are simply another way of applying it in a very impressive manner.

A peculiar value is attached to the sacraments in virtue of their individualizing character. They specialize the word in the individual. While this is true also of the word, it is not always apparent. Preaching is the general application of the word; the sacraments are the special application, conveying to each worthy recipient the direct, personal assurance of blessing. In preaching the word is mediated through speech; in the sacraments through water, bread and wine.

5) THEIR PURPOSE.

The sacraments serve a practical purpose in being external signs of union and fellowship in the Church which is "the congregation of believers, in which the gospel is

rightly taught and the sacraments rightly administered."
Under the old dispensation, circumcision and the observance
of certain festivals, especially the Passover, were divinely
ordained as marks of the true Israel.   Under the new, baptism and the Eucharist take their place.

The real purpose of the sacraments is inward and spiritual.   They set forth great truths such as the cleansing and
the sustenance of the soul.   They are symbolical, but not
mere symbols.   They are the means by which divine grace
is actually conveyed to assure and to strengthen believers.
"Here the witness of those who have used these means in
faith and prayer is too explicit to be denied.   Christian
literature is full of testimony as to the strength and inspiration, the comfort and peace which have come to men and
women as they have publicly committed themselves to
Christ's cause in Baptism, and sat down with their fellow
Christians at the table which commemorates His redeeming love" (W. A. Brown's Theol.   P. 407).

6) Their Necessity.

The sacraments are relatively necessary, in the sense
that they have been divinely appointed as the regular and
ordinary means of grace.   Our Lord declared that a man
must be born of water and the Spirit, and He commanded
His disciples to go into all the world to teach and to baptize.   Nevertheless, it stands to reason that God Himself
is not bound by ordinances, and that where their application is impossible man will not be held responsible for the
omission.   Ordinarily therefore, the observance of the
sacraments is not simply a blessed privilege, but also a
solemn obligation.   They are the expression of man's part
of his acceptance of the grace signified and offered, and
also of his profession of faith before the world.

7) Their Efficacy.

(1) The efficacy of the sacraments when observed in
faith is as real and as sure as the promise of God which
they contain.   They are like the word of God which does
"not return unto him void but accomplishes that which he

pleases and it prospers in the thing whereto he sent it" (Is. 55: 11). They are unaffected by the personal character or intention of the ministrants, for happily the grace of God is not defeated by an unworthy instrument. It is a wicked and disturbing limitation which the Council of Trent puts upon the sacraments, when it says, "If anyone shall say that in ministers, whilst they effect and confer the sacraments there is not required the intention at least of doing what the Church does, let him be anathema."

(2) The sacraments are not effective *ex opere operato*, *i.e.*, by the mere performance of the rite without faith. While it is true that their content and validity are not affected by faith, their value to the recipient is dependent on his faith. The sacraments teach that there must be an intelligent appropriation and trustful assent where blessing is expected. This is ultimately true of infant baptism.

8) THEIR ADMINISTRATION.

The administration of the sacraments is not a peculiar function of the ministry. As an appointed officer of the Church it is ordinarily his duty to attend to the ministry of the sacraments as well as of the word, but in extraordinary cases any pious layman may attend to these, provided he observes the divine directions.

III.   BAPTISM.

1.   The General Doctrine

1) DEFINITION.

Christian baptism is an ordinance instituted by Christ in which water is applied, according to the divine command, by an authorized person, to a believer or his children, with the purpose of bringing the baptized into fellowship with the Father and the Son and the Holy Ghost.

2) HISTORY.

The historical antecedents of baptism cannot be fully traced, for baptism is a very ancient rite practiced by Jew and Gentile. Its connection, however, with Jewish and

Johannine baptism is apparent. The Jews not only circumcised but also baptized converts. John's baptism symbolized repentance or the washing away of sin. Christ gave His baptism the new and richer meaning of the medium of fellowship with God.

3) SIGNIFICANCE.
(1) A Sign of the Covenant.

As circumcision is the sign of the old covenant, so baptism is the sign of the new which is sealed with the blood of Christ. Its application indicates that the recipient accepts the covenant with its rich promises of forgiveness and life.

(2) A Means of Grace.

Baptism is not only a sign and seal but also a vehicle of grace. This is true because of its divine appointment and its purpose. Luther says in his small Catechism, "Baptism is not mere water; but it is that water which the ordinance of God enjoins and which is connected with God's word." Concerning its value he says, "It causes the forgiveness of sin, delivers from death and the devil, and gives everlasting salvation to those that believe, as the word and the promise of God declare."

(3) A Badge of Discipleship.

The baptized can properly be regarded as members of the visible Church. Baptism is in a certain sense a rite of initiation. Without it no one can ordinarily claim to be a Christian. It is one of the marks of the Lord Jesus.

(4) An Assurance to the Believer.

"By this means the individual is saved from the great uncertainty, whether he is warranted to regard himself as called and received by Christ into His communion, notwithstanding that redemption advances only by degrees. Whoever is in earnest about his salvation cannot rest satisfied with the universal proclamation of the Gospel. . . . . Nor can he base the certainty of salvation on what is purely inward alone. For what he seeks is reception into the communion of Christ, the historic, objective, but still actively working mediator. This need is satisfied by baptism in Christ's name, which, since it is done by His command, and is without a doubt merely a continuation of His institution, *is to be regarded as His act* in reference to which the Church simply presents itself as His organ" (Dorner, IV. 286).

4) ITS SUBJECTS.

(1) Adult believers are without doubt proper subjects for baptism, provided they thereby agree to unite with the Church where their faith will be fostered and their service find a field. The only question which may arise is in reference to the maturity of the faith which should be expected in the applicant. Ordinarily there is no need of haste in applying the rite; indeed, a period of instruction should generally precede the rite. A ripe Christian experience cannot be demanded; but a right kind of faith, though it be merely like a grain of mustard seed, alone gives proper fitness for the baptism of an adult.

(2) Children of believers are also entitled to baptism, according to the command of Christ. That the first subjects of baptism were necessarily adults is evident. This is still true in foreign mission work. Perhaps most of what is said on baptism in the New Testament is applicable chiefly to adults. But the grounds for infant baptism are so numerous and firm that it has always been practiced by the vast majority of Christian believers. It should not be regarded as something to be tolerated, but as a sacred privilege and duty. Its rejection or neglect does violence to the plan of grace and deprives the child of a great blessing.

2. The Doctrine of Infant Baptism

1) THE WARRANT FOR INFANT BAPTISM

is found in facts like the following:

(1) The Nature of the Family.

In the Bible and in the conception of the Orient, the family is regarded as a unit, with the father as its head.

This is apparent in the covenant made with Abraham. It is unthinkable that either a Jew or a Gentile would embrace a new faith without bringing his family with him. When he was baptised, his family were baptised. This is clearly apparent in the several household baptisms mentioned in the New Testament, of Lydia, Cornelius, Stephanus, and the Phillipian jailor.

(2) The Nature of the Covenant.

Baptism is a sign and a seal of a covenant. Surely no one would deny that children are embraced in this covenant, nor would anyone affirm that it is a covenant empty of meaning. Why then should a child be deprived of the sign of the covenant in which he is a beneficiary? He received a sign under the old covenant, why not under the new? The exclusion of children from the New Testament congregation by Christ or the apostles would certainly have evoked serious opposition on the part of the Jewish converts.

(3) The Nature of the. Church.

a. The Church of both testaments is one Church, bearing the same name, in Hebrew *kahal*, in Greek *ekklesia*. Stephen says that Christ was in the Church (*ekklesia*) in the wilderness.

b. The blessings of the Church under the two covenants are sealed by an external rite. In the Old Testament it was applied to the male only; but in the broader dispensation of the New Testament there is neither male nor female.

c. Baptism took the place of circumcision as plainly as the Lord's Supper took the place of the Passover.

d. The Church is not only organically one, but its ministries and blessings are for the entire life, from childhood on. It extends its sheltering arms to the little ones in the significant rite of baptism. Deprive them of this and there remains no sacrament for childhood.

(4) The History of the Church.

a. The example and teaching of our Lord are the chief warrant for baptism of children whom He took into His arms and pronounced blessed, and whom He commanded to be baptised when He gave His command.

b.   The apostles baptised five family groups.   It would be singular indeed if there were no children among them. It is most probable also that among the thousand baptised in the apostolic Church there were many children.

c.   In the post-apostolic Church we have the testimony of Justin Martyr and Iraneus in the second century, of Origen (born 185) who was baptised in infancy, of Tertullian (160-240) who opposed baptism on erroneous grounds, of Cyprian and the Council of Carthage in the third century.   Thus a long line of witnesses down to the present proves that infant baptism has always been practiced.

2) OBJECTIONS TO INFANT BAPTISM.

(1) There is no authority for it.   The foregoing statements we trust, will offset this objection.   Christ certainly did command all nations to be baptised.   Were we to look in the New Testament for direct commands in every instance there would be no warrant for the Lord's Day, and probably none for allowing women to participate in the Lord's Supper.   But some things are self-evident or the result of plain deduction.

(2) There is no parallel between baptism and circumcision.   The denial of such a parallel is purely dogmatic and without reason.   The endeavor of some of the early Christians to perpetuate circumcision after baptism precipitated a contention between Paul and Peter; and consequently circumcision was abolished.

(3) Infants   cannot   comprehend   or   believe. Neither could they under the old dispensation.   This objection ignores the patent character of a covenant, under which it was not necessary that all should understand or believe.   Unborn generations were to be its beneficiaries and should finally under its beneficent influence come to faith.

In reference to faith as a requirement for baptism, Dr. A. J. Maclean says: "It is objected . . . that faith is required in the New Testament for baptism, and that infants cannot have faith. But this is not a true objection. If an adult coming to baptism has not faith, he puts the barrier of non-faith between God and himself; he cannot be in a neutral condition, but if he does not believe in God, he must disbelieve in Him. With an infant it is not so. In the age of innocence he cannot put a barrier between God and himself, and therefore the fact that he has not yet learned to have an active faith does not preclude the working of the grace within him." (Dictionary of Apostolic Church. I. 136 b.)

3. Sponsors and Confirmation

1) It has been customary from ancient times for pious persons to take the place of parents under various circumstances to answer for the child at its baptism and to make themselves responsible for its Christian instruction. Such persons are known as sponsors. Where parents are living they are the natural sponsors for their children and they should not delegate this duty to others.

2) Confirmation is an ecclesiastical rite which originated in the laying on of hands. The Roman Catholics have exalted it into a sacrament, but without warrant. In the hierarchical churches confirmation is performed by the bishops, who by the laying on of hands strengthen or confirm the catechumen. In other churches it is interpreted as an appropriate rite in which the catechumen publicly confirms the baptismal promises made in his name, and it is also the recognition of the Church that he is worthy to be admitted to the Lord's Table.

4. The Effect of Baptism

1) THE NEGATIVE ASPECTS.

(1) Baptism accomplishes nothing directly for the body; it has no therapeutic value. Opinions to the contrary should be discouraged as being superstitious.

(2) It does not work as an *opus operatum*, conferring grace simply by the performance of an outward act. It is not a mechanical ceremony endued with magical efficacy.

2) The Positive Aspects.

(1) Conditioned on Faith.

Our Lord says, "He that believeth and is baptised shall be saved" (Mk. 16:16), and "whosoever believeth hath eternal life" (Jno. 3:16). Peter on the day of Pentecost said "Repent ye, and be baptized every one of you in the name of Jesus Christ unto the remission of your sins; and ye shall receive the gift of the Holy Ghost, for to you is the promise and to your children" (Acts 2:38, 39). The word preached or contained in baptism must be united by faith to the hearer or subject to be profitable (Heb. 4:2).

(2) A Means of Grace.

Our Lord connects the new birth with baptism, and Paul calls it a "washing of regeneration." Peter says that baptism saves as Noah was saved in the Ark (I Pet. 3:21). Paul also teaches that baptism means death to sin. The doctrine of the sacraments as expounded above is that they act and effect exactly what the word does.

(3) The Effect on an Adult.

a.   To a person seeking salvation baptism is an aid to faith because of the word of promise. To him it becomes a laver of regeneration. To the disconsolate repentant Saul at Damascus, Ananias said, "Arise, and be baptised and wash away thy sins calling upon his name" (Acts 22:16).

b.   To a person regenerated before baptism it becomes a confirmation and a seal of his acceptance with God, and the means and opportunity of accepting God's covenant and making a profession before the Church.

(4) The Effect on the Infant.

a.   Baptism introduces the child into the Church and signifies the acceptance of the divine covenant, and thus brings him into the way of all the blessings therein signified. To those who look upon the baptism of children as being of no value, Paul's estimate of circumcision is commended. "What advantage then hath the Jew, or what

274   A HANDBOOK OF CHRISTIAN THEOLOGY

is the profit of circumcision? Much every way, first of
all that they were entrusted with the oracles of God" (Rom.
3 : 1, 2).

b. It is an assurance of forgiveness. Original sin is
blotted out through Christ's work. As in Adam all die, so
in Christ shall all be made alive. Baptism being the means
of applying salvation to the child, it becomes the assurance
that the child has been incorporated in the Church, which
is the body of Christ.

c. In reference to baptismal regeneration it may be
said :

(a) Baptism is the means of regenerating all who die
in infancy. This does not mean that the unbaptized are
lost, but that the ordinarily appointed way of salvation is
by baptism. The child being in a state of forgiveness
through the love of God in Christ Jesus, it is no doubt rendered fit by the Holy Ghost to enter heaven. Of this state,
however, the infant is not conscious, nor need it be; for an
active faith cannot be looked for in the mind and heart
of an infant.

(b) Baptism always contains the promise of regeneration, for this is the end of all grace. The significance of
baptism must be chiefly spiritual, and to be spiritual it must
have in view the right personal relation to God and hence
to life in the soul. The consciousness of a spiritual life in
the child is realized only with advancing years and with the
growth of faith. It may never be realized because of the
lack of Christian nurture. Normally, however, when a baptized child is properly taught and trained it will finally have
its Pentecost. One of the errors in regard to baptism is to
limit its effect to the moment of administration, whereas it
is the sacrament for the whole life. Luther speaks of
"creeping back" to one's baptism, and realizing even late
in life the power of life-giving word which it enshrines.

5. Mode of Baptism

1) There is no express revelation of the mode of baptism,
whether by sprinkling, pouring or immersion, indicating
that the mode is a matter of indifference. This is illus-

trated by the mode of celebrating the Lord's Supper. At
its institution the participants received the elements in a
reclining posture. But no one now partakes of it thus.
The bodily attitude is entirely secondary; it has nothing
whatever to do with the sacrament. Even so with baptism.
"The conception of the sacrament as an outward rite depending for its efficacy upon the correct mode of its administration has its most conspicuous illustration in the
view that immersion is necessary to a valid performance
of baptism. This is a relic of the legal conception of Christianity which conceives Jesus as the giver of a new law,
rather than as a revealer of a new principle" (W. A.
Brown's Theology. P. 406).

It is singular that the Baptists, who recognize no sacraments at all, should make immersion of such superlative
importance as to form almost the keystone of their system.

2) The word *baptizo* gives no clue to the mode of administration. For this reason the translators of the Bible
into English very wisely simply transliterated it. The
efforts of some Baptists, who translate the word into "dip"
or "immerse" have not succeeded in producing an acceptable version. Such attempts are purely sectarian.

Baptizo and its cognates occur about a hundred times in
the New Testament and while the original meaning of the
word is "to dip," it is used in a broad sense for the rite
regardless of mode, and it is also used in a figurative sense.
In no case does it require the sense of immersion.

3) PARTICULAR CASES.

When particular cases are examined the result is that
the mode is always found to be secondary, and the emphasis
is on the fact itself. The passages which speak of "baptizing in the river Jordan" may be just as truly rendered "at
the Jordan"; and those which speak of going "down into
the water" and coming "up out of the water" may be rendered "down to the water" and "up from the water." The
"much water" at Aenon, where John baptized, really means
"many springs." Water for the drinking of thousands
was more needed than for baptizing, which could be done

with a few bucketfuls. When Philip baptized the eunuch, it is said that "they both went down into the water" and that "they came up out of the water." This certainly cannot mean that Philip went under the water. The plain signification is that they both went down to the edge of the water or stepped into shallow water, and that Philip either poured or sprinkled water on the eunuch. In the case of household baptisms, as well as that of Saul, immersion seems to be clearly impossible.

4) REFERENCES TO BURIAL.

In the passages which give baptism a symbolical meaning (Rom. 6: 3, 4; Col. 2: 12) as a "burial with Christ," immersionists hold that the figure of speech alludes to the mode of immersion. But the passages seem to have reference not to the mode but to the effect of baptism, which stands for purification and separation from sin, and hence death to sin.

5) THE TESTIMONY OF HISTORY.

Historically three modes of baptism can be traced: immersion, affusion or pouring, and aspersion or sprinkling. In the Didache (120-160) we have the most ancient account of baptism, next to the Bible. It directs the minister to baptize in living water, adding "but if thou hast not living water, baptize in other water, and if thou canst not in cold then in warm. But if thou hast neither, pour water upon the head thrice in the name of the Father and the Son and the Holy Ghost." Affusion is akin to sprinkling. Cyprian in the third century defends the latter against immersionists. A painting in the catacombs at Rome represents John pouring water upon the head of Jesus, while both are standing in the Jordan.

Whatever the antiquity of immersion as a mode of baptism it had gone out of usage until its revival in England in 1641. The Anabaptists during the Reformation did not practice immersion. John Smith, the founder of the English Baptist Church, baptized himself, probably by pouring, about 1605.

6) DIFFICULTIES ATTENDING THE IMMERSION THEORY.

   (1) The improbability that 3,000 were immersed on the day of Pentecost.

   (2) The improbability that household baptism, administered in some cases at night, was by immersion.

   (3) The inconvenience and the impossibility in some cases of applying immersion—in sickness, in frigid climates, in the absence of pools, etc.

   (4) The stress upon the external and accidental.

   (5) The reversal of the Scriptural idea of the application of water to a person. Immersion is the application of the person to water.

7) THE PROPRIETY OF SPRINKLING.

(1) It corresponds with the symbolic acts of the Old Testament such as the sprinkling of blood and of oil (Ex. 24: 8; 29: 21), and of the water of purification (Num. 8:7).

(2) It fulfills the Old Testament prophecies of the pouring out of the Spirit (Is. 32: 15; Joel 2: 28), and of the sprinkling of many nations (Is. 52: 15).

(3) It meets all the conditions of a divine rite or medium of blessing.

(4) It is practicable always and everywhere.

(5) It has the sanction of the oldest tradition, and of the consciousness of its propriety of the great majority of Christians.

IV. THE LORD'S SUPPER.

1. Its Institution

The Lord's Supper was instituted by Christ Himself at the close of the paschal meal on the night of His betrayal. That it was intended to be a perpetual ordinance is evident from the injunction, "this do in remembrance of me" (Lk. 22: 19). Paul also says, "For as often as ye eat this bread and drink this cup, ye proclaim the Lord's death till he come" (I Cor. 11: 26). The Church has observed the Eucharist from the beginning.

2. Its Definition

The Lord's Supper is a sacrament instituted by Christ in which under the form of bread and wine, consecrated by the words of institution, He gives the believer His body and His blood.

3. Its Names

This sacrament is called in Scripture "The Lord's Supper," the "Table of the Lord," "The Communion of the body and the blood of Christ." It is also spoken of in religious literature as the Sacrament of the Altar, the Sacrament, the Eucharist, and also Communion.

4. Its Constituents

1) THE EXTERNAL ELEMENTS.

Our Lord used the unleavened bread of the Passover, and also the wine, which was the fruit of the vine mingled with water. The wafer is a desirable and convenient form of bread, resembling the bread used at the Passover. The wine should be grape juice, fermented or unfermented. The cup should be the "common" or the "individual" cup. These matters cannot be decided dogmatically and have nothing to do with the essence of the sacrament. Change in usage should be made in a congregation only with the consent of the people.

2) THE WORD.

The principal part of the sacrament is the word of God from which alone it derives authority and efficacy. Without the use of the words of institution there is no sacrament, and these also form the true and only consecration of the elements. While prayer is proper, it adds nothing to the consecration, for the supper is God's gift to men.

3) THE PARTAKING.

There is no sacrament where there is no partaking. It is incomplete until partaken of, just as the word has no efficacy apart from the hearer.   After the sacramental action ceases the elements are only bread and wine without sacramental virtue.

5. Its Administration

1) THE MINISTRANT.

The ministrant of the supper should ordinarily be a duly appointed minister of the Church, who may be assisted by devout members, usually officers of the Church.   There seems to be little call for purely lay administration.

2) THE COMMUNICANTS.

The communicants are the baptized and confirmed members of the congregation in good standing.   This includes not only the strong, but also the weak and the fearful, who desire to be strengthened.   This excludes the unbaptized, the indifferent, the hypocritical and the openly wicked. The officers of the congregation including the pastor should encourage the former and exclude the latter.   Communicants should examine themselves conscientiously, but not morbidly.   To this end the Church has appointed a preparatory service; and the pastor should be always ready to counsel the weak.

6. Its Design

1) TO BE A MEMORIAL OF CHRIST.

As the passover was a reminder of a temporal deliverance, so the supper which superseded it is a perpetual remembrance of the person and work of Christ, especially of His death.   Nothing else could more fittingly and impressively preserve the story of our Lord's love and sacrifice.

2) TO BE A SEAL OF CHRIST'S COVENANT.

"This cup is the new covenant in my blood, even that which is poured out for you" (Lk. 22: 20).   Christ's covenant was sealed with blood, even as solemn covenants between men were often signed with pens dipped in their own blood.   The figure of a blood covenant is most realistic and assuring.   Jesus has pledged His life for our redemption.

3) To be a Means of Grace.

The Lord's Supper becomes a vehicle of divine grace to the believer, conveying to him the assurance of pardon and strength to live a Christian life. It brings him into fellowship with Christ, of whose body he eats and of whose blood he drinks. He becomes a partaker of the divine nature. It is the experience of devout communicants that in the supper they receive new revelations of Christ's love and power.

4) To be a Confession.

In the holy supper the communicant confesses Christ and makes an open profession before the world that he is a Christian. The simple act speaks more loudly than words and proclaims the faith of the communicant.

5) To be a Bond of Fellowship.

The Lord's Supper is not only a communion with Christ but also with His people. They constitute the family of God, and their communing together is an expression of a common interest and blessed fellowship.

7. The Doctrinal Construction

1) By Romanists.

(1) The Roman Catholic Church teaches that the elements, bread and wine, are actually changed by the act of consecration, with the intention of the priest, into the body and blood of Christ. This doctrine is known as that of transubstantiation. It is without ground in reason or Scripture.

(2) The Roman Catholic Church also holds that in the Mass the priests actually offer a sacrifice. "The sacrifice of the Mass is identical with that of the Cross," says Cardinal Gibbons, "both having the same victim and high priest, Jesus Christ."

(3) It also teaches that the cup must not be given to the laity, on the plea that it would be difficult to secure enough of pure wine, that it is objectionable for many to use one cup, and especially that there is great danger of

spilling a portion of the wine and thus profaning the blood of Christ. They justify the withholding of the cup by the doctrine of concomittance, which means that as the body contains the blood, so the wafer must also contain the blood.

(4) It also teaches that the consecrated elements which remain after the celebration of the supper continue to be the sacrament. These several distinct points of difference from the Protestant view are so transparently erroneous that they need no answer.

2) By Zwinglians.

Zwingli taught that the Lord's Supper was a purely memorial and symbolical ordinance. It is not a means of grace like the word. This lax view of the supper has no Scripture basis and little confessional authority. Nevertheless, it is the view of some modern churches and of no small number of individuals.

3) By Calvinists.

Calvin taught that Christ really gives Himself in the supper in a purely spiritual and transcendental manner. "This is my body" and "this is my blood" must be understood in a figurative sense only. His body is local in heaven and cannot, therefore, be on earth. Hence, in the Lord's Supper, the communicant is lifted up to heaven and there receives Christ.

4) By Lutherans.

(1) Errors Repudiated.

The Lutheran Church denies and abhors the Romish doctrine of transubstantiation. It also repudiates the doctrine of consubstantiation, which is that the body and blood of Christ unite with the bread and wine, forming a third substance. It teaches that there is absolutely no change in the elements.

(2) Confessional Statements.

The Augsburg Confession (Art. X) says: "Of the Supper of the Lord, they teach that the body and blood of Christ are truly present, and are distributed to those who eat in the Supper of the Lord."

The Formula of Concord teaches that on account of the indivisible unity of Christ's person He is present as the divine human Savior wherever He pleases or promises to be, and that in virtue of a supernatural union (called a sacramental union) of His body and blood with the bread and wine, the communicant receives Him through faith in a heavenly manner.

(3) Interpretation.

The Lutheran doctrine of the Lord's Supper is that the undivided Christ is really and substantially present in the holy supper. His words are to be understood literally and not figuratively. His body and blood are His glorified body and are received in faith. How Christ unites His body and blood with earthly elements we cannot explain any more than we can explain His incarnation. They are mysteries, yet also blessed facts to be received with a joyful faith.

The Lutheran professes to rest his faith on the divine promises, regardless of physical and philosophical objection. Perhaps those who have disputed his belief have betrayed him at times into an attempted explanation of what he holds to be inexplicable. Luther himself was immovable in his faith, though he realized the price it cost him. He might have purchased union among Protestants by accepting a lower view, but he was bound by conscience to maintain his conviction.

(4) The teaching of the Formula of Concord that the unworthy communicant also receives the Lord's body, it seems to us, must be explained by saying that he receives Christ in the supper just as he receives Him in preaching, namely, to his condemnation. In neither case is there the blessed experience of salvation and fellowship with Christ.

V.   THE CHURCH.

The organ for the application of the word and the sacraments is the Church.

1. Its Nature

1) DEFINITION.

The Church is the congregation of saints, in which the gospel is rightly taught and the sacraments rightly administered. (Aug. Conf., Art. VII.) This definition is fairly comprehensive, including an organized society or congregation, made up of professing Christians with a definite purpose and distinct marks—teaching the gospel and administering the sacraments.

2) ITS DESIGNATION.

The New Testament name of the Church is the "assembly" (*ekklesia*) "called out" from the world. This corresponds with the Hebrew *kahal*. The word translated synagogue is *edhah*, which has the idea of an organized body. In the New Testament the Church is identified with the "saints," "the elect," etc.

3) ITS DISTINCTIONS.

(1) The word church is applied to the local congregation as well as to groups of churches in a town, province or nation, to a denomination, and even to buildings where services are held.

(2) The word is sometimes used synonymously with the term the "kingdom of God," but the latter is really a broader term, including God's providence in all departments of human life.

(3) The Church is also spoken of as militant and as triumphant, referring to its struggles here and its final victory yonder.

(4) The Church is thought of also as visible and invisible. As visible the Church has an outward organization with a recorded membership: as invisible it embraces all true believers inside and outside of the organized body. These distinctions should not be unduly emphasized, for it is a high privilege to be enrolled among the people of God. There is danger of promoting fanaticism in over-emphasizing the invisibility of the Church.

2. Its Origin

The Church is a divine institution, founded in Paradise, fostered through the Abrahamic and Mosaic eras, reaching its new birth on the day of Pentecost, working toward its consummation under the direction of the Holy Spirit, and reaching its glorification at the end of the world. The Church is the peculiar property of the Lord Jesus. He said, "upon this rock I will build my church." He is called also the Head of the Church (Mt. 16: 18).

3. Its Marks

The Nicene Creed contains the confession, "I believe One, Holy, Catholic, and Apostolic Church." Unity, holiness, catholicity, and apostolicity are here fittingly recognized as distinct marks of the Church.

1) UNITY.

The unity of the church exists now among all Christians. It is a distinct characteristic of the Church, which is one, not many. Paul says, "There is one body and one spirit, even as also ye were called in one hope of your calling: one Lord, one faith, one baptism, one God and Father of all, who is over all and through all and in all" (Eph. 4: 4-6). Unity, however, is not synonymous with external union. Whether such a union will ever be attained is questionable, even if it were desirable. The numerous divisions into sects, however, cannot be justified from any sensible point of view. They are not only useless but harmful. In many cases separations have occurred without any reasonable excuse. Happily, there is a movement of approach among the several religious bodies. Union cannot be accomplished at the expense of principle and conviction, but co-operation in making the world more Christian ought not to wait upon organic union.

2) HOLINESS.

As God is holy, His family must be holy also. It would be a contradiction to speak of an unholy Church. In so far as it is corrupt, without faith and without good works, it ceases to be the Church of God. The works of the flesh, the propensities of selfishness, and conformity to the low standards and usages of "the world," destroy all holiness and incur divine displeasure. The Church is not a transcendental society, but a religious body characterized by ethical conformity with the highest ideals.

3) CATHOLICITY.

The mark of catholicity implies the possession of "characteristics which make it capable of being a universal religion, adapted to all classes of men, in all parts of the world and throughout all time." Christianity alone meets this just and lofty standard. Any church or denomination which fails to hold this ideal of universal adaptation, and which lacks the missionary spirit is unworthy of the name.

4) APOSTOLICITY.

A church is apostolic in so far as it is true to the doctrine, worship, and discipline committed to the apostles by our Lord and transmitted through the Scriptures. It is by the latter that apostolicity must be judged and not by unsupported traditions and assumptions which are often invoked to support the papacy, so called "apostolic succession," and the like. Of course discrimination must be employed in separating what was purely temporal and local from the abiding fundamental facts and principles. A congregation which departs from apostolic Christianity cannot claim to be a Christian church.

4. Its Design

In general, the design of the Church is to carry on the revealing and the redeeming work of its Founder. This work has many features. The chief functions, however, may be summarized as those of edification and of extension. The former refers to those persons already in the fold; the latter to those outside of it.

1) EDIFICATION.
(1) Instruction.

The members of the Church need constant instruction, for faith and knowledge go hand in hand. Fundamental among the functions of the Church are preaching and teaching. Our Master was pre-eminently a preacher and a teacher. Where instruction is neglected, ignorance, indifference and superstition prevail.

There should also be provision for the religious education of the children in the community under the supervision of the Church. Purely secular training does not satisfy the soul of the child or prepare it for the responsibilities of life.

It is needful also for the maintenance of purity of doctrine and sound learning in the realm of religion that the Church provide its own schools, such as colleges and seminaries in which the ministers may be trained.

(2) Worship.

Edification includes worship and proper provision for it and opportunity for its exercise. Hence the Church must arrange for the holding of stated services and provide suitable hymns, liturgies and other devotional literature. It should also foster family worship. No church can attain its high aim unless there be a deeply devotional and worshipful spirit.

(3) Discipline.

No society can exist without safeguards and penalties. As even the best of men may stray from the path of truth and virtue, the Church has found it necessary to adopt certain religious and moral standards for its own preservation. The persistently wicked must be eliminated and the penitents restored. Persuasion, admonition and penalty are effective only in a society where discipline is recognized and where there is adequate moral sense to maintain it.

(4) The Social Life.

Man is a social being and hence cannot reach his true end in isolation. The hermit and the monk show how disastrous isolation is to the human spirit; and mysticism demonstrates the folly of extreme "other worldliness." The Church is a society or community in which "the lonely gain the sense of companionship, the discouraged new faith and hope, the perplexed fresh insight into duty, the weary renewed strength."

To what extent the church should go beyond the purely religious sphere is a question much discussed. Shall the church become "institutional"? Does it fall within its province to provide a playhouse and entertainment for its people? To a certain extent the social cravings must be satisfied. Shall congregations endeavor to provide social life, or shall it be left to community associations?

It is manifestly impossible for every congregation to meet the cost involved in reading-rooms, gymnasiums, and the like. This is not the place to discuss this matter fully. It is the function of the Church to leaven with the Christian spirit all pleasure, all business, all charities, the whole life, and then to allow them to be directed through individual or corporate enterprises. At all events, the ministry of the word dare not be burdened with mere social administration.

2) EXTENSION.

The second general function of the Church is extension. The purposes of our Lord include the evangelization of the world, and He has appointed His Church as His agent. The world, which is the field of Christian work, extends from the doors of the Church to the ends of the earth. The missionary idea reflects the divine statesmanship of our Lord, and its realization demands the best thought and the richest resources of the Church. The preaching of the word and all that is involved in it is the great business of the Church.

5. Its Ministry

In order that there may be thoroughness in the application of the means of grace, there must be trained agents, who can devote all their time and energy to the great work.

1) THE ORIGIN.

In Old Testament times God instituted the ministry of priests and prophets. When our Lord came, He appointed apostles to proclaim His word, and thus began the Christian ministry.

2) THE PERPETUATION.

The perpetuation of the ministry is one of the chief concerns of the Church, and it should constantly utter the call to the young people, and especially pray the Lord of the harvest that He will thrust more laborers into the harvest.

3) THE NATURE.

The ministry is an "office," not "an order" distinct in its essential character from the laity. It is composed of persons chosen for their fitness and trained for special work, but no peculiar sanctity is attached to the ministry, as Rome teaches.

In reference to the polity of the church, with which the ministry is connected, we are of the opinion that no form of church government has been divinely appointed. All efforts to enforce one or another form have failed. If we may interpret providence by history, democratic forms of government in Church and State are indicated.

PART V

ESCHATOLOGY

THE DOCTRINE OF LAST THINGS

Introduction

The above title is venerable, but somewhat misleading. A better name would be the consummation. There is a tendency to under-estimate this division of theology because of its alleged vagueness, lack of practical value, and speculative character. Such an objection is not well grounded and will not prevent men from thinking about the future, and perhaps from holding unreasonable opinions. There are certain simple postulates that underlie a serious consideration of the future. The first is that the human race with its great past and stirring present will have a future which is necessarily conditioned on the past and present. Secondly, it must be assumed that the purposes of God have a goal, worthy of Himself and of creatures made in His own image. The incompleteness of life on earth seems to demand some kind of a definite consummation.

Christian theology endeavors to answer the questions that arise in reference to life after death. It draws its knowledge on this subject, as on all others within its domain, chiefly from the Bible. It also draws conclusions in harmony with the Scriptures from the consciousness of the people of God. It is true that many problems must wait for answer in the life beyond, because our eyes are holden and the Scriptures are reticent concerning the details of the future life. But enough is revealed to give the believer confidence in the persistence of the soul.

I. DEATH.

1. Its Nature

Death is more than the cessation of life, for life persists after death, as we have elsewhere shown. It is the temporary dissolution of the body and the soul, the earthly psychic body going into the grave, and the soul into the spirit world. Death marks a change in environment, a translation. But the person remains undestroyed. There is no annihilation.

2. Its Cause

The cause of death is sin, whose wages is death. The transgression of law brings merited penalty. However graciously God has overruled death, it carries in it a sting.

3. Its Effect

Death is simply a terminus, it affects no change in the moral character of men, any more than a removal from place to place in this world.

Death derives its significance chiefly from the fact that it emphasizes the settlement of the destiny of men. It marks the end of man's probation, an earthly education. However short the natural life may be it is no doubt long enough for the unerring Judge to assign to each his place on the other side. There is no teaching in Scriptures to lead us to believe in future probation; and there is nothing in the nature of the case to demand it. God has made ample provision for all in this life. Those who have heard the gospel will be judged according to it. Those who have failed to receive it will be dealt with according to the light which they have had (Rom. 2: 11-16).

II.　THE INTERMEDIATE STATE.

1. Its Character

The Scriptures teach that the souls of the righteous are blessed and in a heavenly state immediately after death, and that the souls of the wicked are unhappy and in a state of pain. Nevertheless the departed have not reached a final state until after the resurrection and the judgment. This intermediate state or realm of the dead is presupposed by Christ in the parable of Dives and Lazarus. The former is in a place of torment; the latter is in Paradise.

Whatever indefiniteness may be associated with the Hebrew conception of Sheol, it is not conceived of as a place of unconsciousness, soul-sleeping or uncertainty. Abraham, Moses, and Elijah are spoken of in the New Testament as alive and interested in redemption.

Passages which affirm that "in death there is no remembrance of God" (Ps. 6: 5) are to be interpreted to mean that probation is ended. When Paul speaks of those who are "asleep in Jesus" he refers to the rest which they are enjoying after life's toil.

2. Purgatory

The Roman Catholic Church teaches that "there exists in the next life a middle state of temporary punishment allotted to those who have died in venial sin, or who have not satisfied the justice of God for sins already forgiven. It also teaches that, although the souls consigned to this intermediate state, commonly called purgatory, cannot help themselves, they may be aided by the suffrages of the faithful on earth" (The Faith of Our Fathers. Cardinal Gibbons).

This doctrine is based chiefly upon a passage in II Maccabees (12:43-46), an apocryphal book. Roman Catholics also cite our Lord's words in reference to baptism with fire, and to the forgiveness of sin except that against the Holy Ghost, and also Malachi's words in reference to the refiner (Mt. 3: 11; 12:32; Mal. 3:3; I Cor. 3:15; I Pet. 3: 19-20). These and similar passages do not, according to Protestant teaching, have the remotest reference to a so-called purgatory.

This false doctrine must be rejected because: 1) it is without proof in Scripture or reason; 2) it is derogatory to the complete satisfaction made by Christ; 3) it contradicts the teaching of justification by faith; and 4) it is the source of unspeakable evil, as illustrated by the history of indulgences. Luther called the doctrine "a satanic delusion."

III. THE PAROUSIA.

Our Lord undoubtedly promised "to come again." In what sense He meant this is a subject of much controversy. As His return was to the first disciples a matter of prophecy, which they in some cases misinterpreted, we should be slow in dogmatizing concerning this important matter

The history of the Church bears witness to the harm which a delusion concerning the second Advent may occasion. In spite of the warnings of the past, errors still persist and these should be understood and avoided.

1. Its Certainty

Our Lord speaks of His coming in several senses. He assures His disciples that He will come again through the Resurrection, and that He will meet them in Galilee. He also speaks of a coming to them in a new and spiritual fellowship (Jno. 14:18-24), and also to receive them unto Himself at death (Jno. 14:2, 3). He declares that He will come in temporal judgment upon Jerusalem (Mt. 24; Mk. 13). Some have wrongly concluded that these comings include the entire action and purpose of Christ.

Over against this we have the clear testimony that the disciples looked for His visible, personal manifestation in what they called the parousia, the sudden presence of Christ, His second coming at the end of the age. The clearest exposition of this coming occurs in Paul's Epistles to the Thessalonians.

2. Its Characteristics

1) THE TIME.

The absolute time of the parousia is nowhere revealed, and it is futile to fix any positive date. The relative time, however, is revealed. It is to take place at the end of the world, preceding the resurrection and the final judgment. We may rest in this and not indulge in prophecy. Since the days of the apostles men have been carried away by a passion to fix the day of our Lord's return. They have not heeded the failure and folly of those who have preceded them, but repeat them over and over.

2) THE MANNER.

The second coming is represented in the most striking and figurative language. It will arrive as did the flood in the time of Noah, and the destruction of Sodom in the days of Lot. It will be unannounced, like a thief in the night or the return of the absent householder. There will be divers and terrible convulsions of nature. Our Lord will appear in great glory, accompanied by a host of angels. There will be the voice of the archangel and the sound of a trumpet announcing His presence. These realistic representations convey a correct impression of the sudden, glorious and final coming of Christ.

3) THE SIGNIFICANCE.

The purpose of the parousia is the completion of Christ's earthly redemptive work and the conclusion of the present dispensation. Whatever may be indistinct in the doctrine, the propriety of such a consummation must be apparent. He who once came as a man in Bethlehem in circumstances of deep humility may be expected to come again as king of glory.

4) THE PREMILLENIAL VIEW.

The doctrine of the Church, as above stated in reference to the time of the second advent, is that it will occur at the end of the world. Over against this there is a small minority of Christians who hold that it will take place a millenium or a thousand years before the end. They have invented a varied and wonderful program, the outline of which follows.

(1) The Doctrine.

a.   The world is continually growing worse and will continue to do so until Christ comes.

b.   The coming of Christ is imminent; it may occur at any time.

c.   At His coming Christ will raise the sainted dead, transform the saints living on earth and catch them up into the air. This is designated as the "rapture."

d.   A great tribulation will follow Christ's coming, when He will take terrible vengeance upon the wicked, especially upon apostate Israel, with a view of converting the world. The converted Jews will then be restored to Palestine.

e.   At the close of "the tribulation" Christ and the saints in "rapture" will return to earth. This is called the "revelation."

f.   Christ will then bind Satan and cast him into the abyss and overthrow all wickedness on earth.

g.   Christ will set up an earthly kingdom with Jerusalem as a magnificent capital, restore the ancient sacrifices, and reign over the world for a thousand years.

h.   At the close of the millenium Satan will be loosed for a short time, violence and wickedness will break out and then will follow the resurrection of the wicked and the final judgment.

(2) The Fallacy.

Premillenarianism is rejected by the Church in general on the following grounds.

a.   It is pessimistic.   It is blind to the patent fact that the world is growing better, in spite of wickedness. The world is now in the dawn of a new era of civilization, justice and love.   Missionary activity is growing every day.

b.   It is Judaistic.   Its whole conception of Christ's kingdom is according to the Jewish notion of an earthly kingdom, local and temporal.   History and reason show that the kingdom is one of principle in the hearts of men, embracing all organizations and governments.

c.   It is at variance with Christ's plans.   Our Lord instituted the Church and the means of grace as instruments for the salvation of men.   The world is to be converted by the preaching of the gospel and not by violent judgments.   It is derogatory to Jesus Christ to predicate failure of His spirit and methods.   No one has ever been converted by violence and no one ever will be.

d.   Its history condemns it.   From Montanus in the second century to the present, second adventism has been a source of discord and delusion.   It has diverted people from simple every-day duties to engage in useless speculation as to dates and signs of our Lord's coming.   It has led to fanaticism, paralyzed normal activity in churches, and introduced a divisive spirit.

e.   It is unscriptural.   The fatal objection to premillenarianism is that it has no adequate Scriptural ground.   It rests largely upon a misinterpretation of a single passage in the most obscure book in the New Testament, namely, Revelation 20: 4-6. The language is highly figurative and with our present knowledge difficult of interpretation. The principle that obscure passages should be explained in the light of those that are plain, must be applied here. As our Lord's return is connected elsewhere with the resurrection and the final judgment, the passage in question cannot contradict this fact. The thousand year period mentioned in Revelation must mean something other than an interval between the parousia and the end. It is doubtful whether there is any reference at all to the parousia. The preceding chapters picture the progress of the conquering Christ. The thousand years are a period of triumph. The binding of Satan is the gradual narrowing of his power. Restrictions of the evil of sin, of intemperance, slavery, tyranny, superstition, idolatry, are among the defeats of Satan. The resurrection mentioned is probably that of the revival of the spirit of heroism and martyrdom. If the "millenium" means anything to us it is a picture of continued progress in the kingdom of Christ preceding His coming.

IV. THE RESURRECTION.

1. The Fact

The first great event following the parousia is the resurrection. "For the Lord himself shall descend from heaven with a shout, with the voice of the archangel and with the trump of God, and the dead in Christ shall rise first" (I Thess. 4: 16).

The doctrine of the resurrection, like many other truths is more clearly taught in the New Testament than in the Old. However, there are allusions to it in the latter, particularly in the passages which speak of man's future life (Ps. 16: 11; 17: 15; 49: 15; 73: 24. Job 14: 1-15; 19: 25-29). Isaiah says, "Thy dead shall live; my dead bodies shall arise" (26: 19). Ezekiel 37 pictures a valley full of dry bones which came to life at the voice of prophecy. Daniel says (12: 2), "many of them that sleep in the dust of the earth shall awake, some to everlasting life, and some to shame and everlasting contempt."

A belief in the resurrection was the common doctrine of the Jews in the time of Christ; the Sadducees alone denied it. Martha speaks of the resurrection at the last day as an accepted fact. Christ's own resurrection dispelled all doubt and became the theme of apostolic preaching. We do not thoroughly understand the resurrection, for it is a mystery, but the New Testament is explicit in teaching it.

2. The Nature

1) NEGATIVELY.

By the resurrection is not meant the immortality of the soul, a matter which we have already considered and of which there can be no doubt. Resurrection and immortality are closely connected, but they are not identical.

Neither does resurrection confer upon man a spiritual body in the sense of a body made of spirit, for this is a contradiction of terms. When the Scripture speaks of a spiritual or pneumatic body it uses this language to distinguish it from the natural or psychic body. The spiritual body is one suited to a purified spiritual condition. The new body is still designated by the term *soma*.

2) POSITIVELY.

The resurrection is the restoration of the whole man who goes into dissolution at death. It is not simply the replacing of the body, but the reunion of the two parts which make up the man. It is plainly declared that "if the Spirit of him that raised up Jesus from the dead dwelleth in you, he that raised up Christ Jesus from the dead shall give life also to your mortal bodies, through his spirit that dwelleth in you" (Rom. 8: 11). The Christian is also said to wait for the redemption of the body (Rom. 8: 23). The resurrection, therefore, embraces the replacement of the body lost in death. Man is not normal without a body; it was provided before he became a living soul. It constitutes an essential part of his nature. It is the organism through which he acts. Our Lord in becoming man took a human nature, body and soul, and when He arose from the dead He came forth with His body glorified and thus also He ascended to heaven. The teachings of Paul become meaningless if the idea of a bodily resurrection be eliminated.

When man is redeemed his body and soul share in the redemption. As the body was the instrument of sin as the organism of the soul, man's restoration would be incomplete without the redemption of the body as the organ of the soul in a higher life.

3. The Scripture Details

1) THE SUBJECTS.

It is not simply the good that will be raised, as the Jews thought, but "all that are in the tombs shall hear his voice and shall come forth: they that have done good unto the resurrection of life; they that have done evil unto the resurrection of judgment" (Jno. 5: 28, 29).

2) THE AUTHOR.

The resurrection is ascribed to each person of the Trinity, but particularly to Christ, who says, "I will raise him up at the last day" (Jno. 6: 40).

3) THE TIME.

The resurrection will occur on the last day following the second advent and preceding the Judgment (Jno. 2: 21; 6: 39, 40; 11: 24. I Thess. 4: 15).

4) THE MANNER.

The manner is described in highly figurative language. The dead are said to be raised by Christ's voice and by the voice of the archangel and the trump of God. It is beyond our present apprehension to know how the Lord will accomplish the resurrection. It is one of the mysteries of His inscrutable will. Yet this in no sense denies or disproves the divine power. He who made man can remake him in His own time and way.

5) THE BODY.

It is "spiritual," adapted to the spirit state. It is "immortal," for it is raised in incorruption. It is "glorious," for it is raised in glory. It is "perfect," for it is raised in power. These things Paul writes (I Cor. 15) of the resurrection of the saints. He is not particularly concerned about the wicked. That the wicked are raised is clearly affirmed and is in accord with the idea that having sinned in the body, the wicked suffer in the body.

4. Relation Between the Natural and Spiritual Bodies

1) IDENTITY.

The identity of the two is taught and demanded. Man will certainly not be changed so as to lose his personal likeness. He will always be himself and not another. This follows from the nature of personality, and from the illustrations of the Bible. Moses and Elijah retained their individuality on the Mount of Transfiguration. By identity, however, is not meant unchanged sameness, such as an inorganic substance possesses. We do not lose our physical identity in this life, though the substance of our bodies is in perpetual flux. We are still the same beings, with the same bodies. So we may say that in the future life there will remain an identity with our earthly life and with body and soul which will be peculiarly our own and will distinguish us one from another.

To what extent the substance of the earthly body shall enter into the heavenly no man can tell. It is not impossible for God to refine and glorify some remnant of the old and make out of it the new. He once took the common earth and fashioned it into a human form of marvelous grace and power, and He may again take somewhat of that which is earthly and endow it with still greater glory. While we may not be able to speak with assurance of the process, we are justified in saying that the spiritual body is conditioned by the body of the grave.

2) FALSE THEORIES.

It has been held by some that connected with the natural body is an indestructible germ which produces a new body. But of this there is neither Scriptural nor scientific evidence. It is a mere theory.

Swedenborgians teach that man has two bodies, an external body and an invisible body. The latter envelopes the former, which perishes in the grave. The invisible then becomes the true glorified body.

It has also been maintained after a gross fashion that every particle of the old body will enter into the new, limb coming to limb, though dismembered for centuries.

None of these theories is tenable; all are totally destitute of proof, unphilosophical and unreasonable.

V. THE JUDGMENT.

1. The Fact

It is the universal faith of the Church that after the general resurrection there will occur the general judgment. This is disputed by some who hold that judgment is progressive, taking place all the time and everywhere. Thus Schiller said, "Die Weltgeschichte ist das Weltgewicht." Some hold that the judgment takes place at death. It cannot be denied that there is some foundation for these opinions, for the work of Christ and the preaching of the gospel naturally involve discriminations or judgments. The saving of the believer and the condemnation of the unbeliever imply this. Nor can there be any doubt that death marks the assignment of each person to his own place.

Nevertheless, the fitness of a final judgment at the end of the world and after the resurrection seems almost self-evident. There must be a judgment upon the whole man, body and soul, and an assignment of destiny. The long postponement may be explained by the fact that the fruits of the earthly life maturing slowly, evil and good influences continue long after death of those whom they precede. There may be, therefore, propriety in dealing with them when men themselves see and acknowledge their character. After the manner of earthly courts it would seem proper also that even the guilty who are already in bonds should receive a formal trial. The idea of a final judgment appeals to most men as reasonable, and it certainly serves a high ethical end.

2. Proof of a Final Judgment

A particular day is mentioned: "It shall be more tolerable for the land of Sodom in the day of judgment than for thee" (Mt. 11: 24). "The word that I have spoken, the same shall judge him in the last day" (Jno. 12: 48). "God hath appointed a day in which he shall judge the world in righteousness" (Acts 17: 31). Paul speaks of "the day of wrath and revelation of the righteous judgment of God" (Rom. 2: 5). The connection indicates that a particular and limited period is meant by the word "day," though not necessarily only twenty-four hours.

The revelation of the judgment is in connection with Christ's second advent and the resurrection.   This is taught in the parable of the wheat and the tares (Mt. 13: 37-43). Christ himself declares that "the Son of man shall come in the glory of the Father with his angels; and then shall he render unto every man according to his deeds" (Mt. 16: 27).   In His final disclosure recorded in Mt. 24: 25, Jesus repeatedly affirms a last and general judgment and even gives specific details thereof.

3.   The Judge

Christ is the judge of the quick and dead, for "the Father judgeth no man; but hath committed all judgment unto the Son; that all men shall honor the Son even as they honor the Father" (Jno. 5: 22-25). "God hath appointed a day in which he will judge the world in righteousness, by the man whom he hath ordained, whereof he hath given assurance unto all men, in that he hath raised him from the dead." (Acts 17: 31; II Cor. 5: 10; Matt. 25: 23; Lk. 13: 27).

When Christ says, "I judge no man" and "I come not to judge the world but to save the world" He evidently means that His primary purpose in coming into the world was not judgment, but redemption.   His messianic mission, however, involves judgment.

Some passages seem to place judgment in the hands of the sinner in an automatic manner.   "If a man hear my sayings and keep them not, the word that I spake the same shall judge him in the last day" (Jno. 12: 47, 48).   Back

of all law is personality and an ethical idea. Jesus has set
the standard and he decides whether men have lived up
to it.

4. The Subjects

"The living and the dead," "all nations" great and small
are said to appear before the Judge. Hence there is to
be a universal judgment. Even the fallen angels shall be
judged, as they seem to anticipate, for at Gadara they
cried out, "Art thou come hither to torment us before the
time?" (Mt. 8:29). Peter writes that the angels who sinned
are "reserved unto judgment" (II Pet. 2:4).

When our Lord says about the believer that he "hath
eternal life and cometh not into judgment" (Jno. 5:24),
the word judgment seems to mean condemnation. John declares that those who have "love made perfect" shall "have
boldness in the day of judgment" (I Jno. 4:17). The day
of judgment for those who are in Christ Jesus means that
they will be acquitted, justified and vindicated because they
have the righteousness of Christ.

5. The Ground

The "deeds done in the body" are the matter of judgment. "Deeds" is the concrete expression of the earthly
life in which act and motive are blended. There is no reason to suppose that outward acts rather than the inner
attitude of the soul are meant. To the Jews who asked
Jesus what they must do that they might work the works
of God He replied, "This is the work of God that ye believe on him whom he hath sent" (Jno. 6:29).

The judgment is represented as being minute and comprehensive, including not only deeds but thoughts and
words. The latter show the trend of life and are indic-
ative of character.

6. The Criteria

There must be a standard of judgment by which men
are tried, and this must be known to those on trial. Hence
in the graphic language of Scripture, it is said "books"
were opened (Rev. 20:12). Among these books are the
Bible, the book of God's remembrance, conscience, books

that men have written and read, church books, day books and ledgers—in short, the record of the life. There is also the Lamb's book of life with the names of the faithful. Men will be judged in the light of their opportunities.

7. The Form

The figurative language of the Bible represents the judgment after the manner of a human court. The august judge is seated upon a splendid throne, surrounded by the angelic host. Before Him are gathered the vast multitudes of the human race and of the fallen angels. The judgment proceeds in an orderly, impartial manner and an irrevocable verdict is reached in accordance with the facts and the evidence.

VI. RETRIBUTION.

The judge at last pronounces a sentence from which there is no appeal and which goes into effect at once and forever. Forever! "And he shall separate one from another as the shepherd separateth the sheep from the goats; and he shall set the sheep on his right hand, but the goats on his left. Then shall the King say unto them on his right hand, Come, ye blessed of my Father inherit the kingdom prepared for you from the foundation of the world. Then shall he say also unto them on the left hand, Depart from me, ye cursed, into the eternal fire which is prepared for the devil and his angels" (Mt. 25: 32 f.).

As incarnate spirits men must exist in the future even as now in a place as well as in a state. Hence hell and heaven are both a location and a condition.

1. Hell

The word translated "hell" is "gehenna," the valley of Hinnom, a place near Jerusalem, where a perpetual fire burned to consume the refuse of the city. Hence the word is used figuratively for the place of punishment.

1) ITS CHARACTERISTICS.

The New Testament abounds in highly figurative language concerning the fate of the wicked. They are said to be thrust into a bottomless pit, into a lake burning with fire and brimstone, into unquenchable fire. Their worm dieth not. They are in outer darkness where there is weeping and wailing and gnashing of teeth. From this we gather that the lost are condemned to a state of inexpressible woe. This must include the following:

(1) Loss of opportunity. The period of probation with its inducements and hopes is forever over. Earth will be only a bitter memory to those who failed to use it properly.

(2) Loss of divine favor. Forsaken of God and bereft of the Holy Spirit whom they grieved, the lost are without hope of beholding the face of the Father. The holy influences no longer follow them and His invitation to return is forever withdrawn.

(3) Abandonment to sin and passion. The wicked in this life generally go from bad to worse. In the other world, unrestrained by God and the good, they give themselves to unbridled passion and evil.

(4) Evil company. Jesus declared that those who reject Him shall go to unquenchable fire prepared for the devil and his angels. They and the wicked of earth shall be companions forever. The carnival of evil resulting from the contact of the vile and the debased must be wretched beyond all conception.

(5) Self-accusation. Amid the terrors of perdition nothing can be more dreadful than the accusations of conscience. The moral nature of man becomes an avenging accuser giving its perverter no rest.

(6) Positive punishment. While in a sense sin becomes its own punishment, back of it is a living, holy lawgiver and judge whom the sinner has offended and who is angry with sin, and who punishes the offender.

2) ITS PERPETUITY.

(1) Denied.

a. By Annihilationists. While the common faith of the orthodox church has always been that the punishment of the wicked is endless, there have not been wanting some who deny this.   The annihilationists maintain that at death or at the judgment the wicked will be absolutely blotted out.

b. By Restorationists.   In a variety of forms these teach the universal salvation of men.   This is represented as taking place on the other side through repentance and faith which will finally come to all, though in some cases of extreme wickedness only after a long period of time.   It is urged by advocates of this theory that punishment will have a reformatory effect.   The principle argument in its favor is that multitudes do not have a fair opportunity in this life, and therefore, the justice and goodness of God will not deny them this in the world to come. There is no substantial basis for this belief in Scripture as we shall show.

(2) Affirmed.

a. The language of Scripture.   This seems to teach most explicitly the eternity of punishment.   *Aion* and *aionias* and kindred words are used scores of times in the New Testament.   With few exceptions they express the idea of duration.

a) They are applied to the duration of God. Christ declares, "I am alive forevermore" (Rev. 1: 8).   In I Tim. 1: 16, 17, we have the word *aion* applied to the eternal life of the saints and to the duration of Christ's kingdom and glory.   In Rom. 16: 26, we read of "the eternal God."

b) These words are used to describe the duration of the future life of the saved (Jno. 6: 57, 58; II Cor. 9: 9; Mt. 19: 29; Mk. 10: 30; Jno. 3: 15; Rom. 2: 7).

c) They are used antithetically to describe the life of the saints and the misery of the lost.   "And these shall go away into eternal punishment, but the righteous into eternal life" (Matt. 25: 46).

b. By the nature of sin.   Not only do the words of Scripture preach the eternity of punishment, but the very nature of sin demands it.   We are completely incompetent to judge the demerit of sin, but our compassionate Lord is not.   He has declared that the persistent sinner is worthy of death eternal.   Sin is so terrible an offense to God that

He cannot tolerate it. Having made abundant provision for its pardon in life, He has done all that could be done or justly asked. Those who reject His offers do it at their own peril.

In order to relieve the inexpressible horror of an endless doom it has been suggested hypothetically that if the lost should repent and turn, a merciful God would pardon them in the other world. It is alleged that rational beings must come to their senses sometime, and that when they fully realize the meaning of hell they will naturally turn to God. No doubt God knew that such suppositions are groundless. One never hears of the devil's repenting. It is quite uncommon to see deeply hardened sinners turning to God in old age. When one thinks of the sinner's rejecting a Saviour who gave Himself for him and closing his heart to His indwelling, the conclusion is that his character has been so infected by sin that when once the grave closes over him he can no longer repent even if he would. He keeps on sinning yonder just as he did here.

But is there no mitigation whatever? Shall all suffer alike? The answer is that some shall be beaten with "fewer stripes" than others and their lot shall be "more tolerable."

2. Heaven

Over against the dark picture of the place of doom, the Scriptures delineate in the most alluring and beautiful language the place of reward.

1) THE PLACE.

The word heaven comes from the same root as "heave," or "lift up," and hence signifies that which is high. It is applied to the sky, and also to the exalted place, known as the dwelling of God, and the home of the angels and the saints. It is called the New Jerusalem, the city that hath foundations, the place prepared by Christ.

2) THE SAVED.

The human inhabitants of heaven are those who have accepted or who have not rejected Christ. They come from the east and the west and the north and the south, an exceedingly great multitude, the vast majority of the race. We may say this advisedly, if for no other reason than that the majority of the human family die in childhood.

3) THE BLESSEDNESS.

(1) Exemption from sin. That which makes life miserable here—sin and its consequences—will never be permitted to intrude into the Father's house, for in His presence there is fulness of joy and at His right hand there are pleasures for evermore.

(2) The Vision of God. The saved shall see God's face. The unutterable glory of the divine presence shall surround them. The beatific vision shall thrill their souls, and satisfy them, as they realize in its fulness the love of Christ that passeth all knowledge.

(3) Eternal Life. Heaven is as lasting as God Himself, for the word eternal is applied to both. Duration, however, is not the chief characteristic of eternal life. It is life in its highest degree, its greatest possible fulness and significance. The unfettered soul will be restored to its god-like nature, with vast capacity for knowledge and love.

(4) Fellowship. The saints of all the ages, the choice spirits whom God made great in love and service will be there; and the little children, and the sweet and beautiful characters of the saintly home.

(5) Beauty. From the descriptions of the New Jerusalem we conclude that in the home of the saints will be not only things distinctly spiritual, but such also as minister to the highest esthetic wants and desires of the most cultivated.

"We know not, O! we know not,
What joys await us there,
What radiancy of glory,
What bliss beyond compare."